THE
STONE OF
DESTINY

First Edition 2011

Second Edition 2021

Copyright © Mark Naples and David Bews 2021

ISBN: 978-1-8384308-1-8

THE
STONE OF
DESTINY

In Search of the Truth

Mark Naples F.S.A. Scot.
&
David Bews F.S.A. Scot.

Dedications

To Angela who has had to put up with me for over 40 years
To my son and daughter, Lee and Kerri, who both have turned
into people I love and am extremely proud of
DB

My children Ben, Michael and Amber
My wife Morven
And my parents Eileen and James
I love you
MN

Contents

List of Illustrations

Preface to the Second Edition

Since the release of the first edition of this book in 2011, the story of the Stone of Destiny and its peculiar significance to the politics of the day has continued to evolve with each year that has passed. We figured that at some point there would be a renewed interest in the Stone, prompting the call for a revision. We always expected that this timeline would be determined by an impending coronation ceremony at Westminster Abbey. At the time of writing, Queen Elizabeth II is now the longest reigning monarch of any nation that has ever existed in history. When the time comes for the next coronation, presumably of her eldest son, Charles, the realm under his authority and the faith that he must defend could be very different from that of his mother.

We were, and are, eager to see how events unfold with regards to the Stone. To date, it has not ventured back across the Scottish/English border since its official return to Scotland in 1996. It has been kept at Edinburgh Castle and displayed alongside the Honours of Scotland, but in late 2020 it was announced that in 2024 the Stone will be transferred to Perth. This will be much closer to Scone, from where it was taken in 1296, and is thus an acknowledgement of its symbolic history and influence upon the national psyche of Scotland. It was this announcement that prompted the update for a second edition.

Our research, as you will soon discover, led us to determine that the oft-told tradition of the Stone is perhaps not quite as robust as the historical narrative would like us to believe. It is debatable whether the Stone should be regarded as a Scottish relic taken to England, or an English relic taken from Scotland. The former necessitates that it has a long and provable history in Scotland, whereas the latter implies its significance only became apparent after it was taken to London.

The second edition is, for the first time, available as both digital and printed copy. The printed copy is available with black and white imagery, whereas the digital version contains the same images but in full colour. This is purely down to the high costs associated with colour printing. We are utilising 'print-on-demand' capability to ensure the book is readily available to both the casual reader and the serious historian alike. In addition, we have included new and relevant information that has come to light following our initial publication. Our original intention was to present the findings as we understand them and let the reader decide how to interpret. Hopefully this approach remains valid. There have also been some professional edits and general corrections to the text.

Time will tell if events involving the Stone will inspire us to release a third edition. Until then, we hope you find the following pages an informative and entertaining read.

Mark and David

Introduction

The Stone of Destiny has been the cause of controversy and contention for many centuries. It was taken from Scone in Scotland by King Edward I of England in 1296, and subsequently placed at Westminster Abbey in London, England. Legend claims that it is Jacob's Pillow and spoken of in the Old Testament. If true, it is one of the most important biblical relics on display anywhere in the world. Without doubt it has been used during the coronation ceremonies of the monarchs of England, and subsequently the United Kingdom, since the time of King Henry IV in 1399. However, what is in doubt is the precise history prior to that date and how or why its historical facts became so entwined with legend and myth.

Figure 1: The Stone of Destiny
© Crown Copyright HES

Prior to entering England, the Stone had been used as part of the inauguration ceremony of the Scottish monarchy since time immemorial. There is a long-held belief, at least by some, that the Stone

11

that was taken in 1296 was not the genuine king-making Stone of Scotland. This implies that King Edward was duped with nothing more than an unimportant and insignificant piece of red sandstone quarried from the Scone area. If this is really the case, then what happened to the genuine Stone? Is it possible that it was taken and hidden somewhere in Scotland before the invading armies of England reached Scone, or is this just fanciful thinking? Likewise, if it was taken somewhere, were there guardians of the relic and could they have passed down their secret knowledge through many generations to the present day?

The Stone of Destiny, as it is popularly called, resided in Westminster Abbey for many centuries. It was returned to Scotland in 1996 and placed on display at Edinburgh Castle, marking the 700th anniversary of its removal from Scone. Perhaps a more accurate name would be the Stone of Scone, but for reasons that will become apparent throughout this book we have chosen to refer to it by the more mythical and symbolic name that has been attached to it over the ensuing centuries, namely the Stone of Destiny. Where necessary, and for a coherent narrative, we may choose to use another name for the Stone that better suits the dialogue, but in all cases, what is being described or discussed should be readily apparent to the reader. Likewise, we may use interchangeably the term 'coronation' or 'inauguration' or some other related word when discussing the various king-making ceremonies, even though there are technical differences that a more learned reader might like to have better differentiated. Unless specified otherwise, we are referring to the act of being made a monarch in the way it was best understood for the occasion.

The Stone was returned to Edinburgh Castle on the feast day of Scotland's patron saint – St Andrew. As we delved deeper into the legend of the Stone and researched the official records of both Scotland and England, we became suspicious at the distinct lack of mention of St Andrew, especially as he was seemingly such an important figure in Scottish history. We found it surprising that it was not until the peak of the Wars of Scottish Independence, in the late thirteenth/early fourteenth centuries, that reverence for St Andrew really began to take hold in Scotland. At the signing of the Declaration of Arbroath in 1320, St Andrew was, for the first time, publicly proclaimed as the patron saint of Scotland. What was the situation regarding Scotland's patron saint before that date?

Scotland has an immense history of native, so-called pagan, Pictish tribes being converted by St Columba and his contemporaries. In addition, there are a plethora of Celtic saints that were prevalent throughout Scotland in the early fifth, sixth and seventh centuries. We thought it curious that it was not a Celtic saint chosen to be the patron of Scotland, but instead it was someone who was apparently more in line with the teachings of the Church of Rome.

The more we researched the more we found that the theft of the Stone of Destiny was, on the one hand, a move by the English crown to make the Scottish monarchy subservient. Simultaneously, the church in England, following direction from Rome, was trying to achieve similar subservience from the Celtic church in Scotland. Therefore, it would appear that the theft of the Stone of Destiny, and the establishment of St Andrew as the patron saint of Scotland, were two of the most important events that helped shape the modern-day psyche of Scotland. We decided to look at what was happening throughout Scotland, England, and the rest of Europe before the Stone was taken and for the next hundred or so years afterwards. Our aim was to establish if the legend of the Stone was created for political purposes, or whether its history genuinely extended further back in time.

It was during the Wars of Scottish Independence that the majority of the myths and legends about the Stone were first written down. It is interesting to see how they develop depending on who is writing which account. We even came upon a totally different theory that proposed there never was a Stone used during the coronation ceremonies of Scotland, and that some other artefact may have taken its place. If so, what could this have been and how could such an error have been made?

Today many may see the history of the Stone as largely irrelevant, but for the past few centuries it has been regarded as a symbol of the British Empire. As such, it has been targeted by several organisations looking to establish independence or gain recognition for their cause. These actions were based upon the long-held belief that the Stone was indeed an ancient relic, and that it most certainly did *not* belong in London.

It was this kind of thinking that led to the successful capture of the Stone in 1950 by four Scottish nationalists, whose exploits have been turned into a 2008 feature film titled *Stone of Destiny*. They took the Stone from Westminster Abbey and back into Scotland. It was returned several weeks later in the hope that the British Government and king would see fit to have the Stone permanently returned to Scotland. Unfortunately for them this did not happen, and the Stone was eventually put back on display in Westminster. What their actions did provoke was the debate of whether they had technically stolen the Stone. It was argued by some, that the English monarch, Edward I, had stolen the Scottish Stone so now it was just being reclaimed for Scotland. None of the conspirators was charged by the police for fear of perhaps instigating a more wide-spread backlash in Scotland against the monarchy.

In the present day, the Stone of Destiny is even regarded by some as playing a pivotal role in the propagation of the biblical Apocalypse, as described in the Book of Revelation. To these believers, the Stone is to be used as the foundation stone of a new Temple that they will build on the site of the ancient Temple Mount in Jerusalem. What is it about the legend of the Stone that apparently adds credence to their beliefs?

Whilst researching this book it quickly became apparent that throughout history there has been an amalgamation of various differing stories, histories, and myths in order to try to compile one complete narrative. This has resulted in a historical minefield for anyone attempting to give even a basic overview of the legend, let alone how and why it originated. We have decided to take the two-fold approach of first looking at the legend as is, and then breaking it down to look at how the story became so apparently confused. We consider the impact this has had over the past centuries, and the implications it will likely continue to have into the future.

PART ONE

THE BACKGROUND
TO THE LEGEND

Chapter 1
From Bethel to Scone

For almost 700 years, and until 1996, placed under St Edward's Chair at Westminster Abbey in London, England, was a large block of rough sandstone. Above the chair there was a plaque which read, "This is God's House". This referred to a passage from the Bible that described some of the history of the Stone. The plaque was to inform the passer-by that this was the very Stone upon which God made His covenant with the patriarch Jacob. This was the promise that he and his descendants would be the rightful heirs to the land that is today called Israel. The Stone on display was claimed to be Jacob's Pillow from Bethel in Israel.

The Stone measures 670x420x265mm, weighs 152kg, and features an iron ring at each end. These are presumed to have been used in past times to assist with the movement of the Stone over its vast travels. Aside from a few scratches and a crude Latin cross marked on the surface, there are no distinguishing features to bear witness to its supposed journey from Israel to Scotland, and then to England, over thousands of years.

This Stone, Jacob's Pillow, is also known as the Stone of Destiny, the Westminster Stone, the King's Seat, the Palladium of Scotland, the Stone of Scone, the Coronation Stone, the Covenant Stone, the Fatal Stone, the Marble Throne and the Lia Fáil, amongst several others. The Stone is believed by many to have been used during the coronation ceremony of the ancient kingdom of the Scots, and today it is integral to the coronation ceremony of the British monarch.

English and British coronations have traditionally been held at Westminster Abbey. The Stone is placed in St Edward's Chair, which the soon-to-be monarch sits in whilst they receive the blessing and anointing from the Archbishop of Canterbury. This confirms him or her as the rightful monarch and hence occupier of the British throne. The last time it was used in a ceremony was for the coronation of Queen Elizabeth II on 2nd June 1953.

The Stone is one of the few relics on full public display anywhere in the world with a tradition that spans several millennia, and which claims to have been associated with the royalty of many differing kingdoms from the ancient and biblical world to the present day. It might be expected that a relic that has these claims associated with it would receive many pilgrims each year, and yet strangely this is not specifically the case. The Stone is currently on display in Edinburgh Castle. This welcomes the largest number of tourists per year in Scotland. It would seem that the majority of visitors do not come to see the Stone itself, as many non-Scots have never even heard of its existence, but more because if you visit Edinburgh then the Castle is the prime tourist destination

On display in the Crown Room at the castle are the Honours of Scotland. These are the oldest set of crown jewels in Britain and the second oldest in Europe. They consist of the Crown of Scotland (made in 1540), the Sceptre of Scotland (made in 1494, and remodelled in 1536), and the Sword of State of Scotland (made in 1507). Since 1996, included alongside the Honours of Scotland is the Stone of Destiny.

Jacob's Pillow

The Stone was said to have been the pillow of the patriarch Jacob, whose life is of fundamental importance to both Judaism and Christianity. Jacob was born as the son of Isaac and Rebeka and was thus the grandson of Abraham. He had a twin brother, Esau, and it is said that when Esau was born Jacob followed immediately after him because he was holding onto the heel of his slightly older brother. It is for this reason that the name Jacob is derived from the Hebrew root for the word 'heel' and means 'heel-catcher' or 'supplanter'.

As the second born son, even if only just, Jacob was not the legitimate heir to the Abrahamic legacy, which was traditionally inherited from the father by the firstborn son. It is due to the heel-catching idea that some commentators have argued that Jacob really was the legitimate heir and was simply trying to hold Esau back from being devious and stealing his legacy, pushing Jacob out of the way to be born first.

In a later story of the Bible, we are told how Esau returned from the fields one day, very hungry and in the belief that he was close to dying from starvation. Seizing an opportunity, Jacob agreed to give Esau some of his soup to ease his hunger, but only in exchange for his birth right. Due to the fact he thought he was about to die, Esau agreed to the deal claiming, "Behold, I am at the point to die: and what profit shall this birth right do to me?" (Genesis 25:32). As a result of this statement church doctrine tells us that Esau despised his birth right and that he did not truly believe in the God of Abraham, nor the promises made to him and his offspring. This thus justified Jacob as the legitimate heir of Isaac.

Isaac, the father of Esau and Jacob, lost his sight in later life. When he felt he was close to death, he wanted to bless his eldest son to confer the rights of his divine legacy. The dying man sent Esau out to hunt for some meat in order to prepare a final meal. As a thank you he would bless him upon his return. Rebeka, mother to Esau and Jacob, overheard this exchange. Jacob was her favourite son and she instructed him to go to his blind father, with a meal prepared by her, and receive the blessing reserved for Esau. Jacob and his mother tricked Isaac by disguising Jacob with hairy goatskins. The idea was that the old man would touch his younger son and believe that he was really Esau, who was naturally more hirsute than Jacob. The trickery worked and Jacob received the blessing of Isaac. Coupled with the birth right passed onto him from Esau, Jacob could now claim to be the legitimate heir to the promises of God.

Furious with anger at his brother's treachery, Esau vowed to murder Jacob as soon as his father was dead. Hearing of his murderous intent, Rebeka instructed Jacob to flee to the lands of her brother, Laban, in Haran (in what would later become Israel), and to stay there with him until Esau had forgone his rage.

On route to Haran, we encounter the story of Jacob's Pillow which becomes the start of the Stone of Destiny legend:

"And he [Jacob] lighted upon a certain place, and tarried there all night, because the sun was set; and he took of the stones of

19

that place, and put them for his pillows, and lay down in that place to sleep.

And he dreamed, and behold a ladder set up on the earth, and the top of it reached to heaven: and behold the angels of God ascending and descending on it.

And, behold, the Lord stood above it, and said, I am the Lord God of Abraham thy father, and the God of Isaac: the land whereon thou liest, to thee will I give it, and to thy seed."

Genesis 28:11-13

It is this covenant that God makes with Jacob that has been the cause of controversy ever since, for it is this promise that is held as proof that the land of modern-day Israel belongs to the Jewish people. That Jacob was perhaps not the legitimate heir for the promises of God has proved to be a matter of contention for centuries. It is usually explained away not as being acts of treachery and deviance to get what he wanted, but that the birth right was destined for him all along. Otherwise, God would never have made Jacob the promise. Following Jacob's dream we are told:

"And Jacob rose up early in the morning, and took the stone that he had put for his pillows, and set it up for a pillar, and poured oil upon the top of it.

And he called the name of that place Bethel: but the name of that city was called Luz at the first."

Genesis 28:18-19

Bethel means 'House of God'. The plaque that was placed in Westminster Abbey, above St Edward's Chair that read "This is God's House", refers to the following passage of the Bible:

"And this stone, which I have set for a pillar, shall be God's house: and of all that thou shalt give me I will surely give the tenth unto thee."

Genesis 28:22

20

Figure 2: Early drawing of Jacob's vision as he rested on the Stone

It is the Stone itself that is said to become God's house, almost as though the spirit of God is expected to be resident inside the Stone that Jacob sets up as a pillar. The spirit of God would remain in the Stone regardless of where it would travel throughout the world. The act of setting up memorial pillars is a frequent occurrence in the Bible. Jacob sets up several in a short space of time to mark his conversations with God, as well as to mark his boundaries with Laban, and even as a memorial pillar, or headstone, following the death of his wife, Rachel.

An account of the Jacob's Pillow story is also given in the works of Flavius Josephus in his *Antiquities of the Jews*. His account, from the first century CE (Common Era), is similar to that given in the King James Version of the Bible. The only major difference is that Josephus expands on the promise made by God to Jacob. Josephus wrote that:

> "...he [Jacob] poured oil on the stones, because on them the prediction of such great benefits was made. He also vowed a vow, that he should offer sacrifices upon them, if he lived and returned safe."
>
> **Antiquities of the Jews, Chapter 19:3**

According to Josephus' description of events, the monarchs that have been crowned on the Stone did so sitting atop a sacrificial altar stone. It is also worth highlighting that both of the key authoritative texts for the origin of the Jacob's Pillow legend clearly state that Jacob rested his head on 'stones', plural, and not on a 'stone', singular. That this has gone without remark until now is surely just an oversight on the behalf of other authors and we mention it purely as a point of fact and interest.

Soon after these events, Jacob becomes the father of twelve sons by four different mothers. These sons, and their descendants, were to become known as the Twelve Tribes of Israel. In birth order, the twelve sons/tribes are:

1. Reuben
2. Simeon
3. Levi
4. Judah
5. Dan

6. Naphtali
7. Gad
8. Asher
9. Isaachar
10. Zebulun
11. Joseph
12. Benjamin

Additionally, Jacob was father to a daughter named Dinah. She was born after Zebulun, but before Joseph. Being female, she and her offspring are not counted among the twelve tribes as descent passed from father to son only.

Many people have heard about how the sons of Jacob sold their younger brother, Joseph, into slavery in Egypt. Joseph managed to secure a position of power in the court of the Pharaoh after favourably interpreting his troubling dreams. He predicted seven years of abundance that would be followed by seven years of famine throughout the Pharaoh's kingdom. The Pharaoh was suitably impressed. He gave Joseph the daughter of a Priest of On to be his wife. She was to bear two sons, Manasseh and Ephraim. During the seven years of abundance, Joseph was responsible for keeping stock of the corn levels in anticipation for the ensuing seven years of famine. Part of the preparation plan was to introduce a corn tax on the people.

When the famine finally took hold, Joseph's brothers, with the exception of Benjamin who was left behind, appeared before him to beg for food on behalf of their father, Jacob. They were unaware that the powerful 'Egyptian' viceroy was in actual fact their brother, Joseph. They were sent away and told not to return without their youngest brother, Benjamin. Simeon was held captive to ensure their return. When the brothers finally returned to Egypt Joseph revealed his true identity. Upon recognition, they were regretful of their actions towards Joseph when he was younger. After severe repentance, Joseph forgave his brothers and introduced some of them, along with Jacob, to the Pharaoh. He granted the entire family some land in his kingdom in which to live in peace.

The families settled in Egypt. Many years passed. Eventually, Jacob, Joseph, and all of the brothers died. Their descendants, the Children of Israel, who came to be known as Hebrews, had multiplied greatly. The new Pharaoh did not know of the history of Joseph or of his descendants and grew concerned about the very large number of Hebrews that inhabited his kingdom. He even believed that the native Egyptians were largely outnumbered by them. As a consequence, the Pharaoh decided to enslave all of the Hebrews and to kill all of the new-born sons by throwing them into the river in an attempt to try to contain their population.

One couple, from the tribe of Levi, decided to try to save the life of their son by hiding him. When three months had passed and the infant grew too large to hide, the mother placed her child into an 'ark of bulrushes' and placed it into the river in the hope that the child would be carried to a safe destination, away from certain death. The child was found by an Egyptian Princess and daughter of the Pharaoh. She took the child and raised him as her own. She named the child Moses, because she 'drew him out of the water'.

When Moses had fully grown, he observed the harsh treatment of the Hebrews by the Egyptians and was troubled by what he saw. One day God appeared to Moses in a burning bush to tell him of the promises that He had made to his forefathers, Abraham, Isaac, and Jacob when he rested his head on the Stone. It was God's command to Moses to lead the Hebrews out of Egyptian captivity. Thus begins the story of the Exodus.

Gaythelos and Scota

In the mid-fifteenth century, a manuscript was written on Inchcolm, a small island in the Firth of Forth in Scotland. Inchcolm means the 'Island of Columba', and was home to an Augustinian Abbey. The Abbot and chronicler there was Walter Bower. He wrote a manuscript called the *Scotichronicon*. It is one of the few definitive chronicles of Scottish history that existed in the Middle Ages. It comprises sixteen volumes of work detailing the history of the Scottish nation from the beginning of time until the death of King James I in

1437. The first five books were written by an earlier chronicler named John of Fordun. He died in 1384 before the manuscript was completed, and so the task of finishing the work was taken up by Bower.

The *Scotichronicon* explains that during the time of Moses there was a son of a king from Neolus (or Eolaus), one of the kingdoms of Greece. He was named Gaythelos. Gaythelos was reputed to have been good looking but to be mentally unstable. Consequently, his father would not allow him to hold any position of power in his kingdom. Angered by this decision, Gaythelos, with the support of some of his friends, decided to vent his frustration and fury by inflicting cruelty and destruction throughout his father's kingdom.

This action enraged his father and resulted in Gaythelos being exiled from Greece as punishment. Gaythelos set sail across the Mediterranean Sea and landed in Egypt. Upon arriving, he helped the Egyptian Pharaoh Chencres drive the Ethiopians out of his country as they had over-run it and caused havoc. An alliance was formed between Gaythelos and the Pharaoh, and this alliance was aided by the willingness of Gaythelos to help keep the Children of Israel – the now multitudinous descendants of Jacob – in perpetual servitude in Egypt.

The Pharaoh seeing strength, loyalty and bravery in Gaythelos, and the fact he was of royal stock, gave his daughter, Scota (also known as Scotia), to be his wife. The *Scotichronicon* tells us that Chencres was the Egyptian Pharaoh who drowned in the Red Sea while pursuing the Children of Israel led by Moses in their Exodus. At this time, it was said that the Kingdom of Egypt (originally called Etherea) was the most ancient of kingdoms except for the Kingdom of Scythia. The potential significance of, and an ancient connection to, Scythia will become apparent in a later chapter.

Following the death of the Pharaoh in the Red Sea there was a civil revolt in Egypt by those wishing for an end to the corn tax imposed by Joseph in the times of famine. They saw the death of the Pharaoh as an opportunity for change. With Gaythelos as the son-in-law and heir of the dead Pharaoh, he was seen as a threat to keeping the status quo throughout his leadership and hence the corn tax was likely to remain.

Figure 3: The Legend of the Egyptian Origin of the Stone of Scone
by A. Forester (1911)

For a time Gaythelos remained at Heliopolis, but pressure and dissidence were mounting. Eventually, he and his followers were driven out of Egypt. Those who left with him made Gaythelos their official king, although the problem now was that he had no kingdom or land to rule. Even though he commanded a large army, Gaythelos could not guarantee defeating his many enemies throughout the region. He could not return to his Greek homeland due to his earlier banishment for the crimes he had committed there. He decided that he would seek out a place with no existing inhabitants and claim it as his own. Failing that he would be compelled to take an area by force.

Gaythelos, his wife Scota, and a large army set sail from the African continent to see where the gods would direct them. The people who accompanied Gaythelos on his journey became known as the Scots, so named after the mother of their nation, and wife of their king, Scota. Tradition claims that they took with them the Stone of Destiny.

Spain

During the same period of history that the Children of Israel were said to be wandering in the desert for forty years, so too were the race of Scots, who spent many years trying to find a place somewhere in the world that they could call home. Gaythelos and his followers eventually landed in the vicinity of Cadiz, in southern Spain, and soon they were able to establish a Scots nation. This was at a heavy human cost for they were continually attacked by the natives of the already inhabited area. They managed to conquer a substantial landholding ranging from the south coast to the north. Their tent barrack encampments evolved slowly into more permanent structures, later becoming well-fortified strongholds and towns.

Years passed. Gaythelos and the Scots were continually under attack by the local Iberian inhabitants. They were understandably unhappy about having invaders on their land. This conflict led to a heavy loss of life on both sides.

The *Scotichronicon* relates how Gaythelos and Scota were believed to have carried with them from Egypt a seat that was a "marble throne of very ancient workmanship...on which the kings of the Scottish people in Spain used to sit." This is the seat that is today believed to be the Stone of Destiny. It is curious how a Stone that was reputedly of importance to the Children of Israel (Jacob's Pillow) had come to be in the possession of Gaythelos, who was not a Hebrew. An account from a much later source proposes that it was Moses who gave the Stone to Gaythelos, but this is not in keeping with the narrative flow of the *Scotichronicon*. There is no indication of how, or why, Gaythelos and Scota were chosen to be the keepers of the Stone.

Having to establish and maintain a kingdom by force was not the original intention of Gaythelos. With each succeeding battle to protect his landholding he found his military strength diminished. Deciding that this was too high a price to pay – for without an army to protect his lands he would eventually have no lands to protect – Gaythelos sent out his sailors to explore the oceans in search of an uninhabited island for him to rule as king.

The modern-day town of La Coruña, on the coast of northwest Spain, was known in Roman times as Brigantium. It was a town supposedly established by Gaythelos, and from where an island to the north was spotted from the top of a very high tower. Gaythelos' sailors set out from Brigantium on a bearing of practically due north. They landed on an island deemed much more suitable for the purposes of their ruler, and with far fewer inhabitants who were much easier to subdue than those in Spain. The island was scouted before the sailors returned to Spain to tell Gaythelos of their find. The king was most pleased by all of the accounts of this fertile island, and so he made the decision to settle there as his new kingdom for the Scots. This island, in modern times, is called Ireland.

Ireland

Gaythelos died in Spain before he could follow through with his plans of inhabiting Ireland. Therefore, the task of setting up the new kingdom fell to his son Hiber. He made various skirmishes, but never a full-scale attack with the intention to colonise. In later Roman times, the island was known as Hibernia, possibly after his legacy. Instead of colonising the new island, Hiber decided to go against the wishes of his father and concentrated on trying to secure peace in their landholding in Spain.

Over time the Scots in Spain became a very poor nation as a result of continually being attacked from all sides. Without a proper, safe and secure homeland to call their own the Scots developed a longing for a better life. Eventually a second attempt was made to colonise the island by King Micelius, but this too did not win them any substantial landholding. It was not until many years later, when King Simon Brecc, descendent of Gaythelos, undertook the task that success was finally achieved.

The *Scotichronicon* informs us that Simon Brecc sited the Stone at Tara, the chief place of his new kingdom in Ireland. He received a prophecy about this Stone from the gods, claiming that wherever the Stone is placed the Scots will reign victorious:

Ni fallat fatum, Scoti quocumque locatum
invenient lapidem, regnare tenentur ibidem.
[If destiny deceives not, the Scots will reign 'tis said
in that same place where the stone has been laid.]

An alternative legend mentioned in the *Scotichronicon* suggests that Simon Brecc came to be in the possession of the Stone in a more direct manner. Apparently, he had let down the anchor of his ship and secured it close to the Irish coast. When the winds and storms became too violent for it to be safe, he was forced to pull-up anchor. He only just managed to do so, for when he raised the anchor, he saw that attached to it was a block of marble cut into the shape of a chair. He regarded the chair as a sure omen from the gods that he would reign successfully as king in the new land, and so he decided to use the chair as his throne and placed it at Tara.

Confusingly, in a fifteenth century compilation called the *Cronicon Rythmicum* the marble stone is referred to as the *lapis Pharaonis*, which translates as 'Pharaoh's Stone'. The chronicle also includes the term *anchora vite* meaning the 'Anchor Stone' and it is possible that this is where Fordun obtained his reference for the *Scotichronicon*.

The Stone of Destiny has sometimes been identified with the Benben Stone of the ancient Egyptians, although this was more by fringe writers without any strong evidence to support their claims. The

Benben Stone apparently disappeared thousands of years ago. It is possible that the Benben Stone is what was being described as the *lapis Pharaonis*. In Egyptian mythology, the Benben Stone was believed to have been one of the first objects to appear from the primordial waters and was worshipped for this reason. It was believed to have been set on a podium in the solar temple of Heliopolis, although where it went from there is unknown. Heliopolis was also reputedly the site where Gaythelos stayed for a time following the death of the Pharaoh in the Red Sea. It seems that the reference to both the *lapis Pharaonis* and the *anchora vite* give support to the legend of Simon Brecc coming to be in the possession of the Stone and placing it at Tara.

The Hill of Tara is said to have been the political and spiritual capital of ancient Ireland, and there are many earthworks still visible that associate the place with the old king-making traditions of the area. Whereas the tradition of a king-making Stone being placed at Tara is not disputed, what is contested is how the Stone came to be associated with the place. Whereas the *Scotichronicon* informs us that it was carried there by Simon Brecc, some of the ancient Irish chronicles attest that the king-making Stone – the Lia Fáil – came to Ireland under much more curious circumstances.

The Irish Legends

The ancient history of Ireland is perhaps the best documented of all of the countries of the British Isles. The legends were written down in the *Lebor Gabála Érenn* or *The Book of the Takings of Ireland*. This was compiled by various authors over several centuries. They based their version of events on much older oral traditions. The writings that survive are from between the eleventh to fourteenth centuries. They provide a very detailed and extensive history of Ireland and its inhabitants from long before Christianity reached its shores. Many of the legends are today regarded as merely fables, yet it is interesting that they also chronicle the movements of the Scots people and the Kingdom of Dál Riata, which later becomes important in the legend of the Stone of Destiny.

The *Lebor Gabála Érenn* is narrated by an entity that is known as Tuán, and who seems to represent the spirit of Ireland. Tuán tells the reader of the biblical flood and of the successive invasions of Ireland by all of the peoples that followed. The original inhabitants of Ireland were known as the Fomorians. They are often portrayed as evil, in one instance with them threatening to use magic to tow Ireland to the inhospitable north.

The first set of invaders to come to Ireland were the Parthalóns, who are said to have come from Greece. As Greece was the original homeland of Gaythelos, there may be parallels between the two legends. The Parthalóns had to do battle with the Fomorians and won. Many years later all the Parthalóns died of a plague, leaving the land once more to the surviving Fomorians. Next to come to Ireland were the Nemedians, who also had to fight the Fomorians. This time the battle was much more aggressive. Only 30 Nemedians survived the battle, and their weakened numbers allowed the next set of invaders, the Fir Bolg, to make their subsequent invasion.

The Fir Bolg are said to have escaped captivity in Greece, a story reminiscent of the Exodus of the Children of Israel from Egypt, and again having overtones of the story that involves Gaythelos. They are said to have settled in Ireland having taken their captors' boats as transportation. In the Irish legends it is the Fir Bolg who are credited with the founding of Tara as a royal centre. Their king, Eochaid Mac Erc, married Tailtiu, the last surviving female of the Nemidians. This was said to have happened after he became king at Tara in what would equate to around year 1904BCE (Before Common Era). Moses was said to have been alive during the thirteenth century BCE, and although the dates do not seemingly correlate, neither date can be cited with any certainty and without factoring in a large margin for error.

Eochaid received a vision that forewarned him of another invasion of Ireland by a divine race of beings known as the Tuatha Dé Danann. When the Tuatha Dé Danann invaded, their envoys met with the leaders of the Fir Bolg to negotiate the equal splitting up of Ireland between the two races. At first the Fir Bolg were open to this suggestion,

31

but King Eochaid flatly refused it by stating, "If we once give these people half, they will soon have the whole."

The Fir Bolg fought hard to maintain their kingdom, but eventually they were defeated and killed by the Tuatha Dé Danann. Ireland was now theirs and they continued to use Tara as the chief seat of their kingdom. The date of this is given as 1896BCE. Before they came to Ireland the Tuatha Dé Danann are said to have lived in four mythical cities. From each of the cities was brought a divine gift and placed at Tara.

The first city was called Findias, from which came Nuada's Sword, "from whose stroke no one ever escaped or recovered." From Gorias came the Spear of Lugh that "thirsted so much for blood…when battle was near…it roared and struggled against its thongs; fire flashed from it; and, once slipped from the leash, it tore through and through the ranks of the enemy, never tired of slaying." From Murias was brought the Cauldron of Dagda, called "the Undry, in which everyone found food in proportion to his merits, and from which none went away unsatisfied." Finally, from Falias came the Stone of Fál, otherwise known as the Lia Fáil, which "had the magic property of uttering a human cry when touched by the rightful King of Erin (Ireland)." It is this Stone that was brought from Falias to Tara by the Tuatha Dé Danann that is reputed to be one and the same as the Stone of Destiny.

Throughout all of the invasions the Fomorians were still left inhabiting some parts of Ireland, waiting to strike and reclaim it as their own. They kept a constant pressure on the Tuatha Dé Danann and took every opportunity to attack. There were several battles between the two races. The most notable being the Battle of Moytura, which saw the Tuatha Dé Danann hero, Lugh, raise an army against his father-in-law, Balor, who was also the leader of the Fomorians.

The Fomorians had managed to infiltrate Tara and steal some of their magical relics, such as the Spear and the Cauldron. Also stolen was the Harp of Daghdha. Daghdha was the chief deity of the Tuatha Dé Danann. It is this harp that is still used as a symbol of Ireland in the present day. The Lia Fáil remained in the possession of the Tuatha Dé Danann. Lugh managed to defeat Balor and banished the Fomorians from Ireland forever. He recovered the divine relics and placed them once again back at Tara. The Tuatha Dé Danann ruled for a further nine kings at Tara, until they too had to face an invasion by a race of mortal people known as the Milesians.

When the Milesians landed they met with the leaders of the Tuatha Dé Danann and were determined to take the island by force. They admitted that to invade a country without giving a proper forewarning to its inhabitants did not follow their strict chivalric code of warfare. However, now they were there the Tuatha Dé Danann should submit to them. The Tuatha Dé Danann could see the military strength and might that the Milesians possessed. It was proposed that if the Milesians were to leave the island for three days then in that time the Tuatha Dé Danann would make their decision whether to surrender their kingship or prepare for battle.

The Milesians were not fooled. They had heard of the magical powers that the divine Tuatha Dé Danann possessed. They knew that if they were to leave the island, then some kind of enchanted spell would be put over the country meaning that they would not be able to make a safe landing. Eventually it was decided that the Milesians would retreat from the island to a distance of nine waves, and that if they could land again, and defeat the Tuatha Dé Danann, then the island would be rightfully theirs. It was stipulated in the agreement that whoever won must treat the survivors of the other race with honour and respect.

After a long hard struggle, involving the use of magic and incantations, the Tuatha Dé Danann were defeated, but they were not annihilated. Some of the survivors wanted to leave Ireland altogether, to seek out some other paradise island and make it their new homeland. Most of them wanted to stay in Ireland as this was their home. However, they realised that to live above ground was no longer possible as it now belonged to the Milesians.

The Daghdha, their god-king, decided to give each of those who stayed in Ireland their own *sídhe* (pronounced *shee*), which was to be their entry to an underground realm of paradise. The *sídhe* are the many ancient barrows and hillocks that can be found all over Ireland, even today. Perhaps the most famous of these 'fairy hills' and entrances to the Otherworld are Knowth, Dowth, and Newgrange, near the River Boyne and about 20 miles northeast of Tara. These amazing constructions are thousands of years old, with Newgrange dating back to before 3200BCE, a date which again forces us to read any dating of the legends with a cautious eye. In another early Irish text, known as *The Annals of the Four Masters*, the date given for the invasion of the Milesians is 1498BCE. The Milesians settled in Ireland and continued to use Tara as the principal seat of their kingdom.

The Lia Fáil was to remain at Tara, and was used as the king-making Stone of the Milesians and their descendants for many centuries. Subsequently, it was believed to have been taken to Iona by St Columba in the sixth century CE.

Iona

Iona, or Ycomkill (also spelt Ikkolmkil or Icolmkill), or even just Y, is a small island located off the tip of the island of Mull, which is itself off the western coast of mainland Scotland. St Columba is believed to have taken the Lia Fáil from Tara and carried it to Iona where he crowned some of the kings of the Kingdom of Dál Riata, often referred to as Dalriada. This was the kingdom that spanned the northern shores of Ireland, across the Irish Sea, and onto the western coast of mainland Scotland including many of the surrounding islands. Typically, the main area of the Kingdom of Dál Riata is regarded as the lands of modern-day Argyll in Scotland.

The main source of information for the life of St Columba comes from the *Vita Columbae* (Life of Columba), written by St Adomnan who was the ninth Abbot of Iona following Columba. He wrote his account in the late seventh century, and as an interesting sidenote, he was the first chronicler to reference the Loch Ness monster. The story goes, that many Pictish tribesmen had been killed by some kind of large animal whilst trying to cross the River Ness. One day, Columba managed to save one of these poor unfortunates from the monster by ordering it, by the power of the Cross, to go no further. The monster left the Pictish man alone and troubled the Picts no more. As a result, many Picts converted to Christianity and began to revere Columba's God, and the legend of the Loch Ness monster was born.

Columba is said to have been born in 521 in Donegal, Ireland, and died in 597 on the Island of Iona, aged 75 years. He was also known as Colm Cille meaning 'Dove of the Church'. There is little known about his early life, other than that it was believed he was the great-great-grandson of a fifth century Irish king. At some stage in his life he became a monk and was subsequently ordained as a priest and studied under St Finnian.

Adomnan tells us that around the year 560, Columba had a disagreement with St Finnian over the ownership of a Psalter, which is used to hold copies of holy manuscripts. Columba was making a copy of the Psalter of St Finnian when an argument broke out after Finnian disputed Columba's claim to keep his copy. Finnian wanted to keep it for himself. The argument escalated and resulted in the Battle of Cul Dreimhne in 561, in which many men from both sides were to lose their lives. In penance for the deaths of so many people Columba exiled himself and moved from Ireland to Scotland.

Columba landed on the southern tip of Kintyre, on the south-western coast of mainland Scotland, in the year 563. It is said that he could still see his native Ireland from its shores, which reminded him of his bloody past. He moved further north and preached until he was granted land on the island of Iona. Columba is credited with turning Iona into the hub of Christianity and from where the rest of Scotland would eventually be converted. St Columba travelled with twelve companions who all set out on various missions to help convert the Pictish tribes to Christianity. Several churches were founded in the Hebrides by Columba, as well as a learning centre for missionaries that was based on Iona. His works eventually saw him being regarded as a diplomat amongst the Picts, who held him in high esteem for the miracles he performed.

In the *Vita Columbae* Adomnan writes about a Stone that St Columba used as a pillow when he was dying. This has reminiscences of the Stone being Jacob's Pillow, for we are told that Columba had a vision of angels visiting him shortly before his death. It is St Columba's

Pillow Stone that is reputed to be one and the same as the Lia Fáil, which in turn becomes the Scots king-making Stone.

It is thought that Columba brought this Stone with him from Tara and used it to bless Aedan mac Garbrain, a king of the Kingdom of Dál Riata who ruled between 574 and 608. Adomnan also mentions a certain 'Arturius' that could have been the first written mention of the legendary King Arthur. Arturius was the son of Aedan and therefore also a prince to the Kingdom of Dál Riata. Interestingly, King Edward I of England, who stole the Stone of Destiny from Scotland in 1296, was enamoured with King Arthur and tried to stylise himself on the ancient hero of Britain.

On Iona there is a stone on display that is called St Columba's Pillow, but this was found in a field and named without much corroborating evidence to suggest that it was the Stone mentioned by Adomnan. St Columba is credited with the writing of numerous books, maybe as many as 300 over the course of his life, although these have all been lost during the passage of time. He was a holy man and when he died on 9th June 597 Iona soon became a place of pilgrimage. It remains so to this day for many seeking the peace and tranquillity that can only be found on a remote island of Scotland. The 'pillow' Stone of Columba was said to have been set up as some kind of tombstone that was used to denote the grave of the saint following his death, although it is not known where exactly this is today.

Dunstaffnage

The next part of the journey for the Stone of Destiny moves us from Iona to the western part of mainland Scotland, and the ancient capital of the Kingdom of Dál Riata known as Dunstaffnage. In the present day there still exists a thirteenth century castle at Dunstaffnage, and it is widely believed that this is where the Stone was kept for a brief period of its history. However, the dating of the castle does not match the timing for when the Stone was said to have been held here. It is possible that there was an earlier structure that the castle was built atop, and this is perhaps where the Stone was originally taken.

It is believed that Fergus Mac Erc, alternatively known as Fergus Mac Ferchard, took the Stone of St Columba from Iona to the mainland in order to use it as the chief seat of his kingdom. Fergus is widely held to be the first of the Irish-Scots kings to have been crowned on the mainland of Scotland. He reputedly took the Stone, referred to as the Fatal Chair, and placed it at a town called Beregonium. Beregonium was near to a place called Euonium, and it is said that Evenus, the twelfth king in the line of descent from Fergus, built a town at Euonium. This town is believed to have been at the site of modern day Dunstaffnage. This is reputed to be the place where the coronation ceremonies for the kings of Dál Riata were held.

The Stone was to remain at Dunstaffnage for the crowning of a further 28 kings of Dál Riata until the time of King Kenneth II, also known as Kenneth McAlpin. For his coronation in 843, McAlpin is credited with moving the Stone to Scone. His rule was very important for Scotland as he was the first king to unite the two kingdoms occupying ancient Scotland. The Kingdom of the Dál Riata (the Scots) to the west, and the Kingdom of the Picts to the east.

Scone

Scone is located just a few miles to the north of the city of Perth, in Scotland. The exact meaning of the word Scone is unknown, but it has been suggested that it might be derived from an ancient word meaning 'shadow'. The site was deemed so important that it was regarded as the capital of Scotland with the title *Righe Sgoinde* (Kingdom of Scone). This title was also a term that sometimes referred to Scotland as a whole. Scone was seen as the Scottish equivalent of Ireland's religious and royal centre at Tara.

In the year 843, King Kenneth McAlpin managed to unite the various factions inhabiting ancient Scotland to fight under the same banner. McAlpin's new 'united kingdom' was called the Kingdom of Alba. He was able to unite the two, because he was said to have been descended from Irish-Scots royalty on his father's side, and Pictish royalty on his mother's side. The Scots line of traditional descent was patriarchal, meaning from the father, whereas the Pictish line of traditional descent was matriarchal, meaning from the mother. This made the ancestry of McAlpin agreeable to both parties. Interestingly, McAlpin was known as *Rex Pictorum* (King of Picts) during his reign, and it was not until his grandson, Donald, that the term 'King of Alba' was substituted as the title of the serving monarch.

There are conflicting stories about who McAlpin was and where he originated from. Some accounts have him as a king of Dál Riata who defeated the Picts in a battle and took their kingdom, whereas others suggest that he was a Pictish king who defeated the Dál Riata and the two kingdoms merged in this fashion. All that is really known is that it was he who united the two kingdoms.

One account of his succession states that it was much more underhanded. According to an alternative legend by Flann of Bute, McAlpin, presumably of Dalriadic descent, invited the Pictish nobles to a banquet and then:

> "By him are deceived in the East the fierce ones,
> He shall dig in the earth, powerful the art,
> Dangerous goad-blades, death, pillage,
> On the middle of Scone of high shields."

It would seem that the Pictish nobles were lured to a meeting at Scone. When a signal was given their chairs would be toppled back into deep pits, dug out of the earth and with sharp blades at the bottom, thus killing them all.

When McAlpin merged the two kingdoms he must have felt a need to move his capital from the west coast of Dál Riata to somewhere more central in the country to administer his kingdom. He chose the ancient Pictish capital of Scone to be that centre. Tradition asserts that he also relocated some of the ancient relics of St Columba from Iona and placed them at Dunkeld Cathedral, a few miles north of Scone, that he had built on the banks of the River Tay. These relics consisted of a few small bones of St Columba that were eventually placed inside a small reliquary known as the Breac Bannoch or Monymusk Reliquary. Tradition also claims that McAlpin took with him the Stone from

Dunstaffnage and placed it at Scone. This was to become the location where almost all subsequent monarchs of Scotland would have their coronation.

It is generally believed that the inauguration ceremonies took place at Scone on Moot Hill, or by its other name, Boot Hill. Moot Hill has also been known as *Tom-a-mhoid, Collis Credulitatis* (Hill of Belief) and *Omnis Terra* (Everyman's Land). This mound still exists and the visitor to Scone Palace is quickly drawn to the replica Stone of Scone that is sited on its plateau in commemoration of the history of the site. It was called Boot Hill because of the tradition that each of the lairds of Scotland who came to pay homage to the new king would bring a boot-full of earth from their lands, and pile it together as a mound upon which the new monarch would receive his title. This was to signify that the king could rely on the support of the lairds and that they would acknowledge his rule as king. It is the idea of blood and soil. The king representing the people he was to govern in the land upon which they lived.

This was a different tradition to that practiced in many of the other countries throughout Europe. In England, the presiding monarch held the title 'King of England' and in France they were the 'King of France', suggesting they were the king of the land and therefore by implication also the people. In Scotland, the reigning title was 'King of Scots', meaning that the king could govern the people, but the land could never belong to anyone regardless of their ancestry. This was a very Celtic belief and became a point of contention in later years.

The following is a list of the monarchs of Scotland from the time of McAlpin to the time of John Balliol:

1. Kenneth McAlpin (843-859)
2. Donald I (859-863)
3. Constantine I (863-877)
4. Aed (877-878)
5. Eochaid (878-889)
6. Donald II (889-900)
7. Constantine II (900-942)

8. Malcolm I (942-954)
9. Indulf (954-962)
10. Dubh (962-967)
11. Culenus (967-971)
12. Kenneth II (971-995)
13. Constantine III (995-997)
14. Kenneth III (997-1005)
15. Malcolm II (1005-1034)
16. Duncan I (1034-1040)
17. Macbeth (1040-1057)
18. Lulach (The Fool) (1057-1058)
19. Malcolm III (Canmore) (1058-1093)
20. Donald Ban (1093-1094)
21. Duncan II (May-November 1094)
22. Donald Ban and Edmund (1094-1097)
23. Edgar (The Peaceable) (1097-1107)
24. Alexander I (The Fierce) (1107-1124)
25. David I (1124-1153)
26. Malcolm IV (The Maiden) (1153-1165)
27. William (The Lion) (1165-1214)
28. Alexander II (1214-1249)
29. Alexander III (1249-1286)
30. Margaret (Maid of Norway) (1286-1290)
31. John Balliol (1292-1296)

Balliol was the last Scottish king to be crowned at Scone in 1292 before the Stone was taken in 1296. According to tradition, all except the Maid of Norway will have been seated on the Stone during their coronation ceremony at Scone.

Chapter 2
The Struggle for the Throne of Scotland

The Coronation of King Alexander III

One of the earliest written accounts of a coronation at Scone is that of King Alexander III in 1249. Alexander was only eight years old when he succeeded his father, King Alexander II. Until he came of age, a regent was to be appointed to rule in his place. Infighting meant that the nobles could not agree who would be most suitable and the country suffered internal turmoil. There is little-to-no documented evidence about any of the coronation ceremonies for the earlier Scottish monarchs. The account that exists of the coronation of King Alexander III is not an eyewitness account, for it was written roughly one hundred years after the event by the chronicler John of Fordun in his *Gesta Annalia*. It is possible that the author had access to earlier sources that have not survived to the present day and based the following account on these writings. He states:

> "Alexander, the son of the aforesaid King Alexander, a boy of eight years old, came to Scone with a number of the earls, barons, and knights, on the following Tuesday, the 13th of July. There were present the venerable fathers David de Bernham, Bishop of St Andrews, and Galfridus, Bishop of Dunkeld, a man gracious in many things both to clergy and laity, careful in things temporal and spiritual, one who showed himself amiable to all, both nobles and poor, but terrible to malefactors. There was present also the Abbot of the same monastery of Scone; and, behold, as soon as they were assembled, there arose a great dissension among the nobles. Some of them wished not to make him king on that day, but only a knight, saying that it was an unlucky day; and this was said, not on account of the unlucky day, but because Alan Durward, at that time Justiciary of all Scotland, wished to gird him on that day with a knightly sword. To whom submitting, the Lord Walter Comyn, Earl of

41

Menteath, a man eminent and prudent in council, replied saying that he had himself seen a king consecrated who was yet not a knight, and had often heard of kings who were not knights being consecrated, and added, saying, that a country without a king was without doubt like a ship in the midst of the billows without a rower steersman. He had also always loved the late king, of pious memory, and this king on account of his father. He proposed, therefore, to elevate this boy as speedily as possible to the throne, as it was always hurtful to arrangements already made to defer them. On his advice, the bishops and the abbot, as well as the nobles and the whole clergy and people, gave their consent and assent with one voice to his being made king."

There were a lot of arguments about how the young Alexander should be made a knight before being made a king, and there was further unrest about the coronation being carried out on an 'unlucky' day. In the Middle Ages an unlucky day was also referred to as *Dies Aegypticus*, or an Egyptian Day, in reference to the days that the ancient Egyptian astrologers would advise against carrying out certain major functions. It is likely that the coronation of a king fell into this category. The in-house bickering amongst the nobles was well documented. Opposition to the coronation of Alexander was not due to his young age, or that it was an unlucky day, but solely due to the fact that it was deemed unsuitable for the king to be crowned until he was made a knight.

Eventually the coronation went ahead, and it was not until 1251 that Alexander finally became a knight after receiving the honour from King Henry III of England. As the events unfold, the role of the Stone is revealed:

"And it was done that the same Earl Walter Comyn, when he heard this, and the whole clergy, the Earls, Malcolm Earl of Fife, and Malise Earl of Stratherne, and other nobles uniting with them, they immediately led the future King Alexander to the cross, which stands in the cemeteries or churchyard at the east end of the church; and, having there placed him in the regal chair, decked with silk cloths embroidered with gold, the Bishop of St Andrews, the others assisting him, consecrated him king, the king himself sitting, as was proper, upon the regal chair – that is, the stone – and the earls and other nobles placing vestments under his feet, with bent knees, before the stone. This stone is reverently preserved in that monastery for the consecration of kings of Scotland; nor were any of the kings in wont to reign anywhere in Scotland, unless they had, on receiving the name of king, first sat upon this royal stone in Scone, which was constituted by ancient kings the "sedes superior" or principle seat, that is to say, of Albania. And, behold, everything being completed, a certain Scottish mountaineer [highlander], suddenly kneeling before the throne with bent head, saluted the king in his mother-tongue in these Scottish words – *Benach de Re Alban Alexander, Mac Alexander, Mac William, Mac Henri, Mac David*, and thus, repeating the genealogy of the Scottish kings, rehearsed them to the end."

It is recorded that Alexander III was crowned "with more pomp and ceremony than anyone before him" which suggests that the traditional ceremony, if indeed there ever was a traditional ceremony, had in some way changed. A very similar account is given in the *Scotichronicon* by Walter Bower and it is widely accepted by historians that he took his account of the ceremony from the *Gesta Annalia*, written by John of Fordun. The main difference is that Bower says "...the king was solemnly seated on this royal seat of stone", which is referring to a seat rather than the regal chair that Fordun describes.

At age ten, Alexander married the English King Henry III's daughter, Margaret. During his childhood Alexander established good relations with his brother-in-law, and reigning monarch of England, King Edward I. At this time, Scotland had a population of about 400,000 and was enjoying an age of prosperity.

King Alexander's first wife, Margaret, died in 1274 leaving three children, Margaret (born 1260), Alexander (born 1263) and David (born 1272). There was no cause for alarm at this stage as there was an 'heir and a spare' for the throne if King Alexander should suddenly die. According to early writings, such as the *Lanercost Chronicle,* there might even have been some illegitimate children as well for he was well known for his sexual urges. Following the death of his wife, it was reputed that he visited "nuns or matrons, virgins or widows as the fancy seized him".

Problems began to appear when his youngest son, David, died in 1281, followed two years later by the death of his other son, Alexander, in early 1283. Disaster was to strike again when his daughter, Margaret, died giving birth to her child, also named Margaret, in April 1283. Margaret was married to King Eric II of Norway and her death meant that Alexander had no immediate family to succeed him. His next of kin, and therefore the heir to the throne of Scotland, was his infant granddaughter, Margaret.

This was not really acceptable to the Scots nobles who would have preferred a male heir to a female one, and especially one that was just an infant. Perhaps rather fortuitously, King Alexander was not an old man, being just 42 years old in 1283. This left plenty of time for him to remarry and produce more sons who could rule in his place.

As a contingency and to help to avoid any potential conflict, a meeting of the Estates of Scotland was called at Scone in 1283. It was agreed that in the event of anything happening to the king, his successor to the Scottish throne would be his granddaughter, the young Margaret, unless he was to have another child with his new wife, who would then naturally become the heir. It was agreed that if he died before Margaret was old enough to rule the kingdom then that responsibility would fall to six designated Guardians of Scotland until she came of age.

Alexander married his second wife, Yolande, in late 1285. However, in March 1286 he died suddenly by falling off his horse whilst riding to be with his wife during stormy weather. He fell at Kinghorn in Fife and died at just 44 years of age. A monument was erected on the 600th anniversary of his death to mark the location where his body was reputed to have been found.

Figure 4: Monument to King Alexander III, the last of Scotland's Celtic Kings, at Kinghorn in Fife. Erected in 1886.

Yolande was pregnant at the time of his death and the first problem that the six Guardians had to contend with was the need to proclaim the next heir to the throne. Should it be his granddaughter, Margaret Maid of Norway, or the unborn child of Yolande? The decision was taken out of their hands when Yolande's child died during birth on St Catherine's Day, 25th November 1286. Now the only candidate for the throne of Scotland was the infant Margaret who was soon approaching her third birthday.

This outcome did not suit many of the nobles of Scotland. They were worried that that the kingdoms of Scotland and Norway could now merge, or at the very least, the new Queen Margaret would be advised in political matters by her father which could be to the detriment of Scotland and the benefit of Norway. There were also the distant relatives of Alexander who believed that they had more right to rule Scotland than that of a foreign female infant. Perhaps even more concerning for the nobles of Scotland was the impression that a three-year-old infant Queen would give throughout Europe, and especially in England. Scotland needed to be seen as strong and independent and their predicament made them look extremely weak and vulnerable. However, the agreement that was made at Scone in 1283 was to be honoured, and six Scots nobles would rule as Guardians until the young Queen Margaret came of age, at 18 years, to rule Scotland on her own.

The Heir to the Throne

At the time of Alexander's death his infant granddaughter was still resident in Norway with her father, King Eric II of Norway. The six Guardians of Scotland that were chosen to act on behalf of the young heir to the throne were William Fraser (Bishop of St Andrews), Donnchadh III of Fife (the title passed to his new-born son Donnchadh IV when his father was murdered at Brechin in 1289), Alexander Comyn (Earl of Buchan), Robert Wishart (Bishop of Glasgow), James Stewart (5th High Steward of Scotland), and John Comyn (Lord of Badenoch). Conflicting interests between the Guardians meant that decision making on behalf of the country was proving to be a thankless task. It was decided by the Scottish church leaders that they should seek advice from the brother-in-law of the now dead Alexander III, and fellow monarch, King Edward I of England. Relations had been relatively good between Alexander and Edward, and so he seemed a logical choice to help resolve any conflicts among the nobles.

At the same time, Robert Bruce, 5th Lord of Annandale, who was not one of the Guardians, but who believed he held claim to the throne, joined forces with his son Robert, Earl of Carrick. They raised a rebellion in the southeast of Scotland and took over various royal castles. Bruce was in opposition to the young Margaret being the heir and sought to further his own claims to the throne. The rebellion was soon suppressed. To help appease the situation, a Norwegian Ambassador came to Scotland in the winter of 1286-87 to reaffirm the case for the legitimacy of the Maid of Norway to the throne.

Whilst the Scots were arguing amongst themselves, King Edward I was looking to take advantage of the situation to further his own kingdom. He approached King Eric of Norway, Margaret's father, to open the dialogue for what he saw as an excellent opportunity for both countries. In May 1289 Eric sent ambassadors to Gascony, in France, to meet with the English king. The ambassador was armed with papers referring to the Maid of Norway as "Queen" even before the Scottish nobles had agreed that this would be her title. The Scots were excluded from the meeting and were not informed until Edward met with Robert Bruce and some of the Guardians in October 1289. With Scotland being on the verge of civil war, it was agreed that Margaret would indeed become Queen of Scots. This was officially recognised in the Treaty of Salisbury, also in October 1289. Additionally, it was agreed that Margaret would be recalled from Norway before the 1st November 1290, and that any mention of her marriage was to be deferred until she arrived in Scotland. There were many hopeful suitors waiting in line.

Whether the Scots knew it or not, King Edward and King Eric had already been discussing the marriage between Edward's son, Prince Edward of Caernavon (the future King Edward II of England), and the young Princess Margaret. Ten days after the Treaty of Salisbury, Pope Nicholas IV granted a special dispensation for the marriage. Margaret was six years old and Prince Edward was even younger at just five years old. Edward and Eric had initially approached the Pope to propose the marriage before the meeting at Salisbury, but the Pope only agreed to the marriage if there was the consent from the Guardians of Scotland.

Papal consent was not necessary for the marriage between two children, but rather because Prince Edward and the Maid of Norway were first cousins once removed. Margaret was the great-granddaughter of Henry III and Prince Edward was his grandson.

Even though the Pope had specifically stated that the Scots had to agree to the marriage, Edward and Eric carried on with their plans as though their agreement was guaranteed. The two started to draw up the plans for the marriage, and even the inauguration ceremony of Margaret, before there was any consultation with the Scots. It is possible that some people in Scotland knew of their plans and assisted with the preparations for the coronation to happen at Scone. If Edward could do everything in his power to ensure the marriage went ahead before the coronation, then the Scots would have no choice but to accept that Edward's son would also sit alongside Margaret on the throne of Scotland as husband to the Queen. Edward could see the need to move quickly before the Scots tried to put a halt to the marriage. At great expense, Edward fitted out a ship and equipped it to carry Margaret across the treacherous North Sea. The ship underwent its refit at Yarmouth in England. The project was entrusted to Edward's chief butler, Matthew de Columbariis. The ship was to be fit for a king and his young daughter. It took six weeks to paint, and the English banners were proudly flown.

The ship set sail on the 460-mile journey from Hartlepool in England on 9th May 1290 and arrived at Bergen in Norway on the 25th May. On this ship was Henry de Cranebourne, Abbot of Wellebek, and Henry de Ry, the clerk to the Bishop of Durham, among many others. They stayed in Norway for twelve days before making the return journey to England, albeit without Margaret. The winds were obviously in their favour as they landed at Ravenshore in England on 17th June after just eleven days at sea.

There were rumours that the young Margaret had already left for Orkney before Edward's ship arrived in Norway. At that time, the Orkney Islands were still a part of the Kingdom of Norway. It was not until many years later that they would come under the domain of the Kingdom of Scotland. This would have meant that when Margaret was to eventually journey to Scotland, the distance to travel between kingdoms would have been minimal. If such rumours were true, then we can surmise that King Eric refused to allow Margaret to travel to England for her marriage to Prince Edward before her coronation. This must have infuriated King Edward.

When the Scots agreed to the marriage of the infants, Margaret and Edward, with the signing of the Treaty of Salisbury in October 1289, they made sure that their consent was only given on condition that Scotland was to remain "separate, apart and free in itself without subjection to the English Kingdom" and only if the wedding was to be conducted in Scotland. The Treaty of Birgham was signed on 18th July 1290, which finalised the details of the marriage. However, there were certain clauses in the treaty that raised concern for the Scots. Edward, the son, was to receive a personal right to the Scottish inheritance even if he and Margaret should have no heir themselves, and even if Edward was to subsequently remarry. This would effectively mean that Edward could pass the throne of Scotland to his completely 'alien' heirs, thus breaking the traditional Scottish hereditary line of ascension.

The nobles of Scotland had little choice but to accept the terms of the treaty. It was becoming obvious to the Guardians that Edward had his own agenda with regards to the Maid of Norway. Their fears were allayed, because soon after the treaty was agreed and signed, Margaret, the Maid of Norway, was dead.

The Death of the Maid of Norway

In September 1290, King Eric had sent Margaret on her voyage to Orkney. From there she would make her final sea voyage to the mainland, and then head south by road through Scotland. Edward's envoys, the Abbot of Wellbek and Henry de Ry, headed north towards Orkney in order to meet the Norwegians on their route south, presumably to Scone for her coronation. It is curious to note that King Eric of Norway did not accompany his seven-year-old daughter on what was perhaps the longest and most arduous journey of her short life. Instead, the care of Margaret was entrusted to her lady-in-waiting, Fru

Ingibiorg Erlingsdatter, and her husband, Herr Thore Hakonson, along with the first Bishop of Narve.

An English envoy was to meet the Princess once she arrived in Scotland and escort her to her coronation. Their role was to ensure that nothing could happen that might jeopardise her marriage to Prince Edward. They left Newcastle on 15th September 1290 and arrived at Aberdeen on the 22nd September. By the 1st October they had made it as far north as Meikle Ferry in the county of Sutherland, where they stopped at Skelbo. They met with a messenger of Scotland who was on his way south with important and devastating news. The messenger hurriedly informed the Englishmen that the Maid of Norway was severely ill, and possibly by now even dead.

On 7th October 1290 William, Bishop of St Andrews, wrote to King Edward explaining that he had heard rumours that the Maid of Norway was possibly dead, but reminded the king that this was only a rumour. The main aim of his letter was to warn Edward that the Earls of Mar and Athole were raising their armies and enlisting the aid of other nobles to fight in their respective corners for the title to the throne. Bishop William feared that the situation could escalate into bloodshed unless King Edward would send help to appease the Earls. William mentioned that he, along with the Bishop of Durham and Earl Warrenne, had heard that the Maid of Norway was only ill and on the road to recovery, albeit still very weak, and that Sir Robert Bruce was heading north towards Orkney to find out the truth. William finishes his letter to Edward by stating that if the Maid of Norway were to die, then he should support Sir John Balliol to prevent the shedding of blood. This was obviously a hint from William, that in his mind, the rightful successor to the throne was John Balliol and not Robert Bruce.

Edward must have realised that there was more to this letter than the fact that the Maid was merely ill. He took it to imply that she was indeed already dead. He was also aware of the fact that both Bruce and Balliol were about to seize the opportunity and make a play for the throne of Scotland. This was an ideal chance for Edward to show that he was willing to help prevent civil war by becoming a mediator to help determine the successor to the Scottish crown.

Some accounts state that the death of Margaret occurred at St Margaret's Hope in Orkney, whereas others suggest that she died during her voyage from Norway to Scotland. The circumstances surrounding her death are open to debate and there are many questions that remain unanswered. What is perhaps the only 'fact' is that the young heir to the throne did die, and Scotland was thrown into turmoil as a result.

Margaret's body was returned to Bergen in Norway where her father, King Eric, opened the coffin and identified the corpse as his daughter. With her identification verified, Margaret, Maid of Norway, was buried alongside her mother at Christ's Kirk in Bergen. It is widely accepted that the ship carrying Margaret was always intended to land in Orkney where she would be greeted by both Scottish and English ambassadors, before being escorted on her journey south into Scotland. What has never been resolved is whether any of the ambassadors ever saw the dead child in person. Her death raised a lot of suspicion from all sides, as it was seemingly a convenient way to stop the intended marriage to Prince Edward, without hostilities arising between Scotland and England.

In Scotland, those who would have gained most from the Maid's death were the two families that were the main contenders to the throne – Balliol and Bruce. It must be remembered that very soon after the rumours of the Maid's poor health were announced, Robert Bruce, who was opposed to Margaret being made Queen, set off on a journey to Orkney to try to verify whether she was dead or merely ill. It is possible that she was poisoned to prevent her from uniting Scotland and England through marriage, and although there is no evidence to suggest that this was the case, there was most certainly a motive from more than one corner. If poison was used as the method of choice, then it would have been very easy to make the symptoms of her illness look like a severe bout of seasickness.

Contenders to the Throne of Scotland

The death of the Maid of Norway meant the end of the rule of the House of Canmore. This plunged Scotland onto the verge of civil war. The scenario had not been foreseen that there would be no direct, or legitimate, heir to the Scottish throne. Many felt it their duty to step forward and propose themselves to carry out the role. In all there were thirteen claimants to the throne, six of illegitimate descent from Alexander III, and the rest from slightly more tenuous branches of the family tree. In addition, there was also King Edward I who was claiming that the Treaty of Birgham should be honoured.

The terms of the treaty stated that Edward's son and the Maid of Norway would be married. Edward argued that now she was dead her claim to the throne should automatically pass to his son. The Guardians of Scotland rejected this claim. However, they still wanted the advice of Edward as to who should be the next king, excluding his son.

Edward agreed to act as arbitrator for the next heir to the Scottish crown, but in the interim period he would also have "Sovereign lordship of Scotland and the right to determine our several pretensions." He invited all of the claimants to Berwick Castle on 3rd August 1291 and asked them to put forward their case so that he could decide who had the best claim to the throne. It came as somewhat of a shock to the enthusiastic claimants when, upon his arrival, Edward proclaimed himself as "The Superior and Lord Paramount of the Kingdom of Scotland." This was unethical on the part of Edward and put the Scots in a very vulnerable position.

During the meeting Edward had his army on standby just in case of trouble. He gave the claimants three weeks to agree to his terms. Robert Wishart, the Bishop of Glasgow, who was present at the meeting, told Edward that he thought his manipulations were outrageous and stated, "The Kingdom of Scotland is not held in tribute or homage to anyone save God alone." However, eventually the Guardians begrudgingly acknowledged Edward's right to govern and the hearings were able to get underway. After many months of deliberation Edward decided that the main contenders were John Comyn, Eric of Norway, Robert Bruce (senior) and John Balliol. Each one believed that his claim was superior.

John Comyn claimed upon a dubious descent from Donald Ban, brother of Malcolm Canmore. Eric of Norway claimed upon the right of his now dead daughter Margaret, Maid of Norway. Robert Bruce based his claim on the fact that he was the son of Isabella, the second daughter of King David I. John Balliol, on the other hand, was grandson of the oldest daughter of David, and argued that seniority should outweigh proximity. It was a complete shamble. Eventually it dwindled down to just two claimants – Bruce and Balliol.

The latter was subsequently to gain Edward's favour and John Balliol was proclaimed the next in line to the Scottish throne at Berwick Castle on 17th November 1291. The two claimants and their supporters looked set to do battle, but Edward's choice had been made, and his decision was final.

The Coronation of John Balliol

John Balliol became King of Scots at Scone Abbey on 30th November 1292, St Andrew's Day. He was forced to swear an oath of homage to Edward, who took every opportunity to remind him of such over the coming years. One of the earliest people to write about the coronation of King John Balliol at Scone was William Rishanger. It is possible, although unlikely, that he was present at the coronation in 1292. His *Chronica et Annales* was published around the year 1327 in which he states:

> "John de Balliol, on the following feast of St Andrews, placed upon the regal stone, which Jacob placed under his head when he went from Bersabee to Haran, was solemnly crowned in the church of the canons regular at Scone.
>
> Duncan, son and heir of the late Duncan, Earl of Fife, was under age, and could not perform a certain function in the new creation of the King of Scotland – that of placing him in his royal seat at Scone, incumbent upon him according to the usage of the Kingdom of Scotland – he assigned to John de St John to place, in the name of the said heir, John de Balliol, King of Scotland, to whom he had judicially restored that kingdom in his royal seat at Scone, according to the aforesaid usage."

It was a hereditary privilege for the Earl of Fife to consecrate the king. This might have been a tradition that continued through from the older Pictish times, as Fife was a major Pictish area and Scone was the ancient capital of the Picts. However, as the Earl of Fife was so young, in this instance, the privilege passed to another.

An alternative account of the coronation of John Balliol was written by the fourteenth century English chronicler, Walter of Guisborough, often referred to as Walter of Hemingford. He was definitely not present at the ceremony. He wrote his account nearly fifty years later and states that the Earl of Fife *did* perform his hereditary tasks. He describes how:

> "...on St Andrew's Day John Balliol was made King of Scotland according to the Scottish custom...In the Coronation Chair future kings were set, according to the custom, as the place of their coronation. The placing of the new sovereign in this seat belonged by hereditary right to the Earl of Fife. The King then took the oath that he would protect Holy Mother Church, and his subjects, by ruling justly; and that he would establish good laws and continue the customs and institutions of the nation as long as he lived. When Balliol had been placed upon the Stone, the solemn rites of mass were begun and completed, and he also remained seated upon it during the elevation of the Sacred Host."

He later describes the coronation chair as "a large stone" which was "hollowed out like a round chair." This is a curious description of the Stone, as it does not necessarily depict that which was taken to Westminster Abbey.

Present at the inauguration were countless nobles from all over Scotland, and at least one of the officers of King Edward I, John de St John, as well as the Bishop of Durham. On the whole it was not a happy day. The Scottish nobles who came to pay homage to the new king knew that Balliol was seen as a puppet king of Edward. Even on his coronation day, as King of Scots, Balliol was obliged to pay homage to

Edward, and it could be argued that this was rightly the case. It was down to the choice of Edward, pure and simple, that Balliol now found himself sitting upon the royal seat.

There was very strong opposition coming from the House of Bruce. Their claim to the throne was perhaps even stronger than that of the winning side. Edward must have known this, but ultimately he saw the House of Balliol as being easier to manipulate for his own needs. To further humiliate Balliol, Edward stated that Scotland was not independent and that he was now Sovereign Lord with the right to overturn any judgements made by Balliol. Even though Edward was not king *per se* he was now the person calling all of the shots throughout Britain. This was very much to his liking. When Balliol was crowned at Scone, in effect Scotland became no better than a Princedom of England, much like had recently happened with Wales.

The years passed and Edward continually made a mockery of Balliol. This angered not only the Scottish king, but also the many nobles residing throughout Scotland. In October 1295 Balliol saw the way things were heading and had an agreement drawn up with the King of France, later ratified in February 1296, that if Edward should invade either country then each could guarantee the support of the other. This was known as the 'Auld Alliance' and it lasted off and on until 1746 and the Battle of Culloden. This alliance infuriated Edward, as it could have effectively meant that if he started a war with either Scotland or France then he might have to fight and defend on both his northern and southern frontiers.

After years of humiliation, Balliol decided to make a stand against Edward when he was asked – ordered – to send Scottish troops to support the English war effort against the French in 1296. Balliol's defiance, and his attack on the English castle at Carlisle in March 1296, led to the invasion of Scotland by Edward. The English troops reacted rapidly by killing everyone in the town of Berwick-upon-Tweed before marching further north to Dunbar. Dunbar would be the battleground for what was to be regarded as the first war of Scottish Independence on 27th April 1296.

It has been argued that if the marriage between Princess Margaret and Prince Edward had taken place, then England and Scotland would have been united from that date. The death of the Maid of Norway threw the Scots nobles into disarray and because of the events that followed it would take nearly half a century, and the loss of many thousands of lives, for Scotland to re-establish its sovereignty.

The Return of the Maid of Norway?

King Eric, the father of Margaret, Maid of Norway, died in 1299. His brother, Haakon, became the next King of Norway. The year following his death something unexpected and unusual happened. A mysterious woman and her husband arrived in Norway by ship from Lubeck in Germany. She claimed that she was the Maid of Norway. Recounting her story, she claimed that she was taken to Orkney as a young princess and then immediately sent on another ship to Germany. She said that she was swapped with another child in Orkney and sold by her lady-in-waiting Fru Ingibiorg Erlingsdatter. 'Margaret' went on to describe how she had grown up in Germany and had now returned to her homeland in Norway.

Her story seemed plausible aside from one key problem. The Maid of Norway was born in 1283 and if she were still alive then she would have been about seventeen years old in 1300. However, the 'long lost' Maid of Norway now had the appearance of being a grey-haired 40-year-old woman. Whilst it is possible that she had aged beyond her years, it was unlikely that she would now have looked so aged for a seventeen-year-old girl. King Eric of Norway was born in 1268. This implies that, if correct, then he would have died younger than his long-lost daughter appeared to be!

There was no doubt in King Haakon's mind that this 'Margaret' was a fraud and that she and her husband were either mad or trying to commit a crime. In 1301 they were both found guilty of trying to impersonate the dead Maid of Norway. 'Margaret' was burned at the stake. Her husband beheaded. King Haakon would have had little choice other than to execute the apparent usurper. There was no provision under the laws of Norway whereby 'Margaret' could have made a claim to Haakon's throne. Priority was always given to the closest male heir before a female. It was thus unclear as to what motive the usurper could have had, unless of course she was telling the truth.

The signing of the Treaty of Norburgh in 1281 between Norway and Scotland recognised that Queen Margaret, the Maid of Norway's mother, had the right to the crowns of Norway and Scotland. This right presumably passed to her daughter following her death. Under the terms, 'Margaret' could not make a claim to Haakon's throne, but her husband most certainly could. A major problem for Haakon was that if the Maid of Norway was alive, then under the terms of the Treaty of Salisbury in 1289 she should be married to Prince Edward of England.

By 1301 King Edward I was ruling as the Overlord of Scotland. He could be sure of securing pro-English support from within Scotland to force Haakon in agreeing to the marriage. It had already been sanctioned by the Pope. Prince Edward was still unmarried at the time and it would have suited King Edward greatly to have his son marry the long-lost 'Princess Margaret'. Her existing husband would not be an issue as he could be made to meet an untimely demise, leaving the way clear for 'Margaret' and Prince Edward to marry. If this were to happen then under the terms of the Treaty of Norburgh, Prince Edward, as husband to Margaret, would be able to make a claim for the throne of Norway and also a claim for the throne of Scotland. This would effectively have made the Kingdom of England the largest and strongest in Europe.

With this threat to the reign of King Haakon there was no way that the impostor Margaret could be allowed to live, even if it were to be proven that she was the genuine Maid of Norway. Any forces pushing for this scenario from England would have found strong support from those in Norway who would have loved to see Haakon deposed from his throne.

The death of 'Margaret' in 1301 was not the end of the story. A cult soon appeared and there were many who believed that the heir to the throne of Scotland had been martyred. This 'Margaret' was regarded by some as a saint. There were others who even believed that she was still alive and in hiding, so that one day she would reappear to claim the throne. Very few people believed that she was actually burned at the stake. The stories and hearsay were turned into legends and the following of the 'Margaret' cult grew in size. Eventually, a church was built in Bergen near the site of the execution of the presumed usurper. It was named Margaretaskirk, or St Margaret's Church. It survived until the time of the Reformation.

It is widely believed that the young Maid of Norway died at St Margaret's Hope on the island of Orkney. She was never canonised, and so the references to her being a saint are misleading. The only St Margaret that ever existed in Scotland was Queen Margaret, who died in 1093. To confuse matters further, Queen Margaret never set foot on Orkney as it was not a part of the Kingdom of Scotland during her lifetime. There is another place called St Margaret's Hope near North Queensferry in Fife. It is reputed to be the place where Queen Margaret landed in Scotland in 1068 when fleeing England several years after the Battle of Hastings. The reference to St Margaret's Hope in Orkney possibly resulted from the cult that grew around the supposed impostor Margaret, and the young girl who never fulfilled her destiny as the Queen of Scots. If her marriage to Prince Edward had gone ahead then she would also have been the future Queen of England.

Chapter 3
Hammer of the Scots

Towards the end of the life of King Edward I, he wanted to be remembered as one thing: *Scottorum Malleus,* 'Hammer of the Scots'. This is what he had carved as his epitaph on his tomb at Westminster Abbey. But this was not always so. Until the death of his brother-in-law, Alexander III, King of Scots, in 1286, Edward had a very good working relationship with Scotland. At this time, he still had the voice of reason by his side, filling his life with joy, happiness and love. His wife, Queen Eleanor, was still alive.

The Ideal King for England

King Edward I has often been portrayed in a bad light. Many would argue that this is justifiable since he forcibly tried to take away the sovereignty of countries such as Scotland, Wales, Ireland, and to a lesser extent, France. He did so in pursuit of the dream of becoming the undisputed ruler of the British Isles, believing it to be his birth right.

Edward was born in the night of 17th/18th June 1239. He was son to King Henry III of England and Queen Eleanor of Provence. He was named after St Edward the Confessor, who was the last of the Anglo-Saxon lineage of kings and the favourite saint of both his parents. His mother, Eleanor, was very well educated and she ensured her son would receive the best education. She taught Edward to speak Latin and French, and encouraged him to learn about the arts, music and the sciences of the day. Eleanor and Henry were instrumental in the rebuilding of Westminster Abbey as a shrine to St Edward the Confessor.

Prince Edward was married to Eleanor of Castile, the second child of Fernando III of the former Kingdom of Castile and Leon in Spain. The courting of Edward and Eleanor was not very romantic. Edward's father was having problems with Eleanor's half-brother, King Alfonso X, over the claims to the duchy of Gascony, which was the last holding of the Kingdom of England in France. In 1254 the two kings negotiated and agreed that if Henry's son, Edward, were to marry Alfonso's sister, Eleanor, then Alfonso would transfer all of his claims over Gascony to Edward.

The deal was swiftly agreed and ratified, and the young couple were married on 1st November 1254. Edward was fifteen and Eleanor was just nine. Even then, the influence of his parents' reverence for St Edward the Confessor was becoming apparent. The young Prince Edward insisted that both he and his wife drink the blood of the Saviour from the very chalice that belonged to the saint, in order to consecrate their marriage. Edward and Eleanor were very fond of each other and grew together over the years like a genuine couple in love. Unlike most of the other arranged marriages of the day, they eventually became so enamoured with the other that they were rarely apart.

Edward received the nickname 'Longshanks' because of his great height. He was about 6ft 2in tall, which stood him half a foot taller than the average man of the day. He learned much from his father about piety and perhaps even more from his failures as a king. Edward's father, Henry III, was well known throughout Europe for his long journeys – not necessarily in distance, but in the amount of time he took to complete them. He seized every opportunity to stop and take Mass along his route. This was apparently so tiresome that King Louis IX of France banned all priests from travelling with him, to try to hurry Henry along. Every night he would pray for inspiration to the portrait of St Edward the Confessor that hung above his bed, and again upon waking in the morning. This devotion to the last ruling monarch of the House of Wessex also greatly influenced his son, Edward, who was as much of a devout follower of the saint as his father.

Henry pursued an ill-fated attempt to capture the Sicilian crown for his second son, Edmund, and tried to get it agreed and sanctioned by Pope Innocent IV. This expensive and disastrous affair resulted in anger from many barons in England and Sicily. This included Henry's brother-in-law, Simon de Montfort, whose father, also Simon de Montfort, was the man accredited with the famous saying, "Kill them all, God will know his own!" when asked how to distinguish between the heretic Cathars and pious Christians during the siege of Béziers.

This was the culmination of the Albigensian Crusades of southern France between 1209-1229. It is highly possible that the younger Simon would have fought alongside his father in this crusade, against the supposed heretics. This complete extermination of an entire population would have resounded as a warning throughout Europe of what could happen if you stepped out of line with the Church of Rome.

In later years, King Henry was facing bankruptcy and possible excommunication. He was forced to repay his debts under the Provisions of Oxford, often regarded as England's first written constitution. These were installed in 1258, and forced Henry, as king, to recognise the rights and powers of Parliament. When he overturned the Provisions in 1261 civil war was on the horizon and Henry looked to the French King Louis IX for assistance. During this time, his son, Edward, was tempted to side with his uncle, Simon de Montfort, and hold a Parliament in his father's absence. By the time civil war actually broke out in 1263 Edward was back on his father's side and became a bitter enemy of his uncle.

In 1264 Simon de Montfort won the Battle of Lewes and Edward was taken hostage to ensure his father agreed to the terms of peace. In May 1265 Edward managed to escape from his captors whilst they were out hunting. War was declared yet again. That August, Edward managed to win the Battle of Evesham and Simon de Montfort was killed, thus ending the civil war. Edward was now free to start the reconciliation process between his father and the rebels, and by 1267 England was at peace with both sides suitably placated.

In 1270 Edward embarked on the eighth crusade to the Holy Land, or Outremer as it was also called. He was a very pious man who was deeply committed to securing a place in heaven for himself and his beloved wife, Eleanor. The best way that he knew to ensure this would happen was to fight the good fight and win back Outremer for the Christians by doing 'God's work'.

Edward planned to go to Acre with Louis IX of France and fight to help keep the city out of Muslim control. By the time Edward arrived at Tunis, Louis had died of the plague and the French army refused to take any further part in the crusade. Edward decided to continue and stated, "By the blood of God, though all my fellow soldiers and countrymen desert me, I will enter Acre".

The crusades began following a Muslim victory over the Byzantines at the Battle of Manzikert in 1071. The Byzantine Emperor Romanus was held captive, and in 1095 Pope Urban II called for support from the Christian kings of Europe to help support Byzantium and free the Holy Land from the Muslims. This started a series of campaigns lasting over two centuries in which hundreds of thousands of people died on each side. The crusades would ultimately end in failure for the Christians.

The propaganda of the time insisted that it was 'God's work' to destroy the infidel, the rather unaffectionate term that was used to signify those of the Muslim faith. The objective was to have Christian control of the land whereupon Christ's feet had walked in ancient times. At the same time, the Muslims were doing their work to keep the Christian infidel out of their Holy Land, "In the name of Allah." Christian fever took hold of Western Europe and practically everyone wanted to be a Christian to do 'God's work', thus ensuring their place in heaven and everlasting salvation. The absolution of all past sins was another major incentive.

Forgiveness is what most people sought in the Middle Ages, if not still today. What happens after death was regarded as just as important as how you lived your life. With so many people heading to the Holy Land and willing to fight for the cause, safe passage into previously hostile environments began another industry that would run alongside the fighting – pilgrimage. To go on a pilgrimage would see ordinary people, as well as monarchs and nobles from all over Europe, journey many hundreds, if not thousands, of miles to be as close to the sites mentioned in the Bible as was physically possible, thus bringing them closer to their Saviour. To make such a pilgrimage would show devoutness and this would surely help with entry through the gates of heaven. Maybe it would even provide some physical healing whilst still here on Earth. Holy wells literally sprang up overnight with a nominal fee being charged for each drink of blessed, and fresh, holy water along the pilgrim routes. This was very enriching for the church and soon everyone was trying to cash in, usually with great success.

Edward arrived in Acre in 1271 with about 1,000 knights under his command. This was too few to make a significant assault on the enemy, so his role mainly consisted of defending the city to keep Acre out of Muslim hands. Edward was largely successful and kept a firm hold of the city. However, other Christian crusaders were divided in their thoughts about the best way to tackle the increasing problem of continued loss of lands in Outremer. This led to Edward having to agree to a truce with Baibars al-Bunduqdari, the Mamluk Sultan of Egypt and Syria.

Edward was subsequently attacked by an Assassin who stabbed him with a poisoned dagger. He was nearly killed. The Assassins were an Islamic military sect that operated against the Christians during the crusades. It is said that the term 'Assassin' is derived from 'Hashshashin', which in turn gets its name from the fact that the members of the sect were probably working under the influence of the drug Hashish. It is reputed that the stabbing of Edward is what caused the word 'Assassin' to enter into the English language. One story explains that Edward's wife, Eleanor, sucked the poison out from his wound thus saving his life. Another account suggests it was Edward's friend, Otto de Grandson, whereas another source, which is perhaps a more likely story, is that a surgeon operated on Edward and saved his life whilst his beloved Eleanor sat weeping outside the room. Either way, Edward was severely injured and very close to death.

He was unable to fight for many months and when he had regained enough of his strength, he was forced to abandon Acre and travel to Sicily to continue the healing process. He headed home via Gascony in France. Edward held the duchy of Gascony, but this was not to the liking of everyone in France.

During this period there was a revolt by Gaston de Bearn, who was appealing to King Philip III of France for a jurisdiction against Edward, because he did not like the fact that an English King was the ruler of French lands. The troubles throughout Edward's future kingdom were beginning to make themselves known.

King Henry III died in November 1272. Even though Edward was thousands of miles away there was neither opposition nor opportunist claimants making a play for his throne in England. At the age of 35 he was a veteran of politics, civil war, holy crusades, and was popular with the people of England. However, Edward viewed his crusade as ultimately a failure, for not only had Christianity not expelled the Muslims from Outremer, but he had to return home early because of his poor health. With all that he had done, was it enough to guarantee a place for him and his wife in heaven? Edward could not be sure, and it was always his ambition to one day return to the Holy Land and make sure. As fate would have it, he never got the chance.

He returned to England in August 1274, by which time his barons had already sworn allegiance to him in his absence. He was crowned King Edward I at Westminster Abbey during the same month. It seemed that Edward was the ideal king for England.

Crusading was a very expensive business and during the first few crusades men would quite happily give their land and money to finance a campaign, to help ensure a place in heaven for themselves and their family. For an elderly person this might have been regarded as a bargain. Earthly possessions would last until death, but a place in heaven was for eternity. By the time of the eighth crusade this attitude had started to wane, and people were not as willing to freely give more money to fund another campaign that could not guarantee success. $1/20^{th}$ of every English citizen's goods and possessions was used to finance Edward's campaign of 1271. In addition, he had to borrow money from various other sources. Edward was not an old man when he returned to England in 1274, and so chances are he would live long enough to have to repay his debts in full. These totalled about £100,000 – a vast sum of money in the thirteenth century. Of this amount, Edward had borrowed £23,000 from an Italian banking company. Now that his crusade was over, they wanted their money back. To help with the repayments Edward put a tax on wool and leather exports from England, and then in 1275 he levied a tax of $1/15^{th}$ of the value of all movable property. This was estimated to have raised about £80,000, thus helping the king to pay off his debts and also to fill his coffers.

The need to pay off the debts from the previous campaigning proved to take longer than he had hoped. However, this needed to be done before he could finance any new crusading campaign to the Holy Land. Following his return to England, Edward enjoyed relative peace throughout his kingdom. His relationship with his brother-in-law in Scotland, King Alexander III, was quite good, but his other neighbours, specifically Wales and France, were causing him increasing difficulties. Rather than by being diplomatic and trying to ensure peace throughout his homeland with stability for his kingdom, Edward instead viewed those countries in financial terms. He believed that if he could be their Overlord then he could tax them to raise finance. In addition, he believed that if he could utilise their manpower it would aid his return to Outremer. His place in heaven would be secured.

Of Trojan Descent

Edward grew up believing in the old Arthurian legends about the quest for the Holy Grail and the meetings of honest, true and noble knights at the round table in Camelot. Edward had fashioned similar round tables for himself, around which he held many feasts for the bravest and wisest nobles of the land in tribute to the chivalric ideals of the legendary King Arthur and his knights. One of these round tables is still on display at Winchester Cathedral. It was redecorated by King Henry VIII in 1522.

Edward believed in destiny, and especially that it was his destiny, and his birth right, to be the unifier and king of all Britain. He believed he was a descendant of Brutus of Troy who, according to the popular historian and romancer Geoffrey of Monmouth, had given his name to Britain in the days of the prophets Eli and Samuel. Monmouth is credited with being one of the first writers to detail the history of Arthur and Merlin, and he was the author of *Prophetiae Merlini* (The Prophecies of Merlin). Many would argue that Edward's belief in Arthur was the delusion of a megalomaniac, power-crazed and arrogant man, but by understanding this thought process we can begin to uncover the real motivations of Edward for wanting a unified Britain.

Figure 5: Round Table at Winchester Cathedral
© Stuart Black / Alamy Stock Photo

The legend of Brutus was first chronicled by the eighth century historian, Nennius, in his *Historia Brittonum*. The story was later reinforced in the twelfth century by Geoffrey of Monmouth in his *Historia Regum Britanniae* (History of the Kings of Britain). Both of these early chroniclers, and indeed most others writing at the time, are believed to have concocted many legends in their writings. It is debatable what can be taken as truth and what is pure fiction. Nennius and Monmouth are famed as the major source for the King Arthur legends. Edward was enthused by their writings and wanted to believe as truth what he read. It is possible that Nennius cited sources from the fifth century or earlier, and whilst we may be able to dismiss much of his writing as fable, we cannot dismiss everything. It is quite likely that he was referencing sources that were available to him, but which have not survived through to the present day. The background to Brutus and the Trojan descent of Britain has its roots in Greek mythology and the founding of Rome.

Edward's belief in his Trojan descent was the belief that he was descended from the royal family of the ancient city of Troy. Troy is the location of the legendary Trojan Wars, described in early poems such as the *Iliad* and *Odyssey* by the Greek writer Homer and enhanced by the Roman writer Virgil in his *Aeneid*. The city of Troy was once thought of as merely a mythical creation by Homer. However, in the nineteenth century a German archaeologist, Heinrich Schliemann, identified ruins near the northwest tip of modern-day Turkey as those of Troy.

The Trojans are said to have descended from Electra who was seduced by the god Zeus. Together they had a child who they named Dardanus. The Greek legends have Dardanus originating from Arcadia, whilst the Roman legends have him coming from Italy. When Dardanus died his kingdom was passed to his grandson, Tros, who called his descendants 'Trojans' and his land 'Troad'. It was Ilus, the son of Tros, who founded the city of Troy (also known as Ilium), and to whom Zeus gave a statue of Pallas, upon which the safety of the city was said to depend. This statue is the origin of the term Palladium, which is used to denote an artefact that is believed to ensure the safety and sovereignty of a city or nation of people. Thus, the Stone of Destiny is said to be the Palladium of Scotland.

Illus had a son, Leomedon, and legend claims that he refused to pay Poseidon for the city defences that he had erected for him. Poseidon punished his insolence by flooding the lands and demanded that Leomedon sacrifice his daughter, Hesione, to a sea monster. Leomedon refused and the sea monster destroyed the people outside the city. The city was then attacked by Heracles. He captured Troy and killed Leomedon and all of his sons, with the exception of Priam who then became king. Legend has it that during Priam's reign (around 1190-1180BCE), the Mycenaean Greeks attacked and captured Troy. Thus began the Trojan Wars. All of the Trojan royalty are said to have fled the city and ventured westwards.

The traditional Greek legends claim that the Trojan hero Aeneas, who fled Troy when it was sacked by the Mycenaean Greeks, settled in Italy and built the city of Rome. However, another perhaps more popular legend brings forth Romulus and Remus as founders of the city. The two brothers were abandoned soon after birth near the River Tiber, where a she-wolf saved their lives and suckled them. They were later found by a shepherd who took care of them. The two brothers had an argument that resulted in Romulus killing Remus. It was on the Palatine Hill that Romulus subsequently founded the city of Rome in 753BCE.

The legend claims that there were not enough women in Rome so Romulus abducted women from a neighbouring tribe, called the Sabine, and brought them to Rome – an act which became known as the 'Rape of the Sabine Women'. Romulus then chose one hundred fathers (*patres*) to form a ruling council. This established the Senate, and the men were known as 'Patricians'. As the legends became intertwined, Romulus came to be associated as a direct descendant of Aeneas of Troy.

Brutus, the supposed founder of Britain, was born in Italy, but was said to be of Trojan royal descent. For King Edward to believe that he was descended from Brutus also implied that he believed he was descended from the Greek god Zeus. The legend claims that one day Brutus was playing with some of his friends when he accidentally shot and killed his father with an arrow. As a result, he was exiled from Italy. Being forced to leave his homeland, Brutus initially stayed relatively close to home and sailed to the islands of Corsica and Sardinia in the Tyrrhenian Sea. He subsequently voyaged to the lands of the Gauls and the legend states that he built the city of Turones, believed to be the modern-day city of Tours in France. At a later stage, he decided to leave and make his way to a little-known island to the north-west of the world. There, he staked his claim and named the island Britannia, after himself. The legend claims that Brutus founded *Troia Nova*, or New Troy, which later became *Trinovantum*.

Trinovantum was the chief city of King Lud, or Lludd, from the Welsh Mabinogion. His father was Beli, or Beli Mawr. Some have associated Beli with the Celtic god Belinus. Lud had two or three brothers, depending on which saga is being referenced. Cassivellaunus (Caswallawn), Nenius (Nyniaw), and also included in the Mabinogion, Llefelys. Lud renamed Trinovantum *Caer Lud*, after himself. Nenius objected to the change claiming that this turned them away from their Trojan ancestry, but his protestations were overruled. Shortly after this King Lud died and was superseded by his brother, Cassivellaunus.

Cassivellaunus was king during the invasion of Britain by Julius Caesar. He is largely celebrated as having defeated Caesar in 55BCE and for making the necessary preparations for halting the advance of the second invasion in 54BCE. Nenius clashed with Caesar directly and it is said that during this battle Caesar lost his famed sword, *crocera mors*, meaning 'Yellow Death'. The sword was reputedly forged by Vulcan, the smith of the gods, and originally belonged to the god Mars. It was bestowed to the Trojan prince Aeneas by his mother. Allegedly, this happened on the site of the future city of Rome, and Aeneas heard the words, "With this, conquer" as it descended from heaven.

During the battle between Caesar and Nenius, it is said that Caesar hit Nenius so hard that the *crocea mors* got stuck in his shield and had to be abandoned. Nenius was severely wounded, yet he managed to survive for another 15 days. When he eventually died, he was buried along with the *crocea mors*. Eventually a truce was declared between Cassivellaunus and Caesar. Some have claimed this was a result of the mutual recognition of the others' Trojan descent. Over time, *Caer Lud* was corrupted into *Caer Llundain* and later known by the Romans as *Londonium* – the city of London.

In the city centre of London, located at 111 Cannon Street, there is an ancient stone said to be the Brutus Stone. It is more commonly known as the London Stone and is believed by some to be part of an altar that Brutus built and dedicated to the Goddess Diana. It is said that it was she who safely guided him to the isle of Britain. Allegedly, it is from this stone that the Romans measured all distances in Britain.

For a considerable period, the London Stone was seen as a place where agreements were made and where oaths were sworn. There are also claims that it was the stone from which King Arthur pulled the sword Excalibur. This would have been of particular interest to Edward. The London Stone was even regarded by the poet William Blake as a relic from the ruins of a Utopian Atlantis. There is an ancient proverb that suggests that at one time the London (Brutus) Stone had been regarded as a Palladium of London, if not all of England. The proverb stated, *"So long as the stone of Brutus is safe, so long shall London flourish."*

Figure 6: The London Stone
© John Michaels / Alamy Stock Photo

There is another Brutus Stone in in town of Totnes in Devon, south-west England. This is reputed to mark the place where Brutus first stepped off his ship and onto the British mainland. The foregoing tends to suggest that there was a strong association between the ideas of the founding of Britain and a relationship to stones.

When Brutus landed in Britain, Geoffrey of Monmouth recounts that he divided the land of Britannia into three distinct states. He gave one to each of his three sons – Locrin, Kamber and Albanact. To his eldest son, Locrin, he gave the area that is now largely England

and called it Loegria. Interestingly, in some of the early writings Loegria is the name of King Arthur's realm. To Kamber, Brutus gave the lands now known as Wales, but then called Kambria, or in its Latinised form Cambria, which is Cymru in the modern Welsh tongue. To Albanact, he gave Alba, that is roughly equivalent to modern-day Scotland.

Figure 7: The Brutus Stone
© Westmacott / Alamy Stock Photo

Edward believed he was descended from the eldest son of Brutus, whereas the Scots were descended from his youngest son. However, the Celts of western Britain saw Edward as nothing more than a foreign king who had no real ancestry in Britain before the Norman invasion of 1066. They believed that it was the Celts who were the legitimate heirs from Brutus, and not Edward. If the legends of Brutus and Arthur had even a hint of truth, Edward and his lineage was almost certainly not of legitimate descendant from either. The descendants from the kings of the other old kingdoms of Britain knew this well. Edward did not like this in any way.

The Conquest of Wales

During the 1240s and 1250s there had been conflict between the Welsh and English over who controlled what, and where the boundaries should be drawn between the two countries. Edward's father, King Henry III, had signed the Treaty of Woodstock in 1247 with Llywelyn ap Gruffydd, Prince of Gwynedd. He was also known as Llywelyn the Last for being the last crowned monarch of the Kingdom of Wales. The terms of the treaty stipulated that north Wales would be free from English influence. In 1256 Henry III had granted Edward the lands known as Y Berfeddwald and Gwynedd Is Conwy in the northern parts of Wales. The nobles of this area resented being under English rule and looked to gain support from Llywelyn, who had virtual control in the area.

In November 1256 Llywelyn raised an army and crossed into Edward's designated territory, and by December he controlled most of Gwynedd Is Conwy. Deciding not to stop there, Llywelyn turned south and started to defeat the other Welsh lords until he also had control over Powes and Cardigan. With the exception of the southern coast of Wales, Llywelyn had become the virtual Overlord of the country. This was achieved with the aid of Edward's uncle, Simon de Montfort, who had defeated King Henry III and Prince Edward at the Battle of Lewis in 1264, instigating civil war. After the battle, Henry and Edward were put under house arrest and Llywelyn offered de Montfort 30,000 merks to recognise him as the ruler of Wales and to ensure permanent peace. This was agreed at the Treaty of Pipton in 1265. A marriage was arranged between the Welsh prince and de Montfort's daughter, Eleanor. Prince Edward escaped imprisonment and was enraged by the marriage proposal. Eleanor was a princess of the House of Plantagenet and from the same stock as himself. He paid pirates to intercept the ship carrying her from France to Wales and held her prisoner at Windsor Castle. In her absence Llywelyn married Eleanor by proxy.

Edward raised an army that defeated and killed de Montfort. After the battle, Llywelyn renegotiated with Henry and was recognised as the Prince of Wales following the Treaty of Montgomery in 1267. He was also to pay Henry 25,000 merks in annual 3,000 merk instalments, and if he so desired, he could, for a mere 5,000 merks extra, gain control of Deheubarth. He was allowed to keep all of the lands that he had conquered and this made Llywelyn very unpopular with the other rulers of southern Wales. Edward saw this as Llywelyn taking advantage of his father's perceived weakness due to the civil war. This was something he would not forget when he became king of England.

During his time spent in Acre Edward had made friends with nobles from the Welsh Marches. They would become his loyal followers in the ensuing wars that were on the horizon with Llywelyn in Wales. With the death of Henry III in 1272 the rule of England fell to three men until Edward returned to England from his crusade in the Holy Land. Two of these men sought the return of the lands lost to Llywelyn, who by now had also stopped paying his annual instalments to the English crown, and whose theft of lands from Edward in 1256 was still a matter for contention. War looked imminent.

Llywelyn's brother, Dafydd, made an attempt on the life of his brother, but when this failed, he fled into England to seek refuge from Edward, who agreed, and encouraged Dafydd to conduct border raids against Llywelyn. Edward was crowned in 1274 and Llywelyn was ordered to pay homage to him at Chester. Llywelyn flatly refused, and still claimed the rights of his lands to be free from English rule or laws.

By 1276 Edward had had enough of Llywelyn and declared him a rebel. In 1277 he raised a large army to defeat the Welsh prince once and for all. With Anglesey and northern Gwynedd quickly falling under Edward's rule, Llywelyn soon realised that he had perhaps pushed Edward too far and looked to negotiate a truce. This resulted in the Treaty of Aberconwy and it restricted Llywelyn's authority to just Gwynedd Uwch Conwy. His brother Dafydd gained control of Gwynedd Is Conwy, with a provision that if Llywelyn died then Dafydd would gain a share of his territories. Llywelyn was also forced to pay homage to Edward and recognise him as his own king. Once this was done Edward allowed Llywelyn and Eleanor to officially marry at Worcester Cathedral.

Peace reigned for a time, but Llywelyn had a dispute with Gruffydd ap Gwenwynwyn who had lands given to him by Edward. Llywelyn wanted to settle the dispute by Welsh law, whereas Gruffydd wanted it settled by English law. Obviously, Edward chose the settlement to be by English law, which did nothing to please the other Welsh nobles who had been relatively quiet up till then. Some of those who had supported Edward in 1277 were now turning their back on him and his English ways. In 1282 the once loyal Dafydd attacked the English castle at Hawarden before subsequently attacking Rhuddlan Castle. His actions inspired a Welsh rebellion, and many English strongholds were attacked and captured.

Whilst having nothing to do with his brother's revolt, Llywelyn felt obliged to support him even though he had once tried to assassinate him. The main problem was that Dafydd had planned his revolt in secret with the other lords, which left him little or no time to make adequate preparations for an all-out war. Edward re-enacted the same successful campaign as in 1277, which led to him recapturing Gwynedd Is Conwy and Anglesey. The Archbishop of Canterbury tried to negotiate peace between Llywelyn and Edward, but he was not successful. The terms on offer proposed that Llywelyn should surrender all his Welsh lands in return for land in England. Additionally, his brother, Dafydd, was to go on a crusade and not to return until Edward gave him permission.

The response was the Welsh equivalent of the Scottish Declaration of Arbroath in later years, with Llywelyn refusing to abandon his people, claiming that his ancestors had protected them since the times of Kamber, son of Brutus. Edward was furious that Llywelyn was making an ancestral claim that linked him as a descendent of Brutus of Troy. In Edward's view of the family tree it was *he* who was the legitimate ruler of *all* Britain, having been descended from Locrin, the eldest son of Brutus.

Llywelyn went south to try to raise support for another war but was killed at Builth Wells under mysterious circumstances. He had left his army to confer with some local chieftains and whilst doing so, his phalanx of spearmen was hailed upon by arrows and then charged by English horsemen. It has been suggested that it was a well-conceived plan to decimate his army when he thought he was protected. When Llywelyn saw what was happening to his army he rushed back to assist but was killed in action. His head was severed from his body and sent to King Edward. Edward decided to make a mockery of an old prophecy attributed to Merlin, the sage of King Arthur, which Llywelyn had often used to taunt him. The prophecy claimed that a Welsh king would be crowned in London with the diadem of Brutus of Troy. When Edward received the head of the Welsh leader, he ordered it to be crowned with ivy and paraded through the streets before being set on a pike over the Tower of London. No one was going to make claims of descent that might supersede those of Edward and expect to get off lightly.

With the death of Llywelyn the rest of the Welsh rebels returned home. Dafydd acquired Llywelyn's lands and tried to resist the English for a few more months. He was captured in June 1283 along with his family. His punishment was to be paraded before Edward at Shrewsbury, where Parliament subsequently sentenced him to death. He was dragged through the streets, then hanged, drawn and quartered as a traitor. His head was put alongside that of his brother over the Tower of London.

Edward decided it best to offer no mercy to the rebellious state. He went and stripped Gwynedd Is Conwy of all its relics and regalia, thus ending a dynasty reaching back hundreds of years. Llywelyn's much sought-after Iron Crown, believed to have belonged to King Arthur, was placed in the shrine of St Edward the Confessor at Westminster Abbey, whilst the seals of Llywelyn, Dafydd, and Eleanor were melted down to make a chalice. Edward also took Llywelyn's fragment of the cross of Christ's crucifixion, known as the Cross of Neith ('*croysseneyht*' in Welsh), and placed it alongside King Arthur's crown. The Kingdom of Wales had been subdued and was now a Principality of England. Later, in the summer of 1284, Edward held a 'round table' tournament at Nevin to commemorate his victory, which helped to silence any critics to his claims of being descended from King Arthur and Brutus of Troy.

In 1284 Wales was legally put under the English crown and split into Shires of England. Four weeks after the proclamation of the Statute of Wales, Edward's wife, Queen Eleanor, gave birth to a son at Caernavon. Following the death of his older brother the infant soon became the heir to the throne. King Edward named the child after himself and sixteen years later he would receive the title 'Prince of Wales', an honour that has been given to the first male heir of all subsequent English and then British monarchs up to the present day.

The war against Wales cost Edward about £150,000, much more than his three-year campaign in the Holy Land. The war resulted in Edward borrowing a great deal of money and needing loans from his subjects in lieu of future taxes. Things had become so bad that the money that had been raised by the churches for a future crusade to the Holy Land was seized. The taxes Edward introduced in 1283 had only managed to raise about £42,000. By the end of the campaign he had managed to repay all of his debts, but Edward realised just how costly and time consuming a home campaign could be. However, he was now able to field a larger army than ever before, which included the Welsh archers who would play a prominent part of his military strategies of the future. He could now mobilise at any time 15,000 soldiers and no one could stand in his way. To ensure that his victory in Wales would endure, he spent about £80,000 on fortifying the country with castles and forts, which diverted funds and troops away from his purse. Without money it was unlikely that he would be able to realise his dream of returning to the Holy Land on another crusade.

The Mongol Crusade

Edward was well aware of the costs involved in fighting on various fronts. Having recently subdued the Kingdom of Wales he knew that even the extra revenue now being generated would not cover all of the costs required to mount a new crusade to the Holy Land.

Edward had left Outremer in 1274 to return to England as king, but also because of the injury to his arm. It had always been his intention to return on another crusade and finish the job that his fellow monarchs and soldiers had started nearly 200 years previously. The truce that Edward had negotiated for Acre with the Muslims opened the doors for an alliance to form with another army who shared in the desire to see an end to the Muslim states in the Middle East. The Mongols, as they were known, saw a real opportunity to join with the Christians for one final push towards Jerusalem. They could not raise an army that would guarantee a Muslim defeat, but they could create a joint campaign against the Muslims that would stretch their resources. The intention was to create a situation whereby the Muslims would be forced to fight on two fronts, to the north and east they would be attacked by the Mongols and to the south and west they would encounter the crusading Christian force. Divide and conquer.

In 1287, just three years after Edward had subdued the Welsh, and one year after Alexander III, King of Scots, had died, the Mongols sent emissaries to most European kings. They proposed the idea of a joint campaign against the Muslims to take back the city of Jerusalem. Edward knew how expensive it would be to finance this new crusade, but the motivation was most certainly there, and the money could surely be found from somewhere. The Mongol emissaries returned home in 1288 with positive responses from Pope Nicholas IV, King Philip IV of France and also King Edward I of England. They returned in 1289 seeking a date for when this new campaign could begin. The Mongols were willing to march as soon as the Christian crusaders landed at Acre. Their emissaries were finalising the date in Rome during July to September 1289, in Paris during November to December 1289, and in London during January 1290.

All but Edward seemed enthusiastic. The reality of the situation in his homeland had hit him hard. There was a growing problem to his northern frontier with Scotland. He had tried hard to secure the marriage between his son and Margaret, Maid of Norway, who was now the legitimate heir to the throne of Scotland. The answer to Edward's problem of how he would finance the new crusade could be resolved relatively easily. Soon his son would be married to the Queen of Scots and therefore he could send supplies, money and troops to aid the

English war effort. The problem now was that Margaret was just six years old and was still resident in Norway. Edward knew only too well how easy it was for children to die at a young age, for he had already lost several of his sons and daughters. The Prince of Wales, Edward of Caernavon, was still very young himself and if he were to die then all would be lost. Everything was hanging in the balance for Edward.

Edward could not give a clear commitment to the Mongols. The past troubles with Wales could easily flare up again without proper observance and his concern was growing over what was happening with Scotland. He feared what might happen throughout Britain if he went on a crusade abroad. If a rebellion were to occur in Wales, or his son's marriage did not go ahead for whatever reason, then he could not simply return to England from the Holy Land to resolve the issues, or if opportunists were to make a play for his throne. He needed to ensure that all possibility of unrest was crushed before he could commit himself and his army to a crusade thousands of miles away.

The Year of Change

It can only be imagined what went through Edward's mind as he persuaded himself that the 'lesser' kingdoms of Wales and Scotland were preventing him from carrying out 'God's work' in the Holy Land. In that same year disaster struck and Edward had to face perhaps the toughest mental battle of his life. The death of the Maid of Norway meant that he would not get to control the Scots army and could therefore not support the Mongols in their attack on Outremer. The Mongol plan was to do to the Muslims what Edward was facing himself in his homeland of Britain. To the west he had to heavily garrison the many English castles in Wales to protect against the risk of an uprising. To the south there were many problems with the French who wanted control of his lands in Gascony. To the north there were increasing problems with Scotland.

In 1290, the same year that the young Queen Margaret died, Edward suffered the biggest loss of his life when his much-loved wife and Queen, Eleanor of Castile, died in his arms on 28th November 1290. He questioned if this was God's way of punishing him for not supporting the new crusade. Her death hit Edward very hard, and it is from around that date that he started to noticeably change as a man and a ruler. Shortly after her death Edward wrote in a letter, "My harp is turned to mourning, in life I loved her dearly, nor can I cease to love her in death."

Queen Eleanor died at Harby, near Lincoln, and was to be interred at Westminster Abbey. Wherever the funeral cortege stopped on route with her body a magnificent stone cross was built in her honour. This happened at Lincoln, Grantham, Stamford, Geddington, Hardingstone (outside Northampton), Stony Stratford, Woburn, Dunstable, St Albans, Waltham, and in Westcheap (now known as Cheapside). The final cross was erected in the hamlet of Charing, close to Westminster, and this is the origin of the place name Charing Cross in London. Charing Cross is recognised as the geographic centre of London where all distances to the city started their measure, much like some of the legends attached to the London Stone. Today, only three of the original Eleanor crosses are still intact in their original locations; Geddington, Hardingstone and Waltham. This act of cross building proved how much Edward must have missed his wife. As was the tradition of the day, her organs were given a separate burial. Her bowels were interred beneath the Lady Chapel of Lincoln Cathedral, and her heart was buried in the Blackfriars Church at Bridewell, with a golden angel made by Edward's master goldsmith, Adam of Shoreditch, to mark the site. Her body was buried at Westminster Abbey.

The calming influence on Edward had now gone and it could be argued that this was what pushed him over the edge in his attitudes towards Scotland. Things were to go from bad to worse. Of his four sons, three had died and at the time of Eleanor's death he was left with just one male heir to the throne. That heir was just six years old. Edward was aged fifty-one and an old man by the standards of the day. If his only remaining son were to die, and there was every chance that he could, then who would claim his throne?

The following year, in 1291, his mother, who had played a big part of his life, also died. To compound his troubles, Acre, the last Christian stronghold in the Holy Land was over-run by Muslims. Some

Christians had attacked a Muslim merchant caravan and in retaliation the Muslims attacked Christian pilgrims leaving Acre and demanded compensation. With no response from the Christians about the compensation, the Muslims set siege to Acre, declaring *jihad*, or Holy War, to destroy the last of the Christian strongholds in the Middle East. Acre soon fell. The Muslims now had full control of Outremer and every Christian life that had been lost fighting to reclaim the Holy Land for Christianity was lost in vain. The fall of Acre would initiate the downfall of military units such as the Knights Templar, who had to relocate to Cyprus and decide how to proceed.

As a consequence, Edward had just lost his chance to return to Outremer on another crusade and hence fulfil his vow to ensure a place in heaven for him and his now-dead wife, Eleanor. With all of these events happening within a relatively short space of time, it is quite understandable that he might have instead wanted to turn his crusading ambitions onto his homeland neighbours. The Albigensian crusade of recent years had shown that Christian could legitimately attack Christian with the full support of the Church of Rome in order to oust heretics. If Edward could unify Britain then he would be seen as expanding the domain of the Church. That might be viewed by God as being equally as worthy as a crusade to recapture the Holy Land.

It could be argued – so Edward thought – that Jerusalem and the Holy Land had been lost to Christendom partly because he, Edward, had been unable to send troops. Was he responsible for the fall of Acre in May 1291 for not giving his support? Did he see it as God punishing him with the death of his wife, that of his mother, and that of his soon-to-be daughter-in-law Margaret, Maid of Norway? All of this must have taken a heavy toll on the mindset of Edward. He would take his anger out on those closest to him.

Chapter 4
The Wars of Scottish Independence

The Theft of the Stone

Following the Battle of Dunbar on 27th April 1296, King Edward I of England had pursued John Balliol, King of Scots, further north into Scotland. The two finally met again at Montrose. Edward took the opportunity for one final act of humiliation. He made Balliol surrender the crown and Kingdom of Scotland. Balliol unceremoniously had the royal arms ripped from his jacket by Edward and was subsequently nicknamed 'Toom Tabard' (Empty Coat) by his peers. This effectively ended the reign of John Balliol. He was imprisoned in the Tower of London for his defiance, where he remained until his release into exile in France in 1299.

Edward must have heard stories about the coronation ceremonies of the Scots kings and the importance of the king-making Stone. He knew that if he could obtain the Stone for himself then he would be dealing a harsh blow to the morale of the Scots, who now found themselves without a king. If Edward came to be in possession of their king-making Stone then perhaps the Scots would more readily welcome him as their Overlord and ruler.

On his return south from Montrose, Edward had to pass via Dundee and Perth. It was near Perth, at Scone, where the king-making Stone was kept and where the inauguration ceremonies had taken place since the time of King Kenneth McAlpin in 843. Sometime between 5th and 8th August 1296 Edward sent a force to take the Stone from Scone. What they took was to spend nearly 700 years at Westminster Abbey.

The site of Westminster Abbey was originally known as Thorn Ey (Thorn Island). King Edward the Confessor had selected Westminster to be the place of his burial and built a stone abbey there between 1045 and 1050. It was consecrated on 28th December 1065, which was just a week before his death and subsequent burial. The first time that Westminster was used for a coronation was when Harold Godwinson was crowned King Harold II on 6th January 1066, shortly before the Norman invasion. Westminster also became the burial site of the Norman kings. However, it was not until the coronation of King Henry III on 17th May 1220 that the tradition of Westminster Abbey as the site of English coronations became established.

For many years the Stone had been in the keeping of the Dean of Westminster Abbey, and St Edward's Chair, built to house the Stone, was placed next to the shrine of St Edward the Confessor, along with the crown and sceptre of Scotland. It was here that Edward placed the relics that he had amassed from his conquests of the various kingdoms of Britain, such as the Iron Crown of King Arthur from the Kingdom of Wales and now the Scots king-making Stone. He was also amassing a collection of pieces of the true cross from the crucifixion of Christ. He placed the Holy Rood, or Black Rood of Scotland, that Queen Margaret is supposed to have brought with her when she fled to Scotland in 1068, alongside the Cross of Neith, or *croysseneyht*, that he stole from Wales after the death of Prince Llywelyn. Edward was trying to collect all of the artefacts that conferred some kind of sovereignty, and hence authority, over the people of the various kingdoms of Britain.

With the Stone now on English soil, the battles between Scotland and England continued to rage. The Scots did not accept Edward as their Overlord and fought hard for the recognition of their independence by the Church of Rome. Balliol had been deposed from the throne of Scotland. It remained vacant for several years until Robert the Bruce managed to unite the warring factions of the Scots nobles to fight for a common cause – Scotland.

Robert the Bruce

The Bruce family, who had lost their claim to the throne against John Balliol, had subsequently had one of their sons crowned as King of Scots at Scone in 1306, albeit not on the ancient Scots king-making Stone. King Robert the Bruce was working hard throughout Scotland to try to coerce the warring clans to make a united stand against the English presence in the country.

Bruce was born on 11th July 1274 and was from a Scots-Norman lineage. His father's ancestry could be traced back to Brieux in Normandy, whilst his mother came from Scots-Gaelic descent. He was the great-great-great-great grandson of King David I on his father's side. He was the eldest son of the 6th Lord of Annandale, Robert de Bruce, who died in 1304, and Marjorie, Countess of Carrick, who died in 1292. Legend has it that his mother kept his father a prisoner until he agreed to marry her. Whether this is true or not, their union did bestow on their son a Scots-Gaelic linage which helped to further his claim to the throne.

It was at Turnberry Castle in Carrick, now in modern-day Ayrshire, that Robert was thought to have been born. There are differing accounts suggesting that his birth might have been at Lochmaben in Dumfriesshire. There is even a claim that he was born in Writtle in England, and whilst this might seem preposterous at first, the Bruce family were of Norman descent and are known to have held many lands throughout England. Through his mother, Robert the Bruce acquired the Earldom of Carrick.

It was not until his later years that Bruce decided to make a stand against England and fight for the freedom of Scotland. Before then it has been suggested that he sided with the English to fight against his opponent, John Balliol, at the start of the Wars of Independence. There is little known about his youth other than that he was fluent in Gaelic, French (Norman) and Latin. He was an educated man and was well versed in military tactics and political matters. He married Isabella of Mar in 1295 when still very young. She died shortly after giving birth to their first child, Marjorie Bruce, in 1296.

When Robert was 18 years old he saw his Grandfather, the 5th Lord of Annandale, make a failed attempt at gaining the crown of Scotland. King Edward I had instead picked John Balliol to be the new King of Scots in 1292. Following this humiliating defeat, his grandfather resigned his title as the Lord of Annandale and passed it to his son, who in turn resigned his title as the Earl of Carrick to his son, Robert the Bruce. There was obviously great resentment from the Bruce family about the decision of Edward in favour of John Balliol. When Balliol subsequently turned on the English king in 1296, the

Bruce family were willingly prepared to assist the English in deposing him from the crown.

Contrary to popular belief, the Bruce family and King Edward had a good relationship for many years. The future King of Scots was allowed to visit Ireland for a year and a half and had all his debts to the English Exchequer annulled. It is not certain what the nature of his visit entailed, but he left for Ireland in 1294 and so his return would have been either in late 1295 or early 1296, just before Edward marched into Berwick-upon-Tweed to begin his overthrowing of Balliol. It is possible that Bruce was aware of the intentions of the English king to attack Scotland. Edward retaliated when he was provoked by Balliol after he attacked Carlisle earlier in the year. This could have been viewed by the Bruce family as their chance at ascending the throne of Scotland.

When Edward attacked Scotland in April 1296, the Bruce family swore allegiance to him after he had pursued Balliol deeper into the country, before defeating him at Montrose in August of the same year. It is widely believed that the Bruce family fought for Edward during this campaign, but if so, any oath of allegiance was broken by Robert the Bruce in 1297. Edward sent Bruce orders to support the 7th Earl of Surrey in his plight against the Scots. Instead, Bruce attacked and destroyed the lands of the supporters of Edward. His revolt did not last for very long and in July 1297 Bruce was forced to sign a peace treaty, known as the Capitulation of Irvine. This was effectively a treaty designed to assist the English in their war efforts against the French and meant that the Scots would not be made to fight the French unless they willingly volunteered. In return for accepting the terms, the Lords and Barons of Scotland again swore allegiance to King Edward. They were all pardoned for their past actions.

It seems that when Bruce swore an allegiance it could be taken 'with a pinch of salt'. After the Battle of Stirling Bridge, on 11th September 1297, which the Scots won, Bruce changed sides yet again and decided to fight alongside William Wallace and his supporters. They had been fighting to reinstate Balliol as the monarch. As a result, Bruce's lands of Annandale were destroyed by Edward and in retaliation Bruce attacked the English castle at Ayr. When the English marched through Scotland and faced the Scots army at the Battle of Falkirk on 22nd July 1298, which the Scots lost, Bruce's lands of Annandale and Carrick were seized and given over to nobles who were more loyal to King Edward. However, for some reason Bruce's father decided to remain loyal to Edward and so the lands were only held on a temporary basis, just in case the indecisive Bruce decided to once again fight for the English. This is a rather peculiar scenario. Why would Edward willingly leave the door open for Robert the Bruce to come back through, when it was just as possible that he would stand firm against him? Edward obviously held Bruce in high regard and wanted him on his side.

After the Battle of Falkirk, Robert the Bruce and John Comyn were installed as the Guardians of Scotland following the resignation of William Wallace earlier in the year. However, this was not a good partnership as the two seemed to have different loyalties and each had his own agenda. Bruce wanted the throne that John Balliol had abdicated, albeit under intense pressure from Edward, and Comyn wanted either Balliol reinstated as king, or himself to be seated on the throne.

It was decided that William, Bishop of St Andrews, would be installed as a third Guardian of Scotland to act as a middleman between Bruce and Comyn. Bruce resigned as a Guardian in 1299 and was replaced by Sir Gilbert de Umfraville, Earl of Angus. However, the position obviously had certain drawbacks, as all three resigned in 1301 and were replaced by Sir John de Soules, who was pro-Balliol and active in trying to get him back on the throne.

In 1301 Edward tried to launch another campaign into Scotland, but this achieved very little as the Scots were not keen to have a full-frontal assault in case of another defeat like at Falkirk. The Scots had found relative success with the 'hit and run' tactical approach of launching smaller scale skirmishes into English territory when they were most vulnerable.

In January 1302 a nine-month truce was agreed between the two sides. This resulted in Bruce and various other Scottish nobles changing sides yet again and returning to the fold of Edward's camp. It is possible that each of these nobles were anti-Balliol, who had been released from prison and was rumoured to be making a return to Scotland to try to reclaim his throne. Robert the Bruce would have seen little choice but to make a stand against his Scots enemy and rival to the throne. Perhaps he saw fighting alongside Edward as his only option in the hope of one day winning the title for himself.

That same year Robert the Bruce remarried. This time he took Elizabeth de Burgh to be his wife. She was the daughter of Richard de Burgh, the 2nd Earl of Ulster. They went on to have four children. David, John (who died at a young age), Matilda, and Margaret. Bruce's new father-in-law was a close friend and supporter of King Edward. It is possible that Bruce had to swear allegiance to Edward to convince his father-in-law that he was worthy to have his daughter's hand in marriage.

The Rise and Fall of William Wallace

King Edward decided to invade Scotland once again in 1303 and this time his attack was to be much more successful. He reached Aberdeen by August and then marched his army through Moray and then back down south to Dunfermline. It must have been a humiliating time for the Scots nobles who found themselves yet again having to submit to Edward. John Comyn negotiated the terms of surrender for Scotland. The only Scottish noble still determined to fight against the English was Sir William Wallace.

In all fairness, Comyn negotiated a good deal for Scotland under his terms of surrender. He managed to make Edward agree that all laws and liberties would be reverted back to as they were during the reign of King Alexander III. Essentially, this would mean that the Scots nobles would have all of the rights and most of the privileges that they possessed before 1286. If any changes were to be made to these rights by Edward, then he would have to consult the Scottish nobles for their advice and consent. Why would Edward, 'Hammer of the Scots', agree to terms that essentially meant that he had little power in Scotland without agreement from the Scots? They had been defeated and suppressed, so why not humiliate the country even further?

Edward was, first and foremost, an excellent military tactician. His conflict with France was intensifying and he was also well aware of the vast costs involved with fighting on his home soil. He was still financing the heavy fortification of Wales in case of an uprising there, and the last thing he needed was to be simultaneously attacked from the south by the French and from the north by the Scots. The sooner he could quell the uprisings in Britain, which by then had been going on for many years, the sooner he could think about a possible return to the Holy Land. Even though the laws and liberties of Scotland were as they were before the invasion by Edward, it was still very much the English who ruled over Scotland. The government of Scotland was fronted by the Earl of Richmond who was King Edward's nephew. The only real problem for Edward was how to contend with Wallace and his followers. They had control of Stirling Castle, which was virtually the only stronghold under their control by this time. Edward reasoned, that with the Scottish nobles pacified, his troubles north of the border should be easily manageable and the common folk would soon follow suit. Wallace made sure that this would never happen.

The English laid siege to Stirling Castle in April 1304 and the Scots held out until William Oliphant and 30 others surrendered on 20th July. There are various reasons why the garrison surrendered, but what is interesting to highlight is that a very small number of brave souls stood firm against the might of the English invaders for several months, whilst the rest of the common folk in Scotland had watched in awe at their fantastic effort. Edward saw the admiration in the eyes of the people and decided not to excessively punish the rebels for fear of an uprising by the populace. In retaliation for their blatant act of defiance, Edward decided to execute only one person and imprison their leader, William Oliphant, in the Tower of London. The rest were all pardoned.

Legend has it that Robert the Bruce and William Lamberton swore an oath to each other based on what they had witnessed at Stirling Castle in 1304. It is said that they made an alliance to fight against the English, no matter what, even though they had both previously submitted to Edward. They made the decision to bide their time and wait for an opportune moment to strike back against the oppressive English forces, and if one of them should break the oath then he would have to pay the other £10,000. It was to be another ten years before they would have to fulfil this oath, and only then because the English King Edward II forced them into action at Bannockburn.

Disaster was to strike on 5th August 1305. William Wallace was betrayed by some of the Scottish nobles and with the help of a monetary reward he was captured by John de Menteith, a Scottish knight loyal to Edward. It took seventeen days for Wallace to be frog-marched to London. He was tried at Westminster Hall for treason, an offence for which he was forbidden to plead, and which he proposed was impossible to convict. He had never sworn any allegiance to the English crown and therefore a charge of treason was absurd. He was also charged with murder and robbery.

Wallace was found guilty on 23rd August 1305 and was sentenced to death. He was stripped naked and dragged by a horse through the city of London for four miles. He was taken past the Tower of London and then to Aldgate where his ordeal would reach its conclusion at the gallows 'by the elms' at Smithfield. Here he was hanged by the neck until near death. Then his genitals were cut off. This was followed by his entrails being torn out from his abdomen, whilst he was still conscious, and burned before his dying eyes. Finally, and almost mercifully after what he had endured, he was beheaded, and his body quartered. His head was placed on a pike at the top of London Bridge and his body quarters were separated and sent to the chief cities of the north – Newcastle, Berwick, Stirling and Perth – as a reminder and to dissuade any would-be sympathisers.

The Play for the Throne

The prospects and outlook for Scotland were not looking so good. In September 1305 King Edward ordered Robert the Bruce to place his Kildrummy Castle "in the keeping of such a man as he himself will be willing to answer for." This is perhaps an arrogant statement for the English king to make, but with the surrender of Scotland and the recapture of Stirling Castle, surpassed only by the execution of William Wallace, Edward was now confident that another uprising from the Scots would be virtual suicide for the country. He was indicating to Robert the Bruce that he should hand his castle over into the keeping of someone more loyal or risk losing it. Simply put, Edward was letting Bruce know that he was no longer trusted.

This posed a dilemma for Bruce. Should he defend the titles that he held throughout England and Scotland by conceding to the requirements of Edward's Overlordship, or should he pursue his ambitions of becoming King of Scots and run the risk of starting another war with England? This time the stakes were much higher. If he lost that war then he would lose everything, almost certainly including his own life. Making the decision must have played heavily on his mind. He knew, or at least suspected, that Edward did not trust him. He also knew that most of the nobles of Scotland, including the influential John Comyn, did not trust him either.

John 'the Red' Comyn, Lord of Badenoch, enjoyed good relations on both sides of the border. He was called 'the Red' to distinguish him from his father of the same name, John 'the Black' Comyn. He was highly regarded among the nobility of Scotland, and in this sense, he was more powerful than Bruce as he could leverage greater persuasion to achieve desired results. As the nephew of John Balliol he also had quite a strong claim to the throne of Scotland, and for this reason Bruce regarded him as a major obstacle to his ambitions of becoming king.

On the 10th February 1306 Bruce called a truce and invited Comyn to meet with him at Greyfriars Church in Dumfries. Legend has it that Bruce quarrelled with Comyn over who should become the next King of Scots, and he proposed that they should rise together against the English. Comyn obviously had other ideas, and perhaps felt that a war against Edward would not be particularly beneficial in promoting his own cause. An argument broke out between the two and ended with Bruce stabbing Comyn inside the church. Bruce then fled, telling his companions, Roger de Kirkpatrick, and John Lindsay, that he thought he had killed Comyn, to which his aide, Kirkpatrick, replied, "*I mac sikker!*" meaning "I'll make sure!" Both Kirkpatrick and Lindsay rushed into the church and finished off Comyn once and for all.

It was a heinous crime. However, now Bruce's strongest opposition to the throne of Scotland had been eliminated. For three nights Bruce and his companions were chased by Comyn's supporters. They were never caught. Bruce, Kirkpatrick and Lindsay were excommunicated by the Church for murdering Comyn inside a House of God. Whilst many regarded this as an act of supreme sacrilege, Robert Wishart, Bishop of Glasgow, and staunch supporter of the Scottish church and crown, took Bruce in his arms and absolved him of all accusations. He urged his followers to rise in support of Bruce.

Wishart was perhaps one of the few Scots patriots who remained loyal to Scotland throughout all the Wars of Independence. He was forced to swear allegiance to King Edward on more than one occasion, but immediately after each pledge he would revert back to fighting for the Scottish cause. After Wishart had absolved Bruce at Glasgow the two men travelled to Scone where they met with the Bishops of St Andrews and Moray, as well as other leading church figures in Scotland. It was as if all of the past few days had been planned in advance in order to pave the way for what Bruce had always wanted – to be king.

With no other contender to the throne, Bruce was crowned King of Scots at Scone on 25th March 1306. There was no king-making Stone present, but this did not seem to have had any bearing on his legitimacy as being rightful king – at least in the eyes of the Scots. His popularity with the common folk throughout the country had been steadily increasing over the years.

As an excommunicated king it meant that his kingdom was also outside the influence of the church. The absolution of Wishart could not over-rule the decision of the Pope in Rome. Scotland was now an excommunicated country populated by presumed heretics. Scotland had to be very careful how it made its next move, for fear of possibly incurring the wrath of the church in a similar manner to what had happened to the now-extinct Cathars of southern France.

Bruce had won the hearts and minds of the population across Scotland. The ailing King Edward looked to his son and heir with a sense of dread. Edward would have preferred a strong son with military prowess like Bruce, but instead he would be succeeded by someone who was the laughing stock of the royal court. There was admiration from Edward towards Bruce. They were enemies on the one hand and equals on the other. He knew how adaptive Bruce could be on the battlefield, lending himself to find an advantage whatever the scenario.

Soon after Bruce's coronation the Scots raised an army that was swiftly defeated at the Battle of Methven on 19th June 1306. Wishart was accused of leading it "like a man of war," and following their defeat he was forced to flee. He was captured by the English at Cupar, where he was put in chains and taken south to be executed. His reprieve from execution came from one of the English clerics and is likely to have had the approval of King Edward. Edward took great pleasure in writing to Pope Clement V to inform him all about the exploits of Wishart and of his subsequent capture and imprisonment. It is possible that he was not executed so that Edward could use him as propaganda to the Pope, to highlight the heretical nature of the Scots to the north of his border.

It could have been seen as fortuitous for the English that at a time when Scotland needed the assistance of Rome more than ever, one of their leading figures, for the affairs of both the crown and the church, was a prisoner. Wishart remained in prison for eight more years until after the Battle of Bannockburn in 1314. He was released in exchange for English prisoners, but by this time he was virtually blind and in poor health. He returned to Scotland and took up his old position as Bishop of Glasgow until his death in November 1316. Wishart was a true Scots patriot and is perhaps the most unsung hero of Scotland of the time.

In August of 1306, after the defeat at Methven, Bruce and his followers managed to escape unharmed from a surprise attack by Alasdair MacDougall, Lord of Lorn, at Dalry in Strathfillan. Bruce decided that prudence was the better option and fled to safety on the islands off the west coast of Scotland. Simultaneously, he sent the rest of his family to Kildrummy Castle in Aberdeenshire. This proved to be a grave mistake, because in January 1307 the English tried to capture the castle.

The resident blacksmith was bribed with gold to start a fire in the corn store. The ensuing panic forced the Bruce family to surrender possession of the castle. Robert's brother, Neil, was beheaded, as were all the other men who were captured. Bruce's two sisters, Isabel and Mary, were imprisoned in cages that were hung in full public view over the walls of Berwick and Roxburgh Castles respectively. His daughter, Marjorie, was sent to live out her life in a convent. His other sister, Christina, was also sent to a convent, whilst her husband, Sir Christopher Seaton, was executed. Robert the Bruce's wife, Margaret, who was opposed to his actions against the English, was placed under house arrest at various different locations in England. Along with Bruce's daughter and sisters, she was exchanged and returned to Bruce after the Battle of Bannockburn in November 1314. Bruce had lost most of his immediate family, who had been either killed or imprisoned. Some may have speculated that perhaps this was some kind of divine retribution for him being an excommunicated king.

Things looked bleak for the King of Scots and he decided to go into hiding. Legend has it that he found himself in a cave wondering how he could gain the upper hand over the English. He had continually seen his army defeated and was despairing about the future of Scotland. It is said that he gained inspiration from watching a spider construct its cobweb. The spider had to try several times in order for the cobweb to take hold, and with perseverance and determination it was able to achieve its aims. Not only that, but the cobweb was stronger than it had ever been. Upon seeing this it is said that King Robert the Bruce set out on his mission with renewed vigour. When and where this took place is constantly debated, with virtually every adequately sized cave in Scotland claiming to be the site of the famous spider episode. Whatever the truth, Bruce decided that first he would quell the Scots nobles who were against him and in support of Edward. Then he would concentrate his efforts on keeping the English out of Scotland.

In February 1307 Bruce and his brothers started a new campaign that was to be a guerrilla war in the Lowlands of Scotland.

He split his followers into two groups. Robert and his brother, Edward, would lead one group, and his other brothers, Alexander and Thomas, would lead the second group. Bruce had made a list of those Scots nobles who had supported the English or who harboured the traitors and ordered that they be captured either dead or alive. If alive, then they were to be quickly tried and subsequently executed. Robert and Edward were successful in their campaign with victories at Glen Trool in April and Loudoun Hill in May. His other brothers were not so successful and were captured in Galloway. They were immediately taken to Carlisle Castle and executed.

The Scottish guerrilla tactics forced Edward to raise an army and march north. This was to be his last campaign against the Scots. Bruce had left his brother, Edward, to continue campaigning in Galloway, whilst he headed north to Inverness-shire to suppress the northern pro-English Scots nobles. He captured Inverlochy and Urquhart Castles, and then went on to raze Inverness and Nairn castles before advancing towards Elgin. However, Elgin was not so easy to defeat, and so to avoid losing momentum he decided instead to push on and attack the various castles and estates in Aberdeenshire that opposed him. As he advanced he left a trail of destruction.

On 7th July 1307 King Edward I died, aged 68, at Burgh-on-Sands near Carlisle. He was preparing to launch his final attack on Scotland. In his dying moments he requested that his body should be boiled and all of the flesh removed from the bones. His son, and future King Edward II of England, was instructed to continue the advance and carry his father's bones before the English army until every Scot had surrendered. His heart was then to be transported to the Holy Land to make the final crusade that he had always wanted to lead. If he was unable to ensure his place in heaven during his life then it would have to be ensured after his death.

Edward's son and successor, King Edward II, was not as similarly motivated in defeating the Scots as his father had been. He was more interested in returning to England than leading his army deeper into Scotland. Fulfilling his father's request to defeat the Scots once and for all wasn't a priority. He decided to turn the English army around and head back to London. This would allow him time to suitably prepare arrangements for his own coronation at Westminster Abbey.

Robert the Bruce must have heard about the death of King Edward I and of his son becoming king. This would have been a major morale boost for Bruce and his followers, whilst at the same time it must have sent shockwaves through the Scottish nobles who were loyal to the English crown. By deciding to return to England, King Edward II allowed Bruce the ideal opportunity to concentrate on strengthening Scotland's army and defences in preparation for any future attack from England. This decision would cost Edward II dearly in years to come.

After successful campaigning in Aberdeenshire, Bruce turned back towards Inverness and advanced to the Black Isle. He continued to take back Scottish castles from the English and their supporters. In May 1308, at the Battle of Barra in Inverurie, Bruce defeated the cousin of John 'the Red' Comyn, whom he had murdered in 1306 at Greyfriars Church. Bruce also decided to take back the few remaining English garrisons at Aberdeen and Buchan Castle. With his fortunes seemingly having changed for the better, Bruce returned to the western parts of Scotland to suppress the supporters of Comyn. This occurred at the battle of the Pass of Brander. He then captured Dunstaffnage Castle, which was the last stronghold of the Comyn family. Somehow, Bruce managed to find time to hold a Parliament at St Andrews in March 1309. By the summer of that year, he controlled everything north of the River Tay. By 1314 every English controlled castle had fallen one-by-one to Bruce's army. There was only one obstacle that stood between the Scots and victory. That was the strategic stronghold of Stirling Castle.

The Battle of Bannockburn

Both Edward I, who had died in 1307, and his son and successor, King Edward II, had expended a great deal of manpower, money and effort in first defeating, then securing, a hold on Stirling Castle. Their primary reason for doing so was because the castle defended and oversaw the gateway joining the Scottish southern lowlands and the northern highlands. Whoever controlled the castle on the rock at Stirling could control travel and passage through Scotland. The modern

A9 road follows almost exactly the path of the ancient trading route through the highlands. Over the centuries the land has been extensively cultivated. It was due to the marshy bog-land in the area that the passage below Stirling Castle was the only viable option for travel between south and north.

Laying siege to the castle was left to Robert the Bruce's brother, Edward. King Robert was busy attacking the north of England. It was a deficiency of provisions and supplies that obliged Sir Philip Mowbray, the English governor of Stirling Castle, to agree to surrender the castle back to the Scots on 24th June 1314 – the feast day of St John the Baptist and the Summer Solstice. The surrender would be peaceful unless Edward II would send military support to his aid by that date. The terms of the surrender stated that after 24th June Mowbray and his followers were guaranteed a safe passage through Scotland and back into England. Edward II and his nobles decided that the surrender of Stirling Castle was not an option. The decision was made to raise an army and advance into Scotland. This was an action that many of the English nobles believed should have been done immediately after the death of Edward I in the summer of 1307.

It is unlikely that a full-scale attack would have been able to take place before June. The English army would not have willingly ventured into Scotland until their powerful cavalry, feared throughout Europe for their strength and ability to crush an army, could be guaranteed the provisions needed to sustain such a campaign. Allowing for sufficient supplies was perhaps the key concern for any military tactician planning an attack, especially in Scotland complete with its bog-land, steep mountains and wooded plains. This was excellent for defence, but not for an attack or growing a harvest. June was therefore the perfect time to launch an attack from England.

The English army assembled at Berwick-upon-Tweed, and on 17th June they moved north towards Stirling Castle. The difference in numbers on each side were staggering. There were between 6,000-9,000 Scottish troops facing about 18,000 well trained and armed English soldiers. The English army consisted of around 2,000 cavalry and 16,000 infantry, with some historians claiming the army had 2,000 more men. Some accounts even suggest that the English army was 60,000 strong and consisted of 5,000 heavy and 10,000 light cavalry, with 20,000 archers and 25,000 infantry. On the Scottish side it is reported that there were 1,500 cavalry and 40,000 infantry. These figures are perhaps unlikely, and it is probable that over time the numbers have been exaggerated in order to raise the prestige of the battle.

The vast majority of the nobles from England were prepared to fight. They probably viewed the battle as an easy victory over the smaller Scots army. It was thought that they would surely flee into the highlands or face certain death when confronted by such an immense English army. The English army also consisted of some of the Scots nobles who were opposed to Bruce being king. These nobles were the enemies of Bruce, and therefore Scotland. They had been bribed by being promised more lands and titles in England after a swift English victory. The Scots contingent supporting Edward included Sir John Comyn, the only son of John 'the Red' Comyn, who had been brought up in England. It is possible that he was there to avenge the murder of his father by Bruce in 1306. His father could very well have become King of Scots had Bruce not killed him, and it might be that Sir John Comyn saw himself as the future King of Scots once Bruce was dead.

By the 22nd June the English army had reached Falkirk. They had travelled 82 miles in 6 days. For an army of such immense size this was an outstanding feat. The men had to carry their own weapons and food, and after such a long march they would have been weary and tired. They were now just 13 miles short of their destination and they would need all their energy to reach Stirling the next day.

The Scots had been putting their time to good use. They knew when the English army was at Berwick-upon-Tweed, and that they had only a limited number of routes over which they could travel to reach Stirling. The only viable route open to a large army from Falkirk was via the old Roman Road that led to Stirling Castle. This passed through Tor Wood, crossed over the Bannockburn and then along the edge of New Park. At New Park the road and surrounding area could be observed from Gillies Hill to the west. It was an ideal location for the

Scots to fight from as it had a massive area of woodland to its rear where the Scots could withdraw into retreat if necessary.

Bruce split his army up into divisions that were commanded by Thomas Randolph (1st Earl of Moray), Edward Bruce, and Sir James Douglas, with the king holding the rear. Sir James Douglas was in command of around 500 horsemen. Assuming that the Scots had only had 6,000 foot soldiers, this then implied that each of the divisions held just 1,500 troops. Working in favour of the Scots was that they had been assembling at Bannockburn for a month and during this period they had been training constantly. As a consequence, the Scots now had an idea of what they were to do, where they were to do it, and more importantly, they also had the advantage of knowing that they could escape if defeat was looming. The English, on the other hand, were too busy marching to spend time training. They had no idea where the battle was to be fought or that the terrain was soft, marshy bog-land under foot. More importantly they did not know the numbers in the Scottish army.

The boggy lands between Tor Wood and New Park forced the English to stay near to the old Roman road. Bruce's soldiers dug small, concealed pits which forced the cavalry to remain very close to the road. This resulted in the English infantry line of advance to bunch together. The Scots had also placed stakes in the ground in strategic areas. These would help prevent, or reduce, mounted or surprise attacks. The first advantage in any battle is to pick where you want to fight and try not to let the other side dictate the battlefield. The first mistakes were being made by the English. They were marching straight into battle with little or no time to rest or prepare their troops.

On the morning of 23rd June 1314, Philip de Mowbray arrived at the English camp to advise King Edward II and his commanders that a full-scale attack on the Scots was not needed. He suggested that a parley would be more advisable now that technically Stirling Castle had been relieved. He advised that the English king should seek out a battlefield that was more beneficial to the English than the existing site that was giving the Scots a major tactical advantage.

History tells us that the English commanders of King Edward II were not interested in what de Mowbray had to say. Instead, they were more interested in who was in charge of the army. These disagreements gave rise to an internal war of egos amongst those in the English army's higher ranks. This was all to the advantage of the Scots. Now that the English chain of command was in disarray, with little provocation matters could quickly begin to deteriorate for the English.

Sir Henry de Bohun was riding far in advance of the main English army when he managed to catch sight of Robert the Bruce. Perhaps it was his over-inflated ego, or a simple error of judgement, but de Bohun made the rash decision to attack the King of Scots. He charged with his lance. Legend has it that Bruce was armed only with his axe and had no armour to protect himself. Bruce decided to accept de Bohun's challenge and retaliated against the attack. As the two closed in on each other, and as lances were about to strike, Bruce swerved, rose in his stirrups, and struck de Bohun with a blow to the head that split his helmet and skull in two, killing him outright. This was recorded as having been such a mighty blow that Bruce broke his axe in the melee. Seeing this action would have been a massive morale boost for the outnumbered Scots. They were persuaded that this was to be their day. The first victory was to them.

Following the death of de Bohun, the Scots, headed by Bruce, continued their attack. They advanced on the English who were still making their way slowly along the old Roman road. There was a minor skirmish which saw the English retreating back to Tor Wood, and the Scots moving back to their original position to regroup. At the same time, some of the English cavalry, with the aid and local knowledge of de Mowbray, had found another road to the north of Tor Wood that passed though Bannockburn and led to St Ninian's chapel.

They moved swiftly with a view to outflanking the Scots. However, the Scots noticed this movement and ordered Scottish schiltrons to stop them from reaching St Ninian's. A schilteron is a very long lance, or spear, which could be just a long length of wood sharpened at one end, or it could have a metal point. They were designed to be long enough to prevent a horse or rider from reaching a soldier before the rider could bare his weapons. It is a simple yet effective weapon against cavalry. The only real threat to the person carrying one could be from the archers. However, the English cavalry were looking to attack without the support of their archers and so the attack was doomed to failure.

With all the skill and training learned over the past month, the Scots troops could advance, defend, and attack in formation. This prevented the English cavalry from gaining an upper hand. The horsemen were either killed or forced into retreat. During this skirmish a number of English nobles were captured. At this stage it did not seem to have made a major impact on the mindset of the main English army. The battle could still be won by the sheer number of foot-soldiers. With the first day of battle quickly coming to a close, the English decided that it would be better to set up camp, rethink their strategy and concentrate their attack in the morning.

King Edward II decided that the new attack was to once again be along the route taken the previous day, towards St Ninian's and through Bannockburn. It was probably the worst decision that he could ever have made. Robert the Bruce also had to make a decision, and that was whether to stay and fight the English on the 24th or retire into the woodland to continue fighting using the guerrilla tactics for which the Scots were best known. Bruce's decision was to stand and fight.

The Scots made the advance towards the English, and as the two armies drew closer the Scots knelt in prayer. It was thought by the English that the Scots were praying for mercy, but in fact they were praying to God. Each man had now committed himself to fight and the ensuing day would either see victory or almost certain death.

The English army continued to make errors. King Edward II was advised to hold back by the Earl of Gloucester. Gloucester was subsequently accused of being a coward. This enraged the knight who had fought in more battles than Edward had even witnessed, let alone taken part in. The Earl of Gloucester mounted his horse and rode with his cavalry to attack the Scots schilterons. It was a blood bath, with knight after knight being impaled on the Scots spears. Many English knights lost their lives in this reckless attack, including the Earl of Gloucester himself.

By advancing with a narrow front, the English were restricted in their movements, especially as the English cavalry attacked before their archers could be moved into position. To move fresh soldiers to the frontline meant that they had to pass over the dead and dying, who were lining the path in front of them. The bogs on both sides of the road made it almost impossible to continually replenish the frontline soldiers. This also meant that the retreating cavalry could not move towards safety, but instead had to try to escape across the Bannock Burn (stream). This slowed them down and drowned many who tried.

The Scots were attacking the front of the English column and panic set into the English troops. They had just witnessed their cavalry and knights, the most feared in Europe, being utterly defeated and either lying dead, dying or being desperate to retreat. As the front of the English columns tried to retreat in the face of a Scots onslaught, men were trodden to death underfoot if they happened to fall. Others, realising that they could not escape to the east, decided to head north towards the River Forth where many drowned in an attempt to swim across the river to safety. The remaining English were in a state of panic and started to drop their weapons in surrender, or to find safety by heading south.

If there was any chance of the English recovering from this mayhem, they lost it when Edward II decided to flee for his life. There were reports of the king being panic stricken and only managing to escape with his life thanks to his personal bodyguards. Now his soldiers to the rear were witnessing the flight of the cavalry and their king. They, in turn, thought the battle was lost and also decided to flee for their lives, dropping everything that they had. Any baggage or personal items were left behind, including that of Edward II and his nobles. Many prospered from the subsequent ransacking of anything that was thought to be of value, including from the dead and wounded.

The Battle of Bannockburn was now over, but the killing was not. The English had nearly 100 miles to travel back to the English-Scottish border before they could feel safe and back on home turf.

Those who travelled in large parties were more likely to make it home alive, whereas roving bands of Scots killed those who travelled individually or who formed small groups. It is also probable that those who were wounded were unlikely to have made it back to the border. They would likely have been abandoned by their comrades and left to die of their wounds, or else killed by the revengeful Scots.

It has been estimated that out of the 18,000-20,000 English troops who were at Bannockburn, 700 cavalry and 11,000-12,000 soldiers were killed. Some of the English nobles were captured and held for ransom. The same cannot be said for the poor English foot soldier. He was worth nothing and was more likely to be executed by the Scots. For another week at least, the lowlands of Scotland became a killing field. The Scottish losses were minor in comparison. They lost only a few hundred men and just two knights. The loss of the battle for King Edward II only made his unpopularity even greater. The Scots had now proven that they could defeat the English in battle, even when they were outnumbered three to one.

Whilst the battle was, without doubt, an outstanding victory for Scotland, there are also certain points of contention. Firstly, the location of the battlefield itself has come under scrutiny. At Bannockburn today there is a visitor centre and memorial to King Robert the Bruce on what is widely believed to have been the place where the main battle took place. What is curious, is that whilst there has been some archaeological evidence found there, the volume of finds is not in keeping with the large number of troops who are reputed to have fought and died. It is perhaps more likely that this was the site of one of the smaller skirmishes and that the main battle took place at either Dryfield, a mile or so to the east of the visitor centre, or alternatively a mile and a half to the northeast at the Carse of Balquhiderock.

The main problem with verifying the exact location is that much of what might have been the battlefield has been farmed or urbanised, with any archaeological evidence being either destroyed or built upon. What has never been found is a mass grave of the many soldiers who lost their lives. The bodies would need to have been disposed of, otherwise disease would have spread rapidly throughout the surrounding area. The easiest and quickest way to get rid of so many dead would have been to form a mass grave and set fire to the bodies. This would surely have left evidence of a massive funeral pyre, but neither this, nor the many thousands of discarded weapons, has ever been found.

Another point of contention is whether the Scots were assisted in the battle by the Knights Templar. The Order had recently been attacked and officially disbanded by the Pope. They were widely sought as fugitives throughout Europe. Their involvement is not recorded in any document, but still the rumours persist about their presence on the battlefield. King Robert the Bruce and Scotland had been excommunicated, and so too had the Templars. It is thought that as a result of this excommunication many Templars fled from France to Scotland after King Philip IV of France persuaded the Pope to place all Templars under arrest on Friday 13th October 1307. With Scotland being excommunicated, it was regarded as a safe haven for the now-fugitive Templars who faced an uncertain future if they remained in France. Whether or not this did happen is open to a huge amount of debate, but with Bruce being such a genius military tactician, if there were Templars in Scotland then it is quite likely that he would have enlisted their services. With the order having been officially disbanded, many of the Templar knights found themselves unemployed. Their fighting skills were amongst the best in Europe and it is quite possible that they helped the Scots in return for food, shelter and the chance to live unhindered in Scotland.

In relation to the Battle of Bannockburn, it is reputed that at one point in the battle the English cavalry saw in the distance 500 Scots on horseback, riding with the Templar battle flag being flown. On seeing this the English cavalry are believed to have halted their advance and turned around to leave the battlefield. The English soldiers witnessed this turn-around by their cavalry and thought the battle was therefore lost. They too fled, which resulted in a full-scale retreat.

The problem with this legend is that there is no supporting evidence. It is possible that there were some knights in both the Scottish and English cavalry who were also Knights Templar, but there is no early written reference to any Templar contingent or Templar flag being flown during the battle. This part of the legend of Bannockburn probably originated in the eighteenth or nineteenth century, with a rise in the popularity of both Freemasonry and the Knights Templar.

The third point of contention about Bannockburn is whether the Scots were helped by the sun blinding the advancing English army. It is said that at dawn on the 24th June the Scots lined up on the eastern edge of New Park, and as the English advanced they were blinded by the sun's reflection off the Scots shields. The problem with this is that it was the Summer Solstice and therefore at sunrise the sun would have been rising in the northeast, whereas the English were advancing in the east-to-southeast of the Scots' position. Whilst it is possible that the Scots could have angled their shields to reflect the sun towards the English, it is just as possible that the English could have done the same to the Scots. Also, the Scottish shields were largely made out of wood and leather, which are not the most reflective of materials. A shield could be made in a day by using wood and leather, whereas a metal shield would have taken days to make and even more time to polish. Time was of the essence, so it is just an unlikely scenario. Even as late as 2004 some authors were reporting this as being a 'secret weapon' used by the Scots, supposedly given to them by the Knights Templar. The fact is that Bannockburn was a fantastic victory for Bruce and the Scots, with superior military tactics underpinning the success.

There are several traditions of artefacts having been given by Bruce to his supporters following Bannockburn. It is reputed that the King of Munster in Ireland, Cormac McCarthy, supplied Bruce with 4,000 men to assist against the English. Given the total numbers believed to have been present, this figure is perhaps unlikely. McCarthy owned a castle near Cork in southern Ireland, called Blarney Castle.

There is a certain legend about the 'Blarney Stone' which has been incorporated into the battlements of the castle. After the Battle of Bannockburn, King Robert the Bruce reputedly gave the Blarney Stone to Cormac McCarthy in gratitude for the support of his troops. It is claimed by this legend to be a piece of the genuine Scots king-making

Stone. Although this is perhaps an unlikely scenario, the persisting legend serves to highlight just how important a victory Bannockburn was over the English, even for the Irish.

Legend has it that the Blarney Stone will impart the gift of eloquence in return for a kiss. The visitor to the castle is to lie on their back and stretch out over a hundred foot drop from the top of the castle to kiss the Stone. Doing so attracts a vast number of visitors each year. If the Blarney Stone is a piece of the genuine Scots king-making Stone, then it begs the question, what happened to the remaining piece that, presumably, remained in Scotland and just how big was the king-making Stone originally?

Figure 8: The Blarney Stone.

The victory of the Scots at Bannockburn has gone down in history as perhaps the greatest battle in the Wars of Independence between Scotland and England. The Scots had finally put an end to the English arrogance that seemed to pervade their attitudes towards the rest of Europe. Even though they were vastly outnumbered and less well equipped, the Scots won the battle to once again have control of Stirling Castle. King Robert the Bruce had re-joined lowland and highland Scotland and it has remained as such ever since.

The Declaration of Arbroath

Six years after the Battle of Bannockburn, on 6th August 1320, the Declaration of Arbroath was signed. It was a petition to Pope John XXII by fifty-one of the magnates and nobles of Scotland. It declared the sovereignty and independence of Scotland from England. It was intended to convey to the Pope that Scotland had a lineage dating back to the Kingdom of Scythia, which was believed to have been the most ancient of kingdoms, surpassing even Egypt, and even more so, England. The Declaration also publicly declared that St Andrew, the brother of St Peter, was the patron saint and protector of Scotland. By implication, Scotland was therefore the brother of the Church of Rome. According to ancient legends, it was God Himself who had appointed Scotland as the place where the greatest shrine to St Andrew would be built. It also stated that the matter of independence could only be decided by the Scottish people, and that it could not even be overturned by the King of Scots, and certainly not by the King of England. Indeed, the Declaration even proposed that another king would be chosen if the reigning monarch did anything to threaten Scotland's independence. The petition worked. Rome recognised Christian Scotland as an independent entity, separate from England, and recognised that St Andrew, the brother of Rome's St Peter, was Scotland's patron and protector. In later times the Declaration of Arbroath was used as a basis for the Declaration of Independence of the United States of America. The Declaration of Arbroath was concluded by the famous lines:

> "...for, as long as but a hundred of us remain alive, never will we on any conditions be brought under English rule. It is in truth not for glory, nor riches, nor honours that we are fighting, but for freedom – for that alone, which no honest man gives up but with life itself."

King Edward II

History has perhaps been unkind to Edward II, with the vast majority of people seeing him as a weak and timid character. This was partly due to his reluctance to deal with nobility and administer his kingdom. Instead, he preferred to seek out entertainment from pursuits such as athletics and craft working. Coupled with this were allegations that he was homosexual. This was a far cry from the dominating persona of his father, who was renowned for his strength and military acumen and who saw it as his duty to expand the Kingdom of England for himself and his future generations.

As a young child, Edward was due to wed Margaret, Maid of Norway, and heir to the throne of Scotland. Their marriage would have ultimately made Edward the king in both England and Scotland. However, the death of Margaret in 1290 meant that this union was not to come to fruition. Edward II married Isabella of France, the daughter of King Philip IV of France, on 25th January 1308. It was an arranged marriage and one that was not as happy as his parents had been. The marriage was not welcomed by King Edward II. It was a disaster from beginning to end. Edward was known to neglect Isabella in favour of his male associates, and especially Piers Gaveston. His treatment of her must have left the poor woman feeling isolated and bitter towards her husband.

It is not known whether he had a simple disinterest in governing his kingdom, or whether instead the thought of having to deal with nobles on a daily basis bored him. Either way, that Edward preferred the company of non-nobility is without doubt. This led to a feeling of exclusion on the part of his barons and advisors. Often their better judgements were overlooked in favour of hasty and irrational decisions. His favourite 'advisor' was Piers Gaveston, who was from Gascony in France, which at that time was still part of the Kingdom of England. Gaveston's father was a soldier in the service of King Edward I. Ironically, it was King Edward who encouraged the friendship between his son and Gaveston, and initially he quite liked the Frenchman. It was only when his son tried to grant Gaveston the County of Ponthieu that the king grew to dislike him, as the title was reserved solely for royalty.

Edward began to feel uneasy about the relationship that was developing between his son, a Prince, and Gaveston, who was but a mere knight, and a low ranking one at that. King Edward was enraged when he learnt that Edward and Gaveston had sworn an oath to fight together, protect each other, and share all of their possessions. This was quite unthinkable from the point of view of Prince Edward being the heir to the throne. Would he be expected to share his kingdom with the commoner?

As a result, King Edward had Gaveston banished from England and sent to France. He made him and his son swear never to see each other again without his permission. It was only a short time after this that King Edward died. Almost immediately after his death word was sent to France. Gaveston returned to England and was given the title to the county of Cornwall, which did nothing to please the advisors of the new king who had remained loyal to his father. Many of the advisors rebelled and tried to limit the power of King Edward II by the Ordinances of 1311. They also felt uneasy about how much the new king was relying on his friend. There was a sense of urgency, that if they did not intervene, then the Kingdom of England would surely slide into disrepute. The Ordinances stated that Gaveston should be banished from England once again, but it was never to happen.

The following year Gaveston was killed by the Earl of Lancaster who claimed that he had led the king to folly. Edward was devastated and furious with the death of his best friend and focussed his efforts on exacting revenge on those responsible. He was well advised not to instigate a war with the barons, as he could easily have found himself deposed from his throne. By October 1312 the Earl and his co-conspirators were begging for Edward's pardon. They duly received it.

With Gaveston gone, there was a void in Edward's life that would not be left empty for long. He befriended Hugh Despenser, also known as Hugh the Younger. This resulted in more problems between Edward and his nobles. Hugh Despenser was born in 1286 and was knighted in 1306. He married Eleanor de Clair, the granddaughter of Edward I. This was arranged as a form of repayment by King Edward I, who was in debt to Hugh Despenser's father. It proved to be a lucrative deal for the young Despenser, because when Eleanor de Clair's brother, Gilbert de Clair, was killed at the Battle of Bannockburn, Hugh inherited one-third of his land. When coupled with his own estates it made him one of the greatest landowners in England.

Despenser was one of the nobles who had become concerned about the influence of Gaveston over the English king. He schemed and plotted his way into the court of King Edward II and with Gaveston out of the way he soon became a favourite companion of the king. Once in a position of power he started to seize more land from his brothers-in-law, and indeed anyone else whom he felt had crossed him. There is one story that says he broke the arms and legs of a poor unfortunate lady until she went insane in order to seize her lands. Quite understandably he quickly made enemies with his actions and threats. Perhaps his downfall started when he made an enemy of Queen Isabella. He took Wallingford Castle, which had been given to her supposedly for life by her husband. The Queen was someone who would not forget. She would bide her time in order to exact her revenge.

Queen Isabella of France

During the time that Edward II was campaigning against the Scots, he practically left his poor wife Isabella alone and without proper companionship. His feelings for her cannot have run very deep and it is said that on one of his campaigns to Scotland he abandoned her at Tynemouth. It was only by chance that Isabella managed to escape the advancing army of Robert the Bruce.

Isabella is perhaps one of the most important females in the history of the feuds between England and Scotland. The marriage between Edward and Isabella was arranged when she was an infant, but due to disagreements between the French and English kings over the possession of Gascony the marriage was put on hold. It seems that their marriage was a form of destiny whether they liked it or not, as Pope Boniface VIII had tried to arrange the marriage as early as 1298 when Isabella was only six years old. This 'courting' carried on for nearly ten years before the wedding finally took place at Boulogne-sur-Mer on 25th January 1308. Edward was nearly 24 years old and Isabella was 16 years old. Some sources suggest that she may even have been just 12 years old. If this is true, then it is perhaps understandable why the 24 year old Edward was not particularly attracted to a girl who was just half his age. Their marriage came almost a year after King Edward I had died. It was perhaps because of his death that the marriage was finally able to take place, since Edward had postponed the engagement several times because of his conflicts with France.

Their first child was born in 1312, four years after the marriage, which was something quite unheard of in the Middle Ages and especially with a reigning king who needed to produce an 'heir and a spare' for the throne. The child was named after his father, Edward, and was to become the future King Edward III of England. Over the course of their marriage they were to have a further three children. John was born in 1316, Eleanor was born in 1318, and Joan was born in 1321.

The Death of King Edward II

Time and again, Isabella begged Edward to act more like a king and rule his kingdom instead of behaving like a commoner and associating with all sorts of undesirables. In 1321 Isabella pressed Edward to have Hugh Despenser expelled from the country. She was successful in her plea, because she had also petitioned many of the nobles that also had a disliking of Dispenser. However, he was to return again the following year. This seems to have been the last straw for Isabella and upon his return her hatred for Hugh and his relationship with her husband grew.

Isabella and Edward continued to grow apart, if indeed there was ever a closeness to begin with. The Queen felt that it was her turn to seek alternative companionship. The object of her desires was a man named Roger Mortimer, who had been imprisoned in the Tower of London. Legend has it that Isabella helped Mortimer to escape in 1323, and although it is not known whether the two were lovers before this date, they became that soon after.

In 1325 Isabella was sent to France to try to negotiate a peace settlement for England with her newly crowned brother, King Charles IV of France. He had recently seized the last of the English lands that were held in France. It was perhaps seen as a good ploy by Edward, to send big sister to convince her younger brother to hand back the lands that he had taken. This did nothing to appease Edward's nobles who were disgusted that the king had sent his wife to negotiate terms of peace on his, and England's, behalf.

Whilst in France, Isabella once again met up with Roger Mortimer and they openly became lovers, to the embarrassment of Edward. When word reached the king about the affair of Isabella and Roger, he demanded her return, which she flatly refused. He then demanded that the French king, her brother, return her to England. His reply was that if she had come to France of her own free will then she could return to England of her own free will, and that if she wished to remain in France then she and her lover were welcome. This was a very public embarrassment for Edward. The French king must have revelled in speaking his words.

Isabella and Roger decided not to stay in France, but instead were invited as guests of honour to the court of William I, the Count of Hainaut, in Holland. It seems that the other reigning monarchies throughout Europe also felt a certain satisfaction in seeing the weak English king get his comeuppance. During their stay with the Count, Isabella was forming an army to try to overthrow her husband and arranged a marriage agreement between William I's daughter, Philippa, and Isabella's eldest son, Edward, the future King of England. With this agreement, Isabella received eight war ships from William to assist her war efforts.

On 21st September 1326 Isabella and her army, made up mostly of mercenaries, landed on the coast of Suffolk in England. King Edward had offered a reward to anyone who would kill his wife, and as a rebuke, Isabella said she would double the amount for anyone that would kill Hugh Despencer. In a strange twist of fate this reward was taken up by the estate of Wallingford Castle, which had originally been given by Edward to Isabella for the rest of her life, but which was subsequently taken from her and granted to Hugh Despencer.

Soon after the landing of Isabella and her army, any allies that Edward had started to desert him. He was left to flee for his life. Hugh Despencer was captured and executed, and Edward was held prisoner and forced to abdicate on 25th January 1327. He was succeeded by his eldest son, also named Edward, who was just 14 years old and still too young to rule. In his place, his mother, Isabella, and her lover, Roger Mortimer, acted as his regents until he came of age four years later.

Whilst Edward II was still alive there was always the chance that he could escape his captors and make a play to try to regain power. However unrealistic such a suggestion seemed at the time, the best way to ensure that it could never happen was to murder him and make it look like a natural death. The ambiguous order, "*Edwardum occidere nolite timere bonum est*" was sent by Bishop Adam Orleton. The message could be read in two ways depending on the syntax used. If all was well, then the murderers would read the message as "*Edwardum occidere nolite timere, bonum est*", meaning "Fear not to kill the king, it is good he die." However, if the message were intercepted and the Bishop was held accountable, then he could insist that the message should be read as "*Edwardum occidere nolite, timere bonum est*" which meant the opposite and reads, "Kill not the king, it is good to fear the worst."

What legend testifies happened next was a horrific death, even by the standards of the day, and it is possible that there was at least some connotation in the manner of his death towards the lifestyle Edward chose to lead. Edward was killed at Berkeley Castle and about thirty years after the murder the chronicler, Geoffrey le Baker, wrote a third hand account of what supposedly happened. He wrote:

> "On the night of October 11 while lying on a bed [the king] was suddenly seized and, while a great mattress...weighed him down and suffocated him, a plumber's iron, heated intensely hot, was introduced through a tube into his secret parts so that it burned the inner portions beyond the intestines."

The internal damage that would be caused by a red-hot poker up the rectum would be horrendous and the pain quite unbearable. Geoffrey is said to have heard about the last days of Edward and the manner of his death from William Bishop, who in turn is said to have been told the story direct from the mouths of Edward's murderers, Thomas Gurney and John Maltravers. Although the exact nature of his death is not known for certain, and it has never been proven that it was

111

organised by or on behalf of Isabella, the suffocation aspect of his murder could suggest that it was meant to look more like a natural death than murder. The poker being used as pure malicious torture, if indeed it was used at all.

There is no 'happily ever after' ending to the story of Isabella and Mortimer. When Edward III was approaching the age of 18, when he would officially have taken control of his kingdom, he staged a coup and took both his mother and Mortimer as prisoner. Mortimer was executed on 29th November 1330 and Isabella was sent to Castle Rising in Norfolk to live out her years in forced retirement. She was still allowed to visit her son's court and see her grandchildren, which was perhaps a little mercy for the ageing woman. She died on 22nd August 1358 and was buried at Newgate in her wedding dress. Edward II's heart was placed by her side, under the order of the king. Was this the final act of a loving son, who desperately wanted his father and mother to spend eternity together? Or was it the vengeful act of a troubled son, to torment the souls of his deceased parents? We shall never know.

Chapter 5
The Coronation Stone of the British Monarchs

The relationship between Scotland and England continued to deteriorate during the reign of King Edward III of England. In 1327, the year that Edward ascended the throne, a Scots army led by King Robert the Bruce attacked northern England. This resulted in an English defeat at Stanhope and Weardale in County Durham. At the time of the attack, Edward's mother, Isabella, and her lover, Roger Mortimer, acting on behalf of the young king, started to negotiate a truce with Scotland. The treaty was agreed upon and signed at the Abbey of Holyrood in Edinburgh on 17th March 1328. It was later ratified by an English Parliament at Northampton on 3rd May 1328. This was known as the Treaty of Edinburgh-Northampton. It was a written agreement, or more accurately a concession, that the English monarchy now recognised the legitimacy of the King of Scots and the Kingdom of Scotland as a separate entity that was independent from the Kingdom of England.

It has been suggested that the Stone that was being held at Westminster Abbey would be returned to the Scots as part of the terms of the treaty. This gesture was not included in the official text and so it is unclear whether or not this was seriously considered as an option. The traditional version of events conveys that when Edward III offered the Stone back to the Scots they refused it in favour of having the Holy Rood of Scotland instead, which had also been stolen by King Edward I in 1296. Those who claim it was offered back usually cite a document titled *Vita Edwardi Secundi* (Life of Edward II) that was written sometime around 1326 at the Benedictine Abbey of Malmesbury. According to this document, in previous years the Scots had "demanded that the royal stone should be restored to them, which Edward I had long ago taken from Scotland and placed at Westminster by the tomb of St Edward." If the Scots were demanding the return of the Stone before 1326 then some would argue they must have also been asking for its return in 1328 when the Treaty of Edinburgh-Northampton was signed.

Interestingly, a Writ was issued by Edward III in 1328 to the Abbot and Convent of Westminster for the return of the Stone to Scotland. The Writ states:

"...that the Stone whereon the Kings of Scotland are wont to sit at the time of the Coronation, and which is in their [i.e. the Abbot and Convent's] keeping, be sent into Scotland and the King has ordered the Sheriffs of his City of London to receive from them the said Stone by indenture, and cause it to be carried to [Isabella] Queen of England, his Mother."

Those responsible for the Stone at Westminster were not prepared to give it up under any circumstances, including the issuing of the Writ and demands of the king. Referring to the negotiations and subsequent activity, the chronicler Geoffrey le Baker wrote:

"This stone was now fixed by iron chains to the floor of Westminster Abbey under the royal throne next to the high altar. The Scots asked that the stone should be released and given back to them so that they could consecrate their king [David II, 1329] upon it, as they had done of old. The council of the King [Edward III] gave its assent to this petition and high-ranking envoys were sent to get the stone. But when the abbot of Westminster heard the request of the envoys, we wrote to the king and his council, saying that the stone had once been brought from Scotland with immense effort by Edward, the king's grandfather, and devoutly offered by him to the abbey, so that it now could not and should not be carried off from that church. After this response, the envoys returned to Scotland without the stone."

It is possible that it was at this time that the iron rings were fitted to the Stone in order to secure it and avoid it being taken against the will of the Abbot. If that is correct, then it is evidence of the Stone having undergone major alterations shortly after it was taken to

Westminster. Indeed, the latest archaeological research into St Edward's Chair gathered during its refurbishment between 2010-2012, provides very good evidence that the ends of the Stone have been carved down by approximately 10cm, suggesting that the Stone was altered to fit the chair and not, as previously thought, the chair built to accommodate the dimensions of the Stone.

In conclusion to the negotiations and the signing of the treaty, the Holy Rood was returned to the Scots, but the Stone was to remain at Westminster Abbey for many more centuries.

Figure 9: Bannockburn memorial to Robert the Bruce, King of Scots

A year after the signing of the Treaty of Edinburgh-Northampton, King Robert the Bruce died on 7th June 1329. He was, without doubt, the hero-king of the Scots and is still regarded as such in the present day. His heart was buried at Melrose Abbey, his internal

115

organs at St Serf's Chapel in Dumbarton, and the rest of his remains were buried in Dunfermline Abbey.

Some have claimed that following his death the genuine Scots king-making Stone was taken to the Isle of Skye, off the western coast of mainland Scotland. It was reputedly taken there by John, the eldest son of Angus Og, the Lord of the Isles, in 1329. The Stone is said to have been in the keeping of the Clan MacDonald since then and the location is a secret passed down from father to son. However, this is perhaps just a legend that appeared over time as people sought to bolster their familial connections to Bruce and his significant impact on Scotland's history during the Wars of Independence.

The Union of the Crowns

During its long stay at Westminster Abbey, the Stone featured little in the ensuing history of either England or Scotland. When it was taken in 1296 it was the Scots king-making Stone, but ever since the coronation of King Henry IV in 1399 it was used as the coronation Stone of the English monarchs. With the Union of the Crowns in 1603, the Stone also became the coronation Stone of the monarchs of Great Britain. It remains so to this day.

The Union of the Crowns occurred when James VI, King of Scots, also ascended the throne of England, and assumed the title in England of King James I. After all of the efforts of the English to subdue the Scot's crown, it is perhaps ironic that it should have been a Scottish king who ultimately united the two countries. It is interesting to note that there were six Kings of Scots with the name of 'James', which is the anglicised form of the Hebrew name 'Jacob'. James I, King of Scots, (not James I, King of England), was crowned in 1424. It was as if the Scots were trying to link themselves with the biblical patriarch, even though the Stone, Jacob's Pillow, was now in the hands of the English.

James VI, King of Scots, was the next heir in line to the English throne following the death of his cousin, Queen Elizabeth I of England, who died without any offspring or direct heir. Some will point to this as proof-positive in the *Ni fallat fatum* prophecy concerning the Stone, which claimed:

> If destiny deceives not, the Scots will reign 'tis said
> in that same place where the stone has been laid.

James VI presumably fulfilled that prophecy. Over the following years the British monarchy would sit on the Stone that was believed to have been used by the patriarch Jacob as his pillow, to receive the blessing from God and hence their divine right to reign as monarch. The Stone was widely seen as one of the most important symbols of the British Empire. As such it was a target for any opponents to Britain.

The Irish Rebellion

In 1801 Ireland became a part of the United Kingdom. This was not generally viewed as a happy union, particularly by many of the Catholics in Ireland. The majority in the rest of the United Kingdom, including the monarchy, were Protestant. There were many reasons for Catholic discontent with Protestant rule. Primarily this stemmed back to 1691 when the Catholics in Ireland were barred from voting or being a member of the Irish Parliament. This implied that the country was governed by Protestants, even though they were only one tenth of the population. Just over a hundred years later, in 1798, there was an Irish rebellion. The site chosen for the battleground was historically symbolic. It was the ancient Irish king-making site at Tara.

The Irish rebels decided to assemble at the sacred Hill of Tara, as this was seen as a symbol of Ireland's great past when it was free from rule by any other country. By the morning of 26th May 1798 the rebels had a force of around 4,000 men and women who fought side-by-side. That morning, the rebels attacked a baggage party of the British Army – the Reay Fencibles – who mostly came from Caithness and Sutherland in the most northern part of mainland Britain. They were heading towards Dublin to resupply their regiment. All of the baggage was captured and the Fencibles were defeated. Those who escaped made their way back to their regiment in Dublin and reported the attack. The whole regiment, which consisted of about 700 men, including some Yeomanry, set out to avenge their fallen comrades.

The 700 Fencibles and Yeomanry set up formation at the base of the Hill of Tara to attack the 4,000 rebels who were positioned behind walls and ditches. The rebels defended the hill against the Highlanders but were soon defeated by superior firepower. A bayonet charge finally saw the rebels flee. There were about 400 Irishmen and 30 British soldiers killed. This defeat was a severe blow to the Irish rebellion and prevented it from spreading further. After the battle the Irish placed a large stone on top of the Hill of Tara to commemorate those who fell during the battle. That stone is still there, and it is better known as the Lia Fáil. It is often mistakenly identified as the Stone of Destiny.

Figure 10: The present-day Lia Fáil, sited at Tara, Ireland

The Act of Union came in 1801. This made King George III the king of the United Kingdom of Great Britain and Ireland. Interest in the Stone was growing and the powers-that-be amended the historical notices about the St Edward's Chair. All references to the traditions of the Irish and it being their ancient king-making Stone were omitted.

This did nothing to please the Irish Republicans who wanted their Stone back.

The Clan na Gael, or Clann na nGael (family of the Gaels), was an Irish Republican organisation formed in the United States of America in the late nineteenth century. The support for the Irish cause was strong in the USA and new pro-Irish republican organisations were continually being established year after year. During an anti-British march in March 1868, around 100,000 pro-Irish demonstrators took to the streets of New York. It was widely believed that once the British were out of Ireland then all of the Irish immigrants, that were resident in the USA, would head back to their homeland.

One of the organisations that was established was the Manchester based Irish Republican Brotherhood, who decided to support Clan na Gael in the USA. By the 1880s some of the members were planning to start what would be called the 'Dynamite War'. The aim of this was to make bombing runs to England in order to put pressure on the government to grant Ireland its independence. By 1887 the Irish-Americans had planted around 60 bombs and destroyed at least 10 buildings and monuments. Over 100 people had also been killed. Some of their targets were symbols of the British Empire, such as the Tower of London and the Houses of Parliament. It was their intention to also target the Stone in Westminster Abbey.

Thomas Miller Beach was a British spy who infiltrated some of the Irish-American Republican organisations. He wrote *Twenty-five Years in the Secret Service* in which he recounts how the Irishmen were planning to steal the Stone. In their eyes it was the Lia Fáil of Irish legend and was thus the property of the Irish and not the British. This Irish symbol, which had been used for hundreds of years to crown their own kings at the Hill of Tara, should rightly be returned to Ireland. To steal the Stone would be to strike at the heart of the British Empire. The plan to steal the Stone was quite basic. Someone was going to 'accidently' get locked inside Westminster Abbey. Once the doors had been locked for the night, whoever was inside would overpower any watchmen and steal the Stone by passing it through a window to those waiting outside. Seemingly they waited for months for an opportune moment to put the plan into action, but the chance never came. Eventually the police learned of the plan. They stepped up their patrols of the Abbey and thus prevented any opportunistic theft of the Stone at that time.

The Suffragettes and the Stone

The Stone remained in Westminster Abbey under watchful eyes. The Women's Suffragette movement of the late nineteenth to early twentieth century consisted of a group of political activists. They campaigned to try to secure the right to vote for women. The Suffragette's were frustrated by their social and economic situation. They conducted many protests with the aim of achieving different levels of inconvenience to mainstream society. This included actions such as chaining themselves to railings, disrupting public events, smashing windows, and going on protest marches. There was one instance, however, that really helped their cause to make the headlines.

On 11th June 1914 the Women's Suffragettes targeted St Edward's Chair and the Stone at Westminster Abbey. They placed a back-pack that contained explosives on the rear of one of the pinnacles of the chair and then detonated the bomb. The make-shift bombs were hidden in two bicycle bells that were packed with explosives and surrounded with nuts and bolts. There was considerable damage to the chair, although it was not completely destroyed. The pinnacle on which they had placed the explosives had been blown off completely and the rest of the chair suffered superficial damage. It is possible that this also damaged the Stone, but the bombs were rather small and were perhaps more about making a political statement than attempting to cause major damage. This stunt made little impact for their cause. The following month, on 28th July 1914, war was declared on Germany.

The Stone During the War Years

Soon after the outbreak of the First World War, St Edward's Chair and the Stone were moved to the Chapter House crypt in Westminster Abbey to protect them from any possible German attack. At the end of the war they were taken out of hiding and once again placed on display at Westminster Abbey. They were not to remain on display for long. With the onset of the Second World War in 1939, the chair and Stone were once again hidden in 1940 when an invasion of Britain by Germany appeared to be inevitable.

The Stone was reputed to have been hidden under the floor of the Islip Chapel in the grounds of Westminster Abbey. What is perhaps less well known is that during the war the protection of the Stone was entrusted to the Canadian Forces. Some have suggested that the Stone was secretly flown to Canada. The chances of this are quite slim since aircraft were often shot down and ships were under constant threat of being sunk by German U-Boats. If the plane or ship carrying the Stone had been attacked then there was every chance that it would have been lost forever.

The Stone was a symbol of the British Empire and could not be lost. A map was drawn that located the hidden Stone in the Islip Chapel, and this was then sent to the General Governor of Canada for safety. Alexander Augustus Frederick William Alfred George Cambridge, 1st Earl of Athlone, took over the position of General Governor of Canada on 21st June 1940. He was the brother of Queen Mary and the uncle of the reigning monarch of the day, King George VI. His credentials made him the ideal candidate to know the location of the Stone and recover it should the worst happen in Britain.

The Theft of the Westminster Stone

Very soon after the Second World War had ended, many of the countries that comprised the British Empire were seeking independence and the return of their sovereignty. Independence was granted to most of the countries and yet the pleas of some in Scotland went unheard. Many deemed that this was highly unfair, and they could not understand why the Parliament based at Westminster was directing and controlling the fate of Scotland.

During the late 1940s and early 1950s the political atmosphere in Scotland was being flooded with sentiments of nationalism and separation once again from England. A growing number of Scots believed in *their* elected running *their* affairs, and not to simply follow

121

the order as given by those hundreds of miles away and south of the border in Westminster. This was a bitter argument that had raged since the union of the Scottish and English parliaments in 1707, under the Treaty (or Act) of Union. It was in this political atmosphere that some Scottish nationalists decided to strike right at the very heart of the Empire and steal the Stone from Westminster.

On Christmas Eve 1950 three men and one woman broke into Westminster Abbey and took the Stone from under St Edward's Chair. Their plan was similar to the aborted plan of the Irish Republicans in previous years. The leader of the group was Ian Hamilton. He was a member of the Scottish Covenant Association, which had been established to further the ambition of a devolved Scottish Assembly. His three accomplices were Gavin Vernon, Alan Stuart and Kay Mathieson. Hamilton was studying law at Glasgow University and was a friend and supporter of John MacCormick, founder of the Scottish Covenant Association. MacCormick was elected as the Rector of Glasgow University and became a very influential person throughout Scotland.

The actual taking of the Stone from Westminster reads as a rather comical story, with lady-luck playing her role many times over throughout the course of events. In 2008, the entire saga was made into a feature film titled *Stone of Destiny*.

Hamilton had sneaked into Westminster Abbey and managed to get himself locked inside after closing time. He planned to remove the Stone from the chair, which he thought would be easy. He was caught by the Abbey watchman yet was allowed to walk free after he managed to convince him that he had been locked in by accident. The plan had to be altered to accommodate the unforeseen circumstance of being caught. Hamilton and the others were now faced with the task of having to break into Westminster Abbey from the outside. Thankfully for their cause, security was much laxer in 1950 than in the present day. They were able to park their car at the side of the Abbey and gain entry unnoticed and without too much difficulty.

The Stone was not going to be lifted from St Edward's Chair without a struggle. It was eventually manhandled free. Before anyone realised just how heavy it was, it crashed to the floor and broke into two pieces. It is possible that it was weakened by the Suffragettes bomb in 1914. Rather fortuitously this made it easier to carry and actually aided their efforts. The Stone was dragged across the Abbey floor, using Hamilton's jacket as a sled, and towards the waiting car being driven by Kay.

Ian was first to exit the Abbey with the smaller piece of the Stone. He made it to the car and loaded it into the back before getting into the passenger seat. A policeman was patrolling the area and saw Kay and Ian in the car, which was parked where it really shouldn't be. The police officer approached them to ask what they were doing. The couple feigned affection for each other. They pleaded that they had simply been looking for a quiet place to stop and welcome in Christmas Day, but that in London, and on Christmas Eve of all nights, they were rather limited in their options.

Whilst the officer was listening to the story, Alan and Gavin were still inside the Abbey wondering what was taking so long. When they realised that the police were only a few feet away questioning Ian and Kay, and they were holding one of the most prized relics of the British Empire, they decided that to abandon it might be the better option. Eventually the policeman forced Ian and Kay to drive off. A short distance away, Ian got out of the car, leaving Kay to drive herself to safety, whilst he went to the other get-away vehicle parked close to the Abbey. He went back to load up the vehicle with the larger portion of the Stone. When he arrived at the Abbey he found the Stone, but no Alan or Gavin. Seeing that Ian and Kay had driven off, the two thought that the plan had been compromised and so abandoned the Stone. They decided it would be better to make their way back to Scotland.

Ian managed to lift the larger portion of the Stone into the back of the car on his own. He drove off and eventually came across Gavin and Alan walking down a street. He stopped to pick them up, but there was only room for one more in the car. It was agreed that Gavin would get back to Scotland by train, whilst Ian and Alan would drive south of London to hide the Stone. It would remain hidden until their return to Scotland could be assured of being free from the inevitable police roadblocks that would be set up at all main border crossings between England and Scotland. The pair hid the Stone in a ditch, covered it with leaves, and made the long, arduous journey back to Scotland. They had successfully taken the Stone from Westminster Abbey. The only problem now was how to get it back onto Scottish soil.

When they arrived back in Scotland, they met with several people to decide how next to proceed. With concerns that the Stone might crack and break due to its exposure to the elements, a decision was swiftly made to head back to England and collect it for transportation over the border. When they arrived at the place where they had hidden the Stone there was a camp of Gypsies who had parked on the very site. They had to approach with caution, as the Gypsies could have been the police in disguise. They got talking and realised that the plight of the Gypsies was similar to that of the Scots. There was a mutual appreciation of each situation and so Hamilton told the Gypsies of their adventure. They were able to recover the Stone and leave without any opposition. They eventually managed to cross the border into Scotland, just north of Berwick-on-Tweed, without any police roadblocks to hinder their progress. The Stone was back on Scottish soil for the first time in over 650 years since it was taken by King Edward I of England in 1296.

Over the ensuing weeks there was a major police hunt for the Stone on both sides of the border. The police employed dowsers to look for the Stone. This resulted in the dredging of the Serpentine in London's Hyde Park, much to the amusement of those who knew of the actual whereabouts of the Stone. It was decided that the Stone would have to be returned to the authorities, but only after a letter had been written to King George VI requesting that it remain on Scottish soil.

Eventually the Stone was taken, draped in the Saltire Cross of St Andrew, and placed at Arbroath Abbey where the Declaration of Arbroath had been signed in 1320. The placement was symbolic of the Declaration. It gave a sign to the British establishment that history had not been forgotten and that some in Scotland still wanted independence and the return of Scotland's symbol of nationhood.

Before being returned to the authorities several replica stones were made and it has been an enduring theory that the Stone that was placed at Arbroath was not the original Stone taken from Westminster. In his book, *The Taking of the Stone of Destiny*, in which Hamilton recounts the entire affair, the reader is assured that the Stone returned was the original, but still the rumours have persisted. Either way, King George VI did not heed the call for the Stone to remain in Scotland. It was swiftly taken back to Westminster Abbey and once again placed on display under St Edward's Chair, although this time under much tighter security.

The Coronation of Queen Elizabeth II

The Stone was returned from Scotland to Westminster in time for the next coronation ceremony. On 2nd June 1953, Queen Elizabeth II of the United Kingdom of Great Britain and Northern Ireland, and of Her other Realms and Territories, Head of the Commonwealth, Defender of the Faith, was crowned. She was seated upon the Stone in St Edward's Chair and received all of the anointing and blessing that had to be bestowed as per the traditional rites. Not being inclined to let an opportunity slip, John MacCormick and Ian Hamilton, along with some other Scottish nationalists, challenged the right of the Queen to style herself Elizabeth II. There had never been an Elizabeth I in Scotland. They saw her title as a breach of the 1707 Treaty of Union and took her to court. They claimed that the precedence had been set when James VI, King of Scots (1567-1625) united the crowns in 1603, and so also became King James I of England (1603-1625). In the case of MacCormick vs. Lord Advocate, the Scottish Court of Session ruled against the plaintiffs, finding that the Queen's title was a matter of her own choice and prerogative. Nevertheless, to save further debate, it was announced that all future monarchs with a shared name would use the higher ordinal of any preceding English or Scottish monarch.

The Scottish Knights Templar

It had been widely debated throughout Scotland whether the Stone that had been returned in 1951 and used as the coronation Stone for Queen Elizabeth II, was in fact the original Stone that King Edward I had taken in 1296, or one of the replica stones that had been made. That debate continues, even though Ian Hamilton assured everyone that the genuine Stone had been returned.

One persistent legend is that the modern order of Scottish Knights Templar became the keepers of the genuine Stone, and that they would remain so until the coronation of the next King of Scots in Scotland. There are two versions as to how the Templars came to be the guardians of the Stone. The first legend claims that King Robert the Bruce gave the Stone to the Knights Templar for protection following the Battle of Bannockburn, and they are supposed to have remained the guardians of the relic ever since, even into the present day with only a chosen few knowing its true location.

The second theory is that after Ian Hamilton and his fellow nationalist students took the Stone from Westminster Abbey in 1950 it was replaced by a fake stone that was made by Robert Gray, a stonemason from Glasgow and a future member of *Militi Templi Scotia*, the Scottish Knights Templar.

Militi Templi Scotia is a non-Masonic Chivalric Order of Knights. Their *raison d'être* is to serve God and Scotland in ways that preserve the ancient history and traditions of the Scots. It was said that Robert Gray had made several replica versions of the Stone in the 1930s and it was one of these 'fakes' that was subsequently handed back to the authorities at Arbroath Abbey in April 1951.

In 1965 another Stone miraculously turned up in Parliament Square in Edinburgh. Robert Gray claimed that this was the genuine Stone. Members of *Militi Templi Scotia* decided that the Stone should be kept in the protection of Reverend John Mackay Nimmo. Nimmo was the Chaplin of *Militi Templi Scotia* and his church, St Columba's Parish Church in Dundee, was used for Templar Conclave meetings. The Stone was put in a cage alongside a plaque which read:

"The Stone of Destiny has been set here. An appropriate place for a symbol so venerable and significant in Scottish history. It has been given into the keeping of the Minister and Kirk

Session of St Columba's Parish Church, Dundee, by the 1320 Club in association with Baillie Robert to place the Stone in Arbroath Abbey on 12th April, 1951."

However, in 1990 the church was to be closed. The Stone was moved to Dull Church, near Aberfeldy. From here, and presumably for safekeeping, several members of *Militi Templi Scotia* decided to cut the Stone free from its cage, placed it in the back of a car and drove off. The location of the Stone has remained a secret of the order ever since. Some claim it as part of their private archives known as *Stella Templum*. This is comprised of ancient and historical artefacts, artworks, and documents linking the Templars and their belief systems to Scotland.

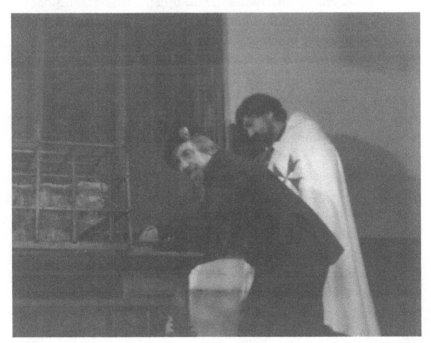

Figure 11: Two members of Militi Templi Scotia remove the Stone from Dull Church, 1990

The Return of the Stone

In 1996 a shock announcement by the Conservative government of the day informed what some people had waited 700 long years to hear. The Stone was going to be returned to Scotland. It was decided that it would be placed on display at Edinburgh Castle, where it could receive the greatest number of viewings and not to Scone from where it was originally taken.

The Stone was only returned to Scotland under strict instruction that for the next, and each succeeding, coronation of a British monarch, it must be returned to England's Westminster Abbey. It will no doubt be an interesting time when this happens, and its return will be hotly debated on both sides of the border.

Many years have passed since the official return of the Stone to Scotland and yet there still continues to be conflict about the Stone and its current place of residence within Edinburgh Castle. On 23rd December 2020 it was announced by the Scottish Government that the Stone would be relocated in 2024 from Edinburgh Castle and placed closer to its ancestral home in Perth. A submission and request was made in 2019 by the Perth & Kinross Council. Following public consultation, the Commissioners on the Safeguarding of the Regalia, who advise the Queen about all matters relating to the Stone, recommended that it should be moved, and the Queen accepted that advice.

The Stone has been revered as one of the most important artefacts in the British Isles for many centuries and possibly even millennia. Its story continues to amaze and there is no doubt that when the time comes for it to be returned to Westminster Abbey, for the coronation of the next British monarch, its importance will continue to rise. However, the history of the Stone is not without controversy and contention. Many argue that the Stone returned in 1951 was not the genuine Stone that Edward I took in 1296. Others claim that the Stone Edward took wasn't the real Scots king-making Stone.

In recent times there have been calls to try to verify once and for all whether the Stone that was taken from Scone in 1296 was in actual fact the king-making Stone of the Scots monarchy. There is a popular theory throughout Scotland, that before the invading army of Edward reached Scone to steal the Stone, some of the monks of Scone Abbey took the genuine Stone and hid it for safety. Accordingly, they replaced it with an unimportant piece of sandstone from the Scone area. It is this piece of sandstone that Edward took and that has resided at Westminster Abbey for nearly 700 years. This begs us to ask the question whether or not it is possible that Edward was duped, and whether he knew about it? If so, how and why did the Stone come to be used as the coronation Stone of the English and subsequently British monarchs? Is it the real the Stone of Destiny?

PART TWO

THE MYSTERY
OF THE STONE

Chapter 6
To Dupe a King

Early in 2008 an article appeared in a leading Scottish newspaper suggesting that the leader of then recently elected Scottish National Party, Alex Salmond, should open an inquiry into whether the Stone that King Edward I of England stole from Scone in 1296 really was the genuine Scots king-making Stone of ancient tradition. This call was significant for a number of reasons. Firstly, it highlighted the sensitivity over the issue that is still felt in the present day, even though many centuries have passed since the theft of the Stone. Secondly, it exposes the fragility of the United Kingdom of Great Britain. The primary goal of the Scottish National Party is to have complete political separation from the governing parliament based at Westminster in London. In essence, they are looking to break away from any form of English control over Scottish politics, economy and law. Thirdly, and perhaps most embarrassingly, it makes one wonder just how foolish the monarchy would feel if it were to turn out that the tradition of being crowned upon the Stone was a complete fallacy.

The very fact that there were calls for the inquiry suggest that there is a strong belief, at least in Scotland, that King Edward was duped. It is therefore worthwhile to re-examine the history to try to uncover whether it is possible that Edward took the wrong Stone, if he had any inclinations that he had, and if so, why did the legends continue to develop around the Stone that was taken to Westminster?

The Genuine Artefact

When the Stone was initially taken from Scone Abbey in August 1296, it was not sent straight to London. On route down south, the Stone was taken and placed at Edinburgh Castle, where it was recorded among the king's jewels in the Wardrobe Accounts for the end of year 24 of Edward's reign (i.e. 19th November 1296) as, *"una petra Magna super quam reges Scotiae solebant coronari"* ("a great stone upon which Scottish Kings were crowned").

It is not known exactly how or when the Stone was taken south to Westminster. It is often claimed to have been recorded by the chronicler, Matthew of Westminster, in his *Flores Historiarum*, that the Stone was presented by King Edward I to the shrine of St Edward the Confessor on 18th June 1297, along with the crown and sceptre of the Scots kings. This would be ten months after the Stone was taken from Scone, and seven months after being recorded in Edinburgh Castle.

What is recorded as having been presented to the shrine by Edward is called the '*tribunal*'. This is claimed by subsequent authors to mean the Stone. However, what is actually written in Latin is, "...*regalia regni Scotiae, tribunal scilicet sceptrumque aureum cum corona*". The word *tribunal* in Latin means a platform for the seat of magistrates, suggesting a position of power from where authority is conferred. It doesn't necessarily mean a physical seat or stone. What is perhaps interesting is the word immediately following tribunal, *scilicet*, which roughly translates as 'that is to say'. Our interpretation of the Latin might therefore be, "...the regalia of the Kingdom of Scotland, from where [regal] authority is conferred, that is to say, the sceptre and crown." This implies that it was not the Stone that conferred regal authority, but other artefacts.

What perhaps supports this interpretation is that in the Edinburgh Castle Wardrobe Accounts for 19th November 1296, the crown and sceptre are also recorded along with the Stone. However, against both the crown and sceptre it is recorded that it was "Offered by the king at the shrine of St Edward in the abbey church at Westminster, 18 June of this year [i.e. 1297 when the account was published]". However, this statement is not written against the entry for *una petra Magna*. When the records are so detailed for the majority of items, about where they were taken from, where they were sent to, to whom they were given, and/or when it was done, it is curious that it goes completely unrecorded for the Stone.

Even more interesting to our story, is that in the Edinburgh Castle Wardrobe Accounts, "remaining in the end of Year 31 [i.e. 19th November 1303] of the jewels which belonged to the former King of Scotland found in Edinburgh Castle in the 25th year [i.e. 19th November

1297]…a great stone on which the kings of Scotland used to be crowned." Amazingly, the Stone is recorded in official *English* records of the era as still being in Edinburgh Castle *seven years* after it was removed from Scone, and five months after it was supposedly presented to the shrine of St Edward in Westminster.

Further to this, it is mentioned by Hunter (1856) that in a subsequent royal inventory for Edinburgh Castle, in the thirty-fifth year of his reign and the year in which he died (i.e. 1307), that the Stone is said to have "been found in the Castle of Edinburgh." If true, this suggests that the Stone remained at Edinburgh for up to *eleven years* after its removal from Scone. However, Hunter argues that this is so contrary to other evidence that it must be an error. Unfortunately, we have not been able to find evidence to support or refute the claim further, so at this stage it is mentioned purely as a curious entry in the saga.

The inclusion of *una petra Magna,* and the style in which it is referred to in the Edinburgh Castle records, has led some (Hodge, 2019) to speculate that perhaps the Stone was always kept in Edinburgh Castle and only moved to Scone for official ceremonies, such as a coronation. Further, he suggests that the various records of the Stone in Edinburgh Castle indicate that the Stone may have been temporarily brought back to Scotland by Edward, even though there is no known record of this having happened. We would argue that perhaps the Stone never left Scotland until after 1303.

In any case, that a Stone eventually ends up in Westminster Abbey is beyond doubt. It is unknown whether the Stone was taken specifically for the purposes of English coronations, or whether it was intended to act as the Bishop's *cathedra* that was required to upgrade Westminster from an Abbey to a Cathedral. Confusion arises due to the fact that in a Westminster inventory account of 1307, where St Edward's Chair is mentioned, the reference to the Stone being used for coronation purposes is struck through on the original. It states:

> "[The stone] was sent by order of the King to the Abbey of Westminster to be placed there next to the shrine of St Edward, in a certain gilded wooden chair which the King ordered to be

made ~~so that the Kings of England and Scotland should sit on it on the day of their own Coronation~~ to the perpetual memory of the matter."

William Rishanger was one of the first to write about the Stone soon after it was placed at Westminster. He says that the chair and Stone were "to be made the chair of the priest celebrant" of Westminster Abbey, which was the *cathedra,* or throne, from where the officiating priest would offer Mass. According to Rishanger, and perhaps supported by the striking through of the wording above, the Stone was never meant to be used in a coronation ceremony but was instead to be used by the clergy. By placing the Stone in the shrine of St Edward the Confessor, it suggests that King Edward I regarded it as nothing more than a trophy of his conquest in Scotland. This was further emphasised by Harding in his fifteenth century *Metrical Chronicle* which states:

> And as he came home by Skoon away,
> The regal there of Scotland that he brought,
> And sent it forthe to Westmynster for ay,
> To ben there ynne a chayer clenly wrought,
> For masse prestes to sitte yn whan hem ought,
> Whiche yit is there stondyng beside the shrine,
> In a chair of olde tyme made ful fine.

There is no definitive evidence to indicate that the Stone was used for any coronation or ceremony of either Edward I or of the future English monarchs, Edward II, Edward III or Richard II. The Stone is first documented as having been used as part of the coronation ceremony in 1399 for the crowning of King Henry IV.

Edward seemingly did not want the Scots king-making Stone so that he could be seated upon it himself, rather he wanted to make sure that no Scots king could be crowned at all, or perhaps without his prior permission. He believed that the Stone held such power in Scotland and that by owning it he could force the Scots into accepting him as their Overlord and ruler, much like the position he now held over Wales.

In 1297 King Edward ordered his master goldsmith, Adam of Shoreditch, to design a chair to house the Stone that had been taken from Scone the previous year. This chair was to be made entirely out of bronze, as a sign of strength and conquest over what Edward regarded, at that stage of his career, as a lesser nation that should openly and gladly accept him as their Overlord. Inexplicably, Edward cancelled the order for the bronze chair several months later on 1st August 1297. This was almost one year to the day after the Stone had been taken from Scone, and when the Stone was still recorded in Edinburgh Castle. Although the project had been scrapped, some of the work had already been carried out on the chair and the design plans were kept on file.

The cancellation of the order for the bronze chair suggests that Edward had perhaps lost interest in his Stone project, and either he could not justify the financing of the chair or he realised that all was not as it should be with the Stone now in his possession. Rather than pursuing his plans of constructing an expensive bronze chair, Edward decided instead to have a wooden chair constructed and gilded in its place.

Some have argued (Rodwell, 2013) that the order to cancel the bronze chair was purely for logistical reasons. The combined weight of a bronze chair incorporating the Stone would have been three-quarters of a ton and therefore virtually impossible to move without causing significant damage to the fragile surrounding area of Westminster Abbey, whereas the wooden chair that was built is just 236Kg when combined with the Stone. This is difficult, but not impossible, to move, just as history has proved.

The wooden chair that is still used in the present day for a coronation ceremony is called St Edward's Chair, or the Coronation Chair. The order for this chair was raised by Edward I in 1299, three years after the Stone was taken from Scone, and two years after the order for the bronze chair was cancelled. It was Walter of Durham, who at the age of about seventy, was requested to make a chair out of wood following the design template drawn by the master goldsmith, Adam of Shoreditch.

The wooden chair was to be gilded and covered in fine imagery, some of which still exists. Most of the gilding, however, has fallen off over the centuries. The frame of the chair is made up of dominating pinnacles and trefoils, all of which were common features of the time period. The chair was to be covered with images of nature as well as images to show the strength of the monarchy. In some of the surviving artwork can be seen the image of a king sitting on a throne resting his feet on a footrest in the shape of a lion. Other areas show the image of the green man, representing the cycle of life, as well as ancient British symbols such as the oak tree.

There would originally have been shields placed in the open quatrefoil tracery where the Stone was housed. This means that the Stone would have been mostly obscured from view when it was positioned in the chair. The chair would have been a magnificent sight when first created, but today it is a mere shadow of its former self. It is covered in what can only be described as graffiti that has been carved into the woodwork by unknown persons over the centuries.

A payment was made to Walter upon its completion in 1300 for the sum of one hundred shillings. He also received a sum of 13s 4d for the carving and painting of two wooden leopards that were to be attached to the chair, although these have not survived that passage of time. The four gilt lions that act as the feet of the chair in its present state were made in 1727. They replaced earlier designs from circa 1509.

Following the most recent renovations to St Edward's Chair, between 2010-2012, an interesting feature was noticed. Rodwell (2013) asserts that there are no traces of original braces to hold a wooden seat above the Stone, which suggests that the original intention was to sit directly upon the Stone itself when seated in the chair. The wooden seat board placed over the top of the Stone is therefore apparently a later addition, presumably to make it more comfortable to sit on.

Figure 12: St Edward's Chair at Westminster Abbey

If it was originally intended to sit directly upon the Stone, then sitting on the iron rings would not really have been practical or comfortable. Rodwell claims that the recesses cut into the top of the Stone, which enable the iron rings to lay flat, were carved once it was no longer necessary to chain the Stone to the floor at Westminster. Presumably this was sometime after the Writ of 1328, and after the threat of the Stone being returned to Scotland, against the will of the Abbot of Westminster, had sufficiently diminished. Around this time, rather than have the iron rings continuously hanging down to the floor, they could be stored out of sight on the top of the Stone. It is therefore likely to have been around this same time that the wooden seat board was added to the chair so that the monarch no longer sat directly upon the Stone. All of this implies that the Stone underwent a major reworking when it was at Westminster, and that what we see today is very different from the Stone that was taken in 1296.

The first signs of contention about the Stone arise when we examine the early references, for no two descriptions of the Stone match. The authenticity of the Stone has been debated for many centuries. What is most interesting, is that the first entry of *"una petra Magna"* in the Edinburgh Castle Wardrobe Accounts of 1296, is one of the earliest references, from either Scottish or English sources, for there ever having been a Scots king-making Stone at all. If Edward believed that he had the genuine Stone, complete with all of its fantastic history, why did he not take it to London sooner? Instead, it was seemingly left at Edinburgh Castle for at least seven years.

Doubters of the importance of the Stone that was taken to Westminster made calls for a proper scientific examination to determine from where exactly it originated. Several studies have been carried out over the centuries, and the results prove to be very interesting, and conflicting. If its composition turned out to be similar to that found in Israel, then it perhaps adds credence that the Stone was Jacob's Pillow that the legend claimed it to be. Likewise, if the results proved it to be from Egypt, Spain, Ireland, Iona or Dunstaffnage then it would at least lend support to the legends surrounding its travels.

The Origin of the Stone

The first study of the composition of the Stone was by John MacCulloch in 1819. He described it as "a calcareous sandstone exactly resembling that which forms the doorway of Dunstaffnage Castle...a piece of Oban sandstone." Whilst this report helps to confirm a general location of origin for the Stone, it does not make for particularly good reading from a historical point of view. If the Stone is exactly the same as is used for the doorway at Dunstaffnage Castle, then can we surmise that this is what the Stone actually is – a door lintel? If so, for what reason would it have become the important king-making Stone of Scotland, unless it was a substitute used to dupe Edward?

The idea of it being of practical usage was further emphasised in the mid-1800s, when Professor Ramsey examined the Stone and concluded, "To my eye it appears as if it had been originally prepared for building purposes, but has never been used." From the first scientific report it seems as though the history of the Stone was coming into doubt, but at least the mention of Dunstaffnage helped to shine a glimmer of hope onto validating the legends.

During the Victorian era there was a revival in the romantic ideals of Scotland. Following the coronation of Queen Victoria in 1838, interest in the Stone began to rise amongst academics, historians, and archaeologists. Later that year, tiny fragments of the Stone were removed with the aim of analysing them to try to identify from where exactly it had originated. In the new age of scientific discovery, the legend of the Stone's travels was not adequate and a more accurate answer was needed.

Initial test results on the fragments of the Stone proved to be inconclusive. It could be from any number of places, and finding an answer proved to be more difficult than first thought. However, a further study in 1865 suggested that it could very well be from Palestine. According to Professor Charles Adelle Lewis Totten (1851-1908) of Yale University, "The analysis of the stone shows that there are absolutely no quarries in Scone or Iona where-from a block so constituted could possibly have come, nor yet from Tara."

This was taken even further by Professor Edward Faraday Odlum (1850-1935), who reputedly found a stratum of sandstone near the Red Sea and Bethel that, according to his research, was geologically the same as the Stone. The mention of the Red Sea is somewhat perplexing, especially in relation to the location of Bethel in Israel. It

141

is possible that he was referring to the Dead Sea and was misquoted with Red Sea.

Odlum chipped some fragments from the rock-face and took them with him to conduct further tests back in his homeland of the USA. According to Odlum, the microscopic tests that he conducted on the sample stone from Bethel perfectly matched the identical test results that had been carried out on the king-making Stone in previous years. He wanted to perform some chemical tests to verify beyond all doubt that the composition of the Stone matched that found at Bethel.

Odlum wrote to one of his English friends and asked him to try to obtain a pea-sized sample of the Stone at Westminster for the tests to be performed. A letter was written to the Dean of Westminster whose reply stated, "I daren't let you have permission. The only way you can get permission would be from the Archbishop of Canterbury." An application was subsequently made to the Archbishop and his reply was rather curter. He said, "To take a piece from that stone no bigger than a pea would require a special act of Parliament to be passed by the House of Commons, endorsed by the House of Lords and signed by the King; and if you get that, then I won't give you permission."

No further tests were allowed to confirm whether the Stone really had come from Bethel or not. Rather bizarrely, the refusal to confirm the origin of the Stone was all the proof that was needed for some that the Stone in Westminster genuinely was Jacob's Pillow, and that it did indeed come from the Holy Land.

An important argument has been put forward against the Stone being transported from the Middle East, through Egypt, Spain, Ireland and Scotland, before eventually being taken to England. The traditional portrayal is that the Stone was transported over this vast distance by way of a long pole being inserted between the two iron rings at each end of the Stone and carried henceforth. However, some have argued that if this were the case then the swinging motion of the Stone, as it was being carried, would have caused the sandstone around the iron pegs, which are imbedded in the Stone, to have eroded it away and that it would have eventually fallen to the ground.

It is hard to imagine the Stone being transported over any meaningful distance by a pole through the iron rings. Indeed, given the uneven way in which they have been set, the balance of the Stone is completely offset from centre which would have made carrying it very awkward. It is also highly likely that an important item such as the Stone would have been transported over long distances by a cart, and only needing to be manhandled over short distances for ceremonial purposes, when a pole through the rings might have sufficed. This all gives good credence to the idea that the iron rings were used for securing the Stone and not for lifting purposes. The most recent evidence available indicates that they were attached to the Stone when it was in England sometime in the 1320-1330s.

Different studies, conducted at different periods in time, have perhaps had different agendas to maintain. All have confirmed that the Stone originated from one of the locations associated with the legend, yet there is disagreement on exactly where that location was. It seems that the Stone originated in all locations and none. It merely depends on which report you want to believe.

The most recent and detailed analysis of the Stone came in October 1998. Dr David Breeze and Mr Richard Welander, of Historic Scotland, were granted permission by the Secretary of State for Scotland and the Keeper of the Regalia to conduct a geological examination of the Stone. Their extensive examinations confirmed that the Stone was lithologically similar to that of the Lower Old Red Sandstone age, which is about 400 million years old. They also conclude that this is the same type that can be found at Quarry Mill, near Scone in Perthshire, Scotland.

Although these findings will be argued by some to be inconclusive, they are based on using the most modern analysis and equipment. The Stone can confidently be said to have originated from the Scone area, rather than the Holy Land or some other location. For a Stone taken from Scone, that is perhaps the most logical conclusion, but it does give rise to the question of how and why it became so important.

Scone was an ancient Pictish capital, and as such it is likely that a Stone that was important to the Picts might have been used during their king-making ceremonies. Therefore, even though a legendary origin of the Stone can be ruled out, the magnificence of its history of being used as a king-making Stone could still be genuine, and as such it is an important part of Scottish, English, and British history.

Return to Scone in 1298

A year after Edward had cancelled the order for the bronze chair, he sent a raiding party to head back to Scone and destroy the Abbey. This happened on 17th August 1298. Although we cannot be sure of the reasoning behind this move, it would be easy to suggest that it was because Edward now thought that the Stone he originally took in 1296 was not the Stone he was after. As a consequence, he sent his army to destroy the Abbey, and kill or torture the monks who had made a fool out of him.

Whilst this is an intriguing scenario, another possible explanation for the destruction of Scone Abbey is that it was the centre of focus for a Scottish uprising the previous year in 1297. Edward had appointed William Ormsby to be the English governor of Scotland whilst he was down south administering the other parts of his kingdom. As a sign of English dominance over the Scottish traditions, Ormsby held his court at Scone in May 1297. The Scots patriot and hero, Sir William Wallace, along with Sir William Douglas, led an attack that saw Ormsby having to flee the country, allowing a Scottish uprising to ensue. The monks of Scone Abbey were very sympathetic to the Scots cause and it is possible that the destruction of the Abbey in 1298 was to silence these critics of the English regime.

A Stone and a Throne

One of the most confusing aspects to try to understand is whether the genuine king-making artefact was a Stone or a seat. The term *lapis fatalis cathedrae instar* was first used by Hector Boece (1465-1536) to describe the Stone upon which Gaythelos was crowned. It often gets translated as 'fatal stone like a chair' and it is for this reason that the Stone is sometimes referred to as the Fatal Chair or Fatal Stone. However, this is not what is actually being described. The Latin term *fatalis* is of similar meaning to 'fate' which is indicating some kind of pre-determined course of action.

It was said that the Stone would reject anyone who was not the rightful monarch, thus meaning it would accept anyone who was fated to be king. This follows the Irish tradition about the Lia Fáil that claimed that the Stone would roar when the true king touched or stood on it. On this reasoning, some authors have identified the *lapis fatalis* with the Lia Fáil that was at one time located at Tara in Ireland. Some slightly less popular accounts state the when the rightful monarch was seated upon the Stone his name would magically appear carved into it.

A more correct translation of *lapis fatalis* would be the 'Fated Stone', in reference to the fact that the next monarch was legitimately the heir to the throne, either through birth right or as designate under the succession rules of tanistry. Succession by tanistry means that the reigning monarch would designate his heir whilst still alive. By this rule of succession, it meant that the next monarch did not necessarily have to be of the same lineage as the previous monarch. This idea gave rise to another, less popular, name for the king-making Stone – the Tanist Stone. It was not until King Malcolm II in 1005 that succession by tanistry was abolished in the Scots monarchy. After this date, succession was by birth right and was typically inherited by the eldest son.

The term 'Stone of Destiny' is a relatively modern way to describe the Stone, and probably the most popular. It is a further corruption of the Latin term *lapis fatalis*. Fate and destiny have often been used interchangeably over the past few hundred years, but this has not always been the case. In ancient times 'fate' was something that could be determined by the gods, whereas 'destiny' was something that could not be altered. You are destined to die but the circumstances surrounding that death can be decided by a plethora of events that collectively make up your fate. Therefore, over time the 'Stone of Fate' vulgarly became the 'Stone of Destiny'.

John of Fordun, in his *Gesta Annalia,* gives an account of the coronation ceremony for Alexander III, King of Scots in 1249. His account was written about 100 years after the event. It is therefore quite possible that he was referencing earlier sources that were describing one thing, whilst trying to liken it to the Stone that was now at Westminster. Rather curiously, he describes the role of the Stone in the following terms:

> "...having there placed him in the regal chair, decked with silk cloths embroidered with gold...the king himself sitting, as was proper, upon the regal chair – that is, the stone – and the earls and other nobles placing vestments under his feet, with bent knees, before the stone."

It takes quite an imagination to view the king-making Stone as anything that could be remotely classed as a 'Regal Chair'. It is almost as though Fordun is trying to reconcile the known artefact in the possession of the English with earlier writings about some kind of other chair or throne.

This confusion about a Stone or a chair/seat has continually stifled any attempts to try to unravel what the genuine Scots king-making Stone actually was. It has even been proposed by the Scottish antiquarian and historian, Dr Joseph Robertson (1869), that there could have been two Stones at Scone used for the purposes of a coronation. One might have been used to represent the king and would perhaps have more of a political bias, and the other to represent the church and more spiritual matters. By using both as part of the coronation ceremony, the king was therefore being crowned in both a temporal and spiritual manner. He further proposes that perhaps there was both a Stone and a chair used for the coronation ceremony in Scotland. This is what happened when the Stone was taken to Westminster, and so it is quite possible that a similar practice was also followed when it was in use in Scotland.

It has long been suggested that Scone was a Pictish religious centre, and so when Kenneth McAlpin also moved his administrative centre there it operated with the dual functions of the royal and religious centre of Scotland. It is also possible that the two aspects of the coronation 'seat' were to signify the union of the Kingdom of Dál Riata and the Kingdom of the Picts. Dr Robertson suggests that the 'Stone of Fate' or Fatal Stone (*lapis fatalis*) of legend was the one that was taken to England in 1296 by King Edward I, whilst the throne in which the Stone was placed during coronations was secreted away by the Scots and has remained hidden ever since.

Even though there have been several studies of the Stone, all with differing conclusions, the most logical theory and conclusion is that the Stone originated from the Scone area. This leads Dr Robertson to suggest that the Stone that was taken to Westminster was of Pictish origin and should be associated with the Pictish king-making rituals and not those of the Kingdom of Dál Riata. However, the Picts have carved many wonderful symbols over a plethora of stones throughout Scotland that were obviously of importance to them. One would expect that if the Stone really was an ancient Pictish king-making Stone then it would have some kind of markings upon its surface in keeping with the known symbols of the Picts. However, this is not the case. It is possible, although unlikely, that if there were any Pictish carvings on the Stone, then they may have been removed at a later date, and possibly when alterations may have been made to the Stone when it was at Westminster.

Evidence to support the 'Stone and throne' theory is from the differing terminology used to describe how the various monarchs are seated during their coronation. Some accounts portray that the king was seated 'on' the Stone and others state they had to sit 'in' the seat. It is impossible to envisage how the Stone could be regarded as a seat that someone could sit *in* as opposed to a Stone that someone would sit *on* unless it was placed inside some kind of receptacle to hold it. This was exactly the original purpose of St Edward's Chair when it was designed. The monarch would sit in the chair, and directly on the Stone. There is no reason to suggest that the practicalities of this design weren't mimicking the setup at Scone.

It is maybe even possible that the Stone didn't play any significant role in the Scots king-making ceremony in the first place. The theft of the Stone in 1296 did not stop the Scots from crowning future monarchs at Scone. King Robert the Bruce was crowned in 1306 and it is therefore possible that at least some aspects of the pre-1296 ceremony was still being used.

On examining the King Seals of Scotland, it is interesting to note that there are few consistencies between the various depictions of the throne, and seemingly no direct representation of them being seated on a Stone. In an article written by McKerracher (1984), he suggests that the depictions of the various seals, prior to the theft of the Stone in 1296, portray a very different Stone to the one taken to Westminster. He claims that what is depicted is much flatter and longer and so this is evidence of Edward having been duped with the Stone from Scone.

A member of our early research team was a gentleman named David Russell. David had some exceptional skills and sadly died in 2007. He pointed out to us that the only correlation between the various King Seals is the footstool that the kings have their feet upon. They all look identical and vaguely similar in size to the Stone that was taken from Scone, especially up to William I. It is an interesting observation, and especially because the king was known as the 'Footstool of God'. Is it possible that the original purpose of the Stone was to be a footstool, and never sat upon? Could this be a continuation of the king-making traditions that were held at Dunadd, having been brought to Scone by the Scots of Dál Riata at the time of Kenneth McAlpin?

When the Stone was taken to London, Edward ordered a chair to be built to house the Stone now in his possession. It must have been realised early on that the Stone was uncomfortable to sit on, and only really big enough for a child to be seated upon due to its low height. Is it therefore just logical that some kind of throne, with a space to receive the Stone, was also an integral part of the coronation ceremony that made up the 'Regal Chair' when it was in Scotland? With the second ransacking of Scone Abbey in 1298, it is possible that Edward realised that he only had one half of the 'King's Seat', and so went back to try to take the other part, and thus have the complete throne.

The only thing that is known for certain is that Edward had a Stone from Scone and was not prepared to give it back.

Figure 13: The King Seals (from top-left to bottom-right) Alexander I (1107-1124), David I (1124-1153), Malcolm IV (1153-1165), William I (1165-1214), Alexander II (1214-1249), Alexander III (1249-1286), John Balliol (1292-1296), Robert I (1306-1329), David II (1329-1371)

Sandstone, Marble, or Meteorite?

Advocates of Edward having been duped with a 'fake' Stone will sometimes claim that the 'real' Stone is made of either of marble or meteorite, and not sandstone. The confusion of this is seemingly down to a translation from Latin to English. During the Middle Ages,

Latin was the main form of the written word in Europe. As often happens, a word can be translated to have more than one meaning, as with our modern-day English language. In an earlier chapter, we encountered the term *'lapis Pharaonis'* or Pharaoh's Stone to describe the Stone of Destiny. It was also discussed how according to the chronicler, William Rishanger, the Stone was to initially be used as the "chair of the priest celebrant", or *cathedra,* when it was first taken to Westminster Abbey. Whenever the Latin word *lapis* is used, such as *lapis Pharaonis* or even *lapis cathedra* it can be read to mean either stone or marble. Therefore, *lapis cathedra* could technically be referring to either a stone chair or marble chair.

Advocates of the Stone originating from Iona, and being St Columba's Pillow, will find instant links with the marble that is common on Iona, even though this is generally green in colour. The 'genuine' Stone is sometimes purported to be white marble and sometimes black marble. Aside from when there is no doubt that it is the Stone taken from Scone by Edward that is being discussed, there is rarely any mention of the Stone as being composed of red sandstone. However, when red sandstone is polished it can have similar looking attributes to marble. This is most noticeable with the Frith Stool in Hexham Abbey, which is likewise composed of red sandstone. The key difference is that the Stone from Scone does not have the appearance of looking like polished marble.

There are even claims that the 'genuine' Stone is made of black meteorite basalt, much like the Kaaba Stone that resides in Mecca. The Kaaba is perhaps the most holy relic in Islam and there are similarities with what is held by some to be the genuine Scots king-making Stone. This is not to suggest that the Kaaba is the 'real' Stone, but merely that the composition is often reputed to be similar. The Kaaba is said to have fallen from heaven during the time of Adam and Eve and was originally white but turned black as a result of all of the sin in the world.

Dunsinane Hill

The idea of the Stone being black marble has its roots in a rather strange event that happened towards the beginning of the nineteenth

150

century. There was a story circulating in the newspapers in 1819, suggesting that a black Stone had been found inside a cavity on Dunsinane Hill. Dunsinane Hill lies three miles east of Scone, and has a particularly interesting history. It is reputed that the top of this hill had an ancient fort that was known as MacBeth's Castle. MacBeth was the Scots king who was made famous by the English play-write, William Shakespeare, in the late sixteenth/early seventeenth century.

On 1st January 1819, a letter was sent to *The Times* newspaper, stating that a cavity had been found on Dunsinane Hill that contained a rather interesting find. It was reported that a few months previously, on 19th November 1818, several workmen that were employed by West Mains of Dunsinane were removing various stones and rubble from a previous excavation at Macbeth's Castle. Apparently, the ground upon which they were standing gave way and they fell into a vault that was about six feet deep, six feet long and four feet wide. Here, they discovered a large black Stone that weighed around 500lb and was described as looking like a meteoric or semi-metallic type of stone. Carefully placed beside the strange Stone were said to have been two bronze round tablets. On one of the tablets there was an engraving which read:

"The sconce of kingdom come until sylphs in air carry me
again to Bethel"

Whoever was reporting the story was in no two minds about it. What had been found was Jacob's Pillow and the genuine Stone that was used as the coronation seat of the ancient Scottish monarchs. It was thought that perhaps this was the Stone that the monks of Scone Abbey had hidden when they first heard of the impending invasion of King Edward I in 1296. The Stone was reportedly sent to London for further tests to validate its authenticity, but mysteriously it has disappeared and has never been seen or heard of since.

There have been various excavations at MacBeth's Castle on Dunsinane Hill, both before and after the publication of the letter, but nothing of such magnitude had been found or reported. The first excavation occurred in 1799 and was followed by another in 1854. Quite what the workmen must have been doing in 1818 simply adds further confusion to the mystery, as there are no reports of any official excavations or digging taking place at Dunsinane Hill around that date. However, the excavation in 1854 did find four vaulted chambers built of old red sandstone, but each of the roofs had fallen in, possibly as a result of a previous excavation. It is possible that one of these chambers was the 'cavity' into which the workmen fell when they found the Stone, but there was no evidence to be found to help back up the story.

Another version of the story suggests the same find but under very different circumstances. Two young men were out walking on Dunsinane Hill after some heavy rainfall. They came upon a small landslide caused by the storm and they noticed a crack in the rock at the side of the hill. The two men each made a flaming torch and entered the crack in the rock. Inside they discovered an old chamber. In the chamber they discovered a large Stone supported by four stone legs. Apparently, the Stone was covered in hieroglyphics and had the words "Where ever this stone rests, the Scots shall reign" carved upon it. This is very similar to the *Ni fallat fatum* prophecy attributed to King Simon Brecc. Another account suggests that the words "Under your protective shadow lies the kingdom until angels carry you back to Bethel" were written on the Stone, hinting towards the Jacob's Pillow legend. The two men are supposed to have left the site and did not report it as they had not realised the importance of their discovery.

Years passed, and the two men had started to hear rumours that the monks of Scone Abbey had taken and hidden the genuine Scots king-making Stone when they had learned that King Edward I and his army was making their way to Scone to take the Stone. Apparently, they had replaced the 'real' Stone with a similar sized stone from the Annety Burn, close to Scone. The rumour persisted that the monks had hidden the genuine Stone somewhere in the local vicinity, which could very possibly have been Dunsinane Hill. When the men heard of this, they became excited by what they had discovered several years earlier. They tried to find the cavity on a subsequent visit to Dunsinane Hill, but they could not locate where the entrance to the cavity was, and so their discovery was lost, left for others to find in the future.

Whilst this may sound fantastical, it is possible that the story was created for another purpose. In February 1818, Sir Walter Scott had been part of a group who had rediscovered the Honours of Scotland (Scottish Crown Jewels) that had been hidden, or lost, in Edinburgh Castle since the Treaty of Union in 1707. As the Honours of Scotland had no symbolic function to perform following the establishment of the new Parliament of Great Britain that was then based at Westminster in London, the Honours were placed in a chest, locked up in Edinburgh Castle and forgotten about for over a hundred years. Their rediscovery became an event of Scottish significance and re-kindled a wave of national pride. This was six months before the black Stone was reputedly discovered at Dunsinane Hill, and it is highly possible that the story of the 'find' was nothing more than a publicity event, in an attempt to try to reinstate a passion for Scottish sovereignty. Regardless, the rumours persisted about the genuine Stone being composed of black stone, possibly meteorite. The confusion continues to this day.

Whatever the Dunsinane Stone was, if indeed it was anything, that it has gone missing is rather unfortunate. In early 2008, it was reported in the UK *Daily Express* newspaper that the present owner of Dunsinane may have known of the whereabouts of the genuine Stone. According to their sources, in the 1970s the then owner of Dunsinane House reputedly claimed that he could "reach out and touch" the Stone if he wanted. Whatever the truth, which they have kept to themselves, the suggestion of a Stone being found at Dunsinane and the enduring legacy of that find has served only to add intrigue to the legend of the Stone of Destiny. If the Stone was indeed of a black meteoric substance, then it is perhaps easy to understand how and why it came to be revered as a sacred stone because it 'fell from the heavens'. Such a Stone would perhaps be more appealing, and mystical, than a piece of red sandstone from a quarry not too far from Scone.

The Confusion of a Legend

There are no references to any Scots king-making Stone, seat, or description of a Scottish coronation ceremony that is written from before the Stone was taken from Scone in 1296. This is a rather curious fact and as such we must look to later sources to try to identify how the legend of the Stone became established.

The reference that is most commonly used when detailing the travels of the Scots race is that which is found in the *Scotichronicon,* written by John of Fordun, and enhanced by Walter Bower around the year 1440. To recap from an earlier chapter, in the *Scotichronicon* version of events it was written that the Greek Prince Gaythelos went to Egypt and eventually married Scota, the daughter of the Egyptian Pharaoh, Chencres, who, along with his army, was drowned whilst pursuing Moses and the Children of Israel across the Red Sea. It was Gaythelos who then led some of the remaining followers of the Pharaoh, who had not drowned, through Africa and eventually across the Mediterranean Sea by boat. They are believed to have landed around Cadiz in Spain. The reference to Africa is most likely indicating the country of modern-day Libya and/or Tunisia, and it is possible that they made their way to Spain by crossing the sea at the Straits of Gibraltar, often described as the Pillars of Hercules.

Many years passed, and the Scots, who now lived in Spain, were regularly attacked by the local inhabitants. Gaythelos decided to try to find an uninhabited island where he could rule as king, so he sent his sailors in search of somewhere more suitable to the north. When they returned from their voyage the sailors informed Gaythelos of their find and he decided that this would be the new Kingdom of the Scots.

Gaythelos died before he could journey to the intended island and many years passed without any of his successors making plans to fulfil his wishes. It was not until his descendent, Simon Brecc, came to power that serious efforts were made to colonise the island. Brecc took the "marble throne on which the Scottish kings in Spain used to sit" and placed it at the site that was to be the chief seat of his kingdom. He called this place Tara.

For many years the Scots race lived on the island in relative peace, as any natives could be easily subdued. However, as generations passed the nature of the kingdom changed and eventually there were various factions competing for the throne. Fergus, the first King of Dál Riata, is said to have taken the stone chair that Simon Brecc placed at Tara and took it with him to Argyll to be crowned upon.

The Kingdom of Dál Riata extended from the north-eastern parts of Ireland and across the sea to modern-day Argyll in western Scotland. Many more kings were crowned in Argyll, with the last being King Kenneth McAlpin. He united the Scots of the Kingdom of Dál Riata with the Picts of the eastern parts of Alba (modern day Scotland) in 843. In that year he moved his chief seat from Argyll to Scone, and legend states that he brought with him the king-making seat. This Stone seat was used in the coronation ceremonies of each succeeding monarch of the Kingdom of the Scots and was last used to crown King John Balliol in 1292. When Balliol instigated a conflict with King Edward I of England, the English king went to Scone and took away what he believed to be the Scots king-making Stone in 1296.

Following soon after the *Scotichronicon* was the work of Hector Boece (1465-1536). His account was of a similar vein, but some key facts were included that were omitted by Fordun. Instead of Gaythelos and Scota travelling across Africa (Libya and/or Tunisia) towards Spain, Boece has them travel over the Mediterranean Sea to Portugal, where they founded their kingdom at Brigantium on the northern coast. This area of the northern Iberian Peninsula is called Galicia and still retains very strong Celtic links.

Boece is also the first person to introduce Dunstaffnage Castle into the legend of the Stone. It is often told that Dunstaffnage was the place where the Stone was taken and the coronations took place once it had been removed from Tara by Fergus, the first King of the Scots who dwelled in Scotland. However, this appears to be incorrect.

The confusion arises with the early translations of the works of Boece by various writers. Boece says the Fatal Chair was taken from Ireland and placed at Beregonium. The original works of Boece clearly state that Beregonium was *near to* a place called Euonium, that was subsequently called Dunstaffnage. His work was translated by John Bellenden, Archdeacon of Moray, in 1531, and whereas Boece continued to refer to the site as Euonium, Bellenden continuously refers to it as Dunstaffnage.

As a respected member of the clergy, Bellenden's account was more influential than the original. A few years later, another writer, William Stewart, assumed Beregonium and Dunstaffnage to be the same place and later historians, such as the sixteenth century John Monipennie, took his assumptions and stated them as fact. Whilst it is possible that Dunstaffnage superseded Beregonium as the capital of Dál Riata, there is no evidence to suggest that this was the case. Therefore, it is unlikely that the Stone was ever specifically taken to Dunstaffnage for the purposes of a coronation. This direct link between Dunstaffnage Castle and the Stone was first introduced by Monipennie and it has been retold as part of the legend ever since. The actual location of Beregonium has never been identified, and until it is found Dunstaffnage and the surrounding area will remain intimately tied to the story of the Stone of Destiny.

With the Dunstaffnage location for the Stone being presumably a 'red herring', it brings into doubt the idea that the Stone is of a similar material as the door lintel to the castle. Perhaps the only part of the story that can be verified with other sources is that it was Fergus who took the Stone from Ireland in the fifth or sixth century, and it was to be used as the chief seat of the Kingdom of Dál Riata. Boece identifies this Fergus as Fergus Mac Ferchard, of whom history has no record. He says Fergus placed the Stone in Argyll, but whereas other accounts would agree on the name, they would not agree on the place where the Stone was taken.

Before this came the work of Andrew Wyntoun (1350-1420). He was a canon and prior of St Serf's Church on Loch Leven before becoming a canon at St Andrews. He wrote the *Orygynale Cronykil of Scotland* at the request of his patron, Sir John of Wemyss, of Wemyss Castle in Fife. It was to be a history of Scotland from the earliest of times until King James I in 1406. It is widely believed that he took his chronicle from older manuscripts that have not survived to the present day.

Wyntoun identifies the person responsible for moving the Stone from Ireland as the historical Fergus Mac Erc, who is mentioned in the Irish accounts as the first king of Dál Riata. However, confusion arises in the fact that Wyntoun does not have Fergus taking the Stone to Argyll but rather to a place known as Ycomkill. Ycomkill, also spelt Ikkolmkil or Icolmkill is widely believed to be the island of Iona, but interestingly it was also an old name for the Island of Inchcolm in the Firth of Forth in the east of Scotland. Inchcolm literally means 'Island of Columba'. Is it possible that Iona was misread for Inchcolm and the Stone has no associations to the island on the west coast of Scotland at all, but rather has closer links to the Pictish island of Inchcolm?

The Stone is composed of sandstone from around the Perthshire area, and so it is possible that its original history started with Pictish traditions that were later incorporated into the story of the travels of the Scots race coming in from the west. The Irish-Scots traditions of king-making were more akin to those that were held at Dunadd, just south of Dunstaffnage, on the western coast of mainland Scotland. Here, carved into the rock that protrudes from the flat plain there is a hole in the shape of a human footprint from an unknown date. Tradition asserts that part of the inauguration ceremony at Dunadd required the next monarch to place his foot into the footprint, and if it was an exact fit then he was seen as the rightful heir to the throne. This is a similar concept to that which appears in *Cinderella* and the story of the glass slipper, originally written by the French author Charles Perrault and later popularised in the film by Walt Disney. The foot that fits the slipper is the chosen one. As previously mentioned, the chosen king was often described as the 'Footstool of God', much like the position that the Pope in Rome is held in the eyes of Catholic believers. Also, the placing of the foot in the footprint was to signify that the new king was 'following in the footsteps of his father'.

We do not know what king-making traditions the Picts followed, but it is possible that the idea of being seated on a Stone originated with them and not from Dál Riata. If this is the case, then it

157

is easy to see how the confusion between Iona and Inchcolm could have come about when later historians tried to tie in the wanderings of the Scots race through Spain and Ireland with the traditions of the Picts who were always resident in the lands of modern-day Scotland. By the time that the accounts were being written down, the Scots and the Picts had already been merged for several centuries, and their respective histories would have been intermingled to create one complete story of the history of the Scots race. Wyntoun also describes the Stone in rather peculiar terms:

> A gret Stane this Kyng than had;
> That fore this Kyngis Sete was made;
> And haldyne wes a gret Jowale;
> Wyth-in the Kynryke of Spayne hale.

The above seems to be referring to a Stone seat that held a great jewel. Is it possible that in Wyntoun's day it was believed there were two parts to the throne that made up the 'Coronation Seat'? One part as a throne and the other as a Stone/jewel that was to be placed inside the throne, as previously discussed. Perhaps one part, for example the chair, belonged to the Irish-Scots and the other, the Stone/seat, belonged to the Picts and bringing them together signified their unity.

There is yet another chronicle from around the same time as Wyntoun which also suggests that it was Fergus who took the Stone. However, in this account, Fergus placed it at yet another location. The *Scalacronica* was written by Sir Thomas Gray of Heaton, who was an Englishman being held as a prisoner in Edinburgh between 1355 and 1362. He too mentions Simon Brecc taking the "stone on which the kings of Spain were wont to be crowned" and placed it at Tara, before it was later removed by Fergus. Instead of Fergus taking it to either Dunstaffnage or Iona, Heaton bypasses all mention of Dál Riata and has him take it directly to Scone.

Following several years later was the account by Blind Harry (1440-1492) in his *The Actes and Deidis of the Illustre and Vallyeant Campioun Schir William Wallace*. This is believed to have been written

158

around 1477. Blind Harry's poem of William Wallace was supposed to have been based on the Latin works of Bishop William Sinclair of Dunkeld, who died in 1337. He is believed to have received the information from John Blair, a monk of Dunfermline Abbey, and the confessor of William Wallace. It is generally assumed that it was the intention of Bishop Sinclair to use the story as proof of the English aggression during the Wars of Independence and send it to the Pope in Rome to aid the Scottish cause.

Bishop William was angry with the English and would have done what he thought was necessary to keep them out of Scotland. After the death of Matthew de Crambeth, Bishop of Dunkeld Cathedral, in 1309, William was elected as the person who would succeed him. However, King Edward II of England decided to put forward his own candidate, John de Leck, for the position. William then went to Avignon to put his case forward to Pope Clement V who was also hearing the case from the English candidate. Eventually the dispute was resolved in 1311 when John de Leck was made Archbishop of Dublin, thus leaving William free to become the Bishop of Dunkeld uncontested. It is possible that Bishop William was one of those present at the coronation ceremony of John Balliol, although this is not known for certain.

Blind Harry wrote his poem about the inauguration of King John Balliol nearly two hundred years after the theft of the Stone, and his account almost mirrors that of Heaton in the *Scalacronica*. He says:

> The crown he took upon the self-same stane,
> That Gadales sent with his son from Spain;
> When Iber Scot first into Ireland come.
> At Canmor syne King Fergus has it won,
> Brought it to Scone, and stable made it there,
> Where kings were crowned eight hundred years and mair,
> Before the time that King Edward it fand,
> This jewel he garttuise into England.

Again, both Dunstaffnage and Iona are excluded from the account, with Fergus taking the Stone directly to Scone in the fifth century.

Perhaps the oldest mention of the Stone as a legend, appears in the writings of a Scottish lawyer named Baldred Bisset in 1301. Bisset was sent to Rome, along with William Frere and William of Eaglesham, to plead the cause of the Scots to Pope Boniface VIII in 1301. This was to prove that the Scots had a different and older linage than that of the English, and accordingly they had no right to oversee or rule Scotland. They were armed with a document that had been approved and prepared by the Scottish Government, known as the *Instructiones* that stated:

> "The ancient people of the Scots, thus called after Scota, daughter of Pharao, king of Egypt, went from Egypt, and first occupied Ireland; they occupied, secondly, Argyll in Scotland, and having driven the Britons out of Scotland, the part of Britain thus occupied was called by them by the new name of Scota, from that first Scota, queen of the Scots, according to the line; *a muliere Scots vocitatur Scotia tota.*"

At the time, King Edward I of England was trying to prove his Overlordship of Scotland by claiming that the English were descended from Locrinus, the eldest son of King Brutus of Troy, whereas the Scots were descended from Albanactus, the youngest son. In response to this, the Scots had to ensure that they could claim an older and more ancient heritage that superseded that of the English. By taking their history back through Ireland to Egypt they were doing just that. However, for Bisset the *Instructiones* did not emphasise the point far enough, and so he added to them some irrefutable proof of their voyage by including a certain artefact. His *Processus Baldredi contra figmenta rigis Anglie,* or *Processus* for short, now included the Stone that Edward had stolen from Scone. The *Processus* says:

> "The daughter of Pharao, king of Egypt, with an armed band and a large fleet, goes to Ireland, and there being joined by a

body of Irish, she sails to Scotland, taking with her the royal seat which he, the king of England, with other insignia of the Kingdom of Scotland, carried with him by violence to England. She conquered and destroyed the Picts and took their kingdom; and from this Scota the Scots and Scota are named, according to the line: *a muliere Scots vocitatur Scotia tota.*"

In the *Processus*, which is perhaps the oldest written account of the travels of the Scots and the Stone, there is no mention of Spain, Tara, Fergus, Dunstaffnage, Iona, or with it having any biblical association whatsoever. Even the Britons are replaced by the Picts, who by then had been completely amalgamated into the Kingdom of Scotland and who, for some reason, were regarded in a different light to the Britons. History had now been written and was stated as 'fact', but which account are we to believe?

It is interesting to note that missing from both the *Instructiones* and the *Processus* is any mention of St Andrew, who is largely presumed to have been the patron saint of Scotland at the time. It seems strange that Bisset does not mention the 'first Apostle' in 1301, yet he is mentioned in 1320 in the Declaration of Arbroath, when strangely the Stone is not mentioned.

At the time of the *Instructiones* and *Processus*, we have the start of the legend of the Stone, and the tit-for-tat written war between Scotland and England, each trying to prove a more ancient heritage than the other. At the time that the *Processus* was delivered to the Pope in 1301, Edward had also written to him demanding that the Scots Bishop, Robert Wishart, be removed from his position as the Bishop of Glasgow. The response from the Pope was to rebuke Edward and accuse him of being "the prime mover and instigator of all the tumult and dissention which has arisen between his dearest son in Christ, Edward, King of England, and the Scots."

Edward was having the English religious clerks search for any evidence of the English being the superior race of the British Isles. He was utilising the myths and legends from works such as *Historia Regum Britanniae* by Geoffrey of Monmouth (1100s), *Historia Britonum* by

Nennius (800s), *Historia Ecclesiastica Gentis Angorum* by Bede (700s), *De Excidio Britanniae* by Gildas (500s), as well as any and every other document that his clerks could find to help support his beliefs. However, with Bisset came the first written Scottish reference to suggest that the Stone now in England had historical links with other locations, rather than just Scone.

Several years after Bisset published the *Processus,* a poem was written in French titled *La Pierre d'Ecosse,* in 1307. What is of special interest with this poem is that for the first time the Stone is linked to having been present during biblical times. It is said that it was at the time of Moses that Scota left Egypt with the Stone, but in this there is no mention of Jacob or his pillow.

With all of the different versions of events appearing around the same time, it is easy to suggest that there were oral traditions being told, and that when they were eventually written down certain aspects of the story would have been included in some and excluded in others. Naturally, some aspects would have been omitted depending on which version was being told. What is perhaps not so convincing with this suggestion is that the timing of the release of many of these stories coincided with major political events happening between Scotland and England, and their many petitions to Rome. Each was trying to establish a more ancient heritage that linked them to the land upon which they lived. It is therefore highly possible that the creation of the legend of the Stone was to further the claims for the independence of Scotland by associating the Scots with some of the most ancient kingdoms and known history of the day, but whilst at the same time still keeping true to the Christian faith.

The site of the actual king-making ceremonies is itself also a contentious issue. Surprisingly, what is not described in any of the early accounts is where the actual coronation ceremony took place. Today we accept that the crowning of Alexander III and all the other ancient kings of Scotland since Kenneth McAlpin took place on Moot Hill at Scone. However, this can be likened to the depiction of Jesus being born in a stable. It should be recognised that there are no written references to this in the Gospels, only that he was placed in a manger, which the authorities assume to have been in a stable. Although it is widely believed it does not make it documented fact.

In the *Scotichronicon*, Fordun does not mention the coronation ceremony taking place on Moot Hill, but rather in a cemetery at Scone Abbey where a large cross was situated. The mausoleum that is located on top of Moot Hill today was not constructed until 1624, some years before the coronation of Charles II in 1651. This suggests that unless the present Moot Hill is built on an old cemetery, of which there is no written or archaeological proof, then the site of the coronation of King Alexander III, and therefore presumably so too of all of the other monarchs who preceded him, was at least 150 yards south-east of the centre of the present Moot Hill. So what is a Moot Hill?

It was previously discussed how Moot Hill is sometimes referred to as Boot Hill, in respect to the idea that the nobles of Scotland would bring a boot-full of earth from their lands in order to pay homage and show respect to the new monarch. 'Moot', as in a 'moot point', is something that is brought up for discussion, or in other words, a debate. The term Moot Hill is actually referring to a debating or parliamentary hill rather than a king-making hill. However, it is possible that Moot is also referring to a Moat/Motte which implies a stronghold that was surrounded by a ditch, with or without being filled with water. To date, there is no archaeological evidence to support any defensive structures around Moot Hill, and it therefore has to be assumed that it was just a meeting place used to 'moot' over ideas and issues of the day.

What is interesting to highlight is that there are Moot Hills sited all over the British Isles, and not just at Scone. All of the other Moot Hills are associated with the justice courts or some kind of meeting place, and Scone should not be regarded as being any different. Another tradition that later becomes potentially important to our story, is that it was seemingly common to call people to the Moot Hill by the ringing of a bell. Bells were used hundreds of years beforehand for calling people to the places of worship, and the tradition is carried on even today. Town criers, churches, schools and Parliament all use bells to call people to the meeting place. It is therefore logical to accept the possibility that there would have been a special ceremonial bell at Scone.

There has even been the suggestion that the Moot Hill replaced the Stone Circles of the ancient Druids as a place of holding courts and administrating the law. Over time, Moot Hill at Scone became the centre of the Pictish and then the Scottish kingdoms. However, again there is no hard evidence that Scone or Moot Hill was a sacred or king-making centre before King Kenneth McAlpin in 843. Therefore, it is perhaps more logical to assume that any coronation ceremony at Scone would have been held at, or even inside, Scone Abbey.

The Founding of a Legend

The history of the Stone appears to be verging on the fantastical – from Israel to Egypt, Spain to Ireland, then Scotland to England. It appears more probable that the ancient histories written about the Stone were created to suit different purposes. The coronation of King Edward III of England occurred at Westminster Abbey on 1st February 1327. Released in the same year, was a chronicle by the English writer, William Rishanger, titled *Chronica et Annales*. His chronicle is responsible for one of the most enduring legends associated with the Stone of Destiny.

It is the first time that the Stone stolen from Scone by King Edward I in 1296 is reputed to be Jacob's Pillow. This was published 31 years after the Stone had been taken. Before 1327 there is no surviving written record or tradition associated with the Scots king-making Stone identifying any artefact from Scotland with the biblical patriarch Jacob. If there was indeed a tradition associated with such an important biblical relic that was widely believed in Scotland before this date, then it is very curious that it was never recorded or promoted. Indeed, there are only scant references to any such coronation Stone, seat, or chair in the Scottish records, which in itself is a curious fact for such a supposed ancient sacred relic. If it is to be assumed that the creation of the Jacob's Pillow legend began with Rishanger in 1327, as might appear to be the case, then for what intents and purpose would an English chronicler have been inspired to create such a myth?

The first pro-English reference to the Stone occurs in 1307, when *La Pierre d'Ecosse* was published. This is from an English viewpoint of the legends surrounding the Stone and was printed in French. It emphasised the capture of the Stone and its placing in Westminster Abbey by King Edward I. It was to be used as propaganda to show the might of the Kingdom of England to the other monarchies throughout Europe. The main body of the text apparently came from Scottish sources, such as the Scottish lawyer Baldred Bisset's *Processus* from 1301. This claimed that the Stone was carried by Scota from Egypt, but according to the author of *La Pierre d'Ecosse,* Scota and the Stone, now in the possession of the English, were present during the time of Moses. Thus, begins the biblical associations of the Stone.

The year was 1307. The supposed Scots king-making Stone had been at Westminster Abbey for several years, and yet Robert the Bruce had been crowned King of Scots at Scone. It seems that a legitimate King of Scots could still be crowned even without the Stone. This appears to contradict popular tradition being promoted in England at the time. For what purpose would it serve the English to make up and promote a false history of the Stone now in their possession?

The timing of the release of *La Pierre d'Ecosse* and *Chronica et Annales* perhaps lends a clue, for each of the dates coincide with the coming to power of an English king. King Edward II in 1307, and King Edward III in 1327. The first was a weak and feeble king, and the other is a young king who is unable to rule his kingdom. Both are supposedly crowned upon the ancient object, or so the traditional story goes, even though there is no written proof to substantiate this claim whatsoever. It would seem that when the Stone came to be in the possession of the English it took two giant steps towards God, and virtually overnight it became a holy and Christianised object. Why?

The church in England had been trying for many years to make the church in Scotland subservient. The Stone object now in their possession was ideal for serving their needs. For many years, the Stone had been in the keeping of the Dean of Westminster Abbey, and along with St Edward's Chair that was built to house the Stone, they were placed next to the shrine of St Edward the Confessor. Rishanger informs us that the Stone was "to be made the chair of the priest celebrant" of Westminster Abbey. This would suggest that the chair was not originally intended to be used for the purposes of a coronation, but rather for the use of the Abbot or priests. There is no evidence to suggest that the Stone was used for any English coronation ceremony before 1399 with the coronation of King Henry IV of England.

With the signing of the Declaration of Arbroath in 1320, the Scots had publicly stated their position of having moved away from the Celtic church and officially adopted St Andrew as their patron saint. Scotland had distanced itself from any potentially heretical beliefs that were associated with its Celtic past and could now be relied upon to faithfully follow the Christian teachings of the Church of Rome. The reverence of a Stone had pagan connotations and it could be that they were quite happy for such a thing to now be out of their hands and with the English, whose patron saint at the time, St Edmund, was a long way behind St Andrew in the order of saintly rankings. The church in England now had a problem. The theft of the Stone from Scone was meant to humiliate Scotland and show the Scots that England and the English kings held superiority over their country and monarchs. It was never foreseen that the taking of the relic could work in Scotland's favour by distancing them from a pagan past. A damage limitation exercise was desperately needed by the church in England, and soon!

Whether or not the Stone that was taken by Edward in 1296 was the Scots king-making Stone, or indeed whether there was ever even a king-making Stone in Scotland to begin with, when it arrived in England it was actively promoted by the English as being an integral part of the coronation ceremony of the Scottish monarchs. With the coronation of King Robert the Bruce in 1306, the Scots had shown that the Stone was not needed. The Church of Rome reinforced this by making Bruce the first Scottish monarch *ever* to receive official recognition, albeit not a blessing, in 1320 from Pope John XXII when his excommunication was lifted.

Now that Robert the Bruce was officially recognised as king, and more importantly as a Catholic king, England could not backtrack on its claims about the 'pagan' Stone, as this would have led to great humiliation throughout Europe for the already weak and unpopular King Edward II. A plan was needed to transform the pagan Stone into an acceptable Christian holy relic. In 1307 the foundation of the legend was set. This was probably concocted by some in the English church and not necessarily by the crown, as most of those who could write were in the clergy.

In 1301 the Scots had claimed an ancestry going back through Ireland, Spain and Egypt to the time of Scota, and they had said that the Stone had travelled with them throughout their journey. The English, in 1307, now associated Scota and the Stone with the time of Moses, thus inferring biblical associations with the Stone. The 'biblical' Stone was now in England and was under the protection of King Edward II of England. The English king could be relied upon by the Church of Rome to look after such an important relic for the Christian faith. He would defend it from the pagan ceremonies that the Scots had subjected it to over the years. Then, in 1327, the second phase of the plan was put into action and this time a simple association with the time of Moses was not enough.

The Scots had the upper hand over the English by officially claiming St Andrew as their patron saint, as declared in the Declaration of Arbroath in 1320. With the assistance of a respected chronicler, the English would cement the standing of the English monarchy forever. Rishanger promoted the idea that the Stone at Westminster had been the very Stone upon which Jacob had rested his head whilst he journeyed from Beersheba to Haran, and when he received the covenant from God about his offspring.

It was a daring plan that succeeded, for not only was England now in the possession of one of the most important biblical relics, backed up by a tradition that the Scots themselves had promoted to the Pope, but they also had something that Scotland would like to have owned. Over the years, as the propaganda grew and the legend transformed into 'fact', the Scots forgot about their own traditions and coronation ceremonies and saw the Stone as a political symbol that should, by right, be back on Scottish soil. It could be argued that this is true, as it is a Stone from Scotland. However, it is a Stone that seemingly has no provable associations with any sort of ceremony, purpose or history relevant to Scotland until after it was taken to England.

Chapter 7
The Britain Rulers

Why was King Edward so interested in having the Stone in his possession in the first place and what, in his mind, was so significant about the monarchs of Scotland being crowned upon a Stone? In answering this question we must look back over many centuries to the Dark Ages of Britain, and what was considered in the thirteenth century to be a magical and mystical age of heroism and honour. Edward I held the ancient monarchs of the British Isles with an almost divine regard. His idol, King Arthur, was believed to have ruled during this time.

The House of Wessex

In the fifth or sixth century, the Saxon King Cerdic founded the Kingdom of Wessex in the south and southwest of England. Interestingly, Cerdic has sometimes been identified as being one and the same as King Arthur. The Arthurian legend seems to be a recurring theme throughout our understanding of the history of Britain and how it relates to the beliefs of King Edward I. The descendants of the House of Wessex laid claim to holding suzerainty, or lordship, over all the other princes and kings of Britain. This meant that they had a certain level of superiority over the other kingdoms in the British Isles. It is uncertain how or why they got this suzerainty, but it was even recognised by the Romans when they were in Britain between the first and fifth centuries. Therefore, its tradition must have extended long before the founding of the House of Wessex by King Cerdic.

It is from the seventh/eighth century historian Bede in his *Ecclesiastical History of the English People* that we are told how the monarchs of the House of Wessex are the heirs of an ancient Roman *imperium* over all the southern English kings. King Edward I was well aware of the writings of Bede, as he was of all of the popular romancers from the past, such as Nennius and Monmouth. They had chronicled the history of the British Isles and are even famed with having written the first accounts of King Arthur. Bede makes a special mention of the

Wessex King Ceawlin who ruled from 560-591 and who was the grandson of King Cerdic. Ceawlin and his descendants from the House of Wessex were referred to by Bede as *bretwalda*, meaning 'Britain Ruler'.

In later centuries, Saxon kings also had traditions of being crowned upon a stone that resemble the traditions associated with the Stone of Destiny. In the London borough of Kingston-upon-Thames there still remains to this day a stone upon which tradition claims the following seven Saxon kings were crowned between the years 902 and 979:

- Edward the Elder (902)
- Athelstan (924)
- Edmund (940)
- Edred (946)
- Edwy (955)
- Edward the Martyr (975)
- Ethelred II The Unready (979)

Figure 14: The Kingston Stone
© Greg Balfour Evans / Alamy Stock Photo

170

The tradition of Saxon kings being crowned upon a stone must have its origins in the ancient world and this is something that King Edward I would presumably have known. The West-Saxon kings, including those crowned on the Kingston stone, are described by Bede as *Gewissæ*. The term was used to describe the people belonging to the Kingdom of Wessex – the chosen people to rule Britain, the *bretwalda*. The similar sound between '*Gewissæ*' and '*Jew*', and the connection to a chosen people, should not go unnoticed and perhaps becomes more relevant as our story unfolds.

The only empire outside of Gascony that Edward coveted was the British Isles, through which the history and blood of his hero, King Arthur, had flowed. To be able to stake his claim as the king who united all of Britain, to replicate what Arthur is credited with having done, was something to which Edward attached a great deal of importance. His problem was that the *bretwalda* bloodline was still prevalent during his lifetime and it was perpetuated in the Scottish monarchy.

1066

In 1066, before the Battle of Hastings when the Normans came to conquer England, the descendent of Cerdic and king of the Wessex kingdom was Edward the Confessor. He reigned between 1042 and 1066. Edward the Confessor was the last reigning king of the House of Wessex and the penultimate Anglo-Saxon King of England. Edward, or in its alternative spelling *Eadweard,* was born in 1003 in Islip, Oxfordshire, in England. He was the son of Ethelred the Unready and Emma of Normandy. He spent a great deal of his youth in Normandy, and this served to influence his decisions in later years, before the Normans and William the Conqueror made their invasion of England in 1066.

Edward's coronation occurred a year after he ascended the throne, and he was crowned King of England on 3rd April 1043. This was at the royal seat of the West Saxons at Winchester Cathedral. Winchester has been held in high regard ever since and especially by the English monarchy due to its ancestral links to the ancient kingdoms of Britain. In the present day there exists at Winchester Cathedral a round table that was made by King Edward I in honour of the round table of King Arthur fame. The table even depicts an image of King Arthur on it, although this was painted under the instruction of King Henry VIII some centuries later.

Edward the Confessor was responsible for building a chapel on the ancient site where Westminster Abbey in London is now located. He decided that this would be the place where he would like to be buried. A week after the chapel was completed, Edward the Confessor died. His reign had been relatively peaceful, and it was not until his death that the Normans made their invasion of England. He was canonised in 1161 by Pope Alexander III and is regarded as the patron saint of kings, difficult marriages and separated spouses. Interestingly, he is also the patron saint of the British monarchy, even in the present day. Edward the Confessor was childless and so his nearest heir was his nephew, Edward the Exile, so called because he spent most of his life outside of Britain.

As an infant, Edward the Exile was sent to live with his half-brother, Olof of Sweden, supposedly to be murdered, even though that murder never happened. He was secretly sent to Kiev and then managed to make his way to Hungary where he had three children. A son, Edgar, commonly known by his hereditary title, the Ætheling, a daughter, whom he named Margaret, and a second daughter, Cristina.

Edward the Confessor saw that troubles were brewing in his country and contestants were coming to the fore, ready to stake their claim to his throne when he died if an heir could not be found. He therefore sent word to Edward the Exile to return from Hungary so that he could be the heir to the throne and continue the line of descent. Edward the Exile and his family returned from Hungary in 1057, but disaster was to strike as he died very shortly after arriving back in England. This meant that his only son, Edgar Ætheling, was the last surviving male heir to the House of Wessex and the line from King Cerdic.

Edgar was only fourteen years old. Edward the Confessor died in 1066 and the Ætheling was simply too young to defend his country from the impending Norman invasion led by William of Normandy.

Therefore, Harold Godwinson, the brother-in-law of Edward the Confessor, was elected as his successor by a *witenagemot*, meaning a meeting of wise men. He was subsequently proclaimed King Harold II. William defeated and killed King Harold by an infamous arrow to the eye at the Battle of Hastings on 14th October 1066. That battle changed the face of England forever.

William the Conqueror, as he was commonly called, subsequently proclaimed himself William I of England. Following the death of Harold, Edgar Ætheling was proclaimed King Edgar II by another *witenagemot*. He was never crowned and several weeks later he submitted his throne to William the Conqueror. For reasons that are unknown, William did not have the Ætheling killed. This allowed him to rally support that led to a failed attempt at recapturing his crown in 1068. The failed coup resulted in the Ætheling and his family fleeing to Scotland for protection under King Malcolm III, also known as Malcolm Canmore. The reign of the House of Wessex and the *bretwalda* bloodline had come to an end in the monarchy in England.

Queen Margaret

Before they fled to Scotland, Edgar, his mother and two sisters are thought to have stayed in Northumbria from where they made plans to find refuge in their original homeland of Hungary. Following their departure, their ship is said to have blown off course and landed in Scotland at the site that is today called St Margaret's Hope, near North Queensferry in Fife. It is widely believed that Margaret brought with her the Holy Rood of Scotland, also known as the Black Rood, which was reputed to be a piece of the true cross upon which Jesus was crucified.

The true cross was reputedly found in 312CE in Jerusalem by Helena, mother of the Roman Emperor Constantine I. The legends claim that at the age of 80 years old, Helena was put in charge of a Christian relic-hunting mission for her newly converted son and Emperor. Helena and her entourage travelled to a Jerusalem that was still largely in a ruinous state after the destruction of the city by the Roman Emperor Hadrian in the second century CE. This was the same

Hadrian that had built Hadrian's Wall in Britain that runs east to west across England and was supposedly built to keep the barbarian Picts from entering the civilised Roman England.

Hadrian had crushed a revolt by the Jews in Jerusalem, but at a heavy price to the Romans. The casualties were high on both sides. The Romans were believed to have lost their entire Legion XXII and around 580,000 Jews were reputedly killed. Hadrian destroyed 50 large towns and about 1,000 villages but did not stop there, for he wanted to eradicate the Jewish religion once and for all. He banned the Torah (the Five Books of Moses that make up the first five books of the Bible), the Hebrew Calendar and executed all of the Jewish Scholars that he could find. Not only that, but he also ceremoniously burnt the Sacred Scroll on the Temple Mount and installed a statue of Jupiter and himself in the Temple sanctuary. He subsequently removed the name Judea from all maps and replaced it with Syria-Palaestina, in memory of the Philistines who were the ancient enemies of the Jews. He built a Temple of Venus over the site of Jesus' tomb at Calvary and his last insult was to rename Jerusalem to Aelia Capitolina and forbid all Jews from entering the city.

When Helena arrived in Aelia Capitolina, nearly 200 years had passed since its destruction and yet the city was still being rebuilt. She visited the Tomb of Jesus at Calvary and began excavating. The legend states that she discovered three wooden crosses. Believing that one of them was the true cross on which Jesus was crucified, the other two presumably belonging to the two thieves crucified by his side, she took the crosses to the sick and allowed the people to touch them. When a woman touched one of the crosses and was immediately cured of her ailment, Helena declared the cross to be the true cross of Jesus. Not only that, but she also excavated the nails allegedly used during the crucifixion of Jesus. One of these nails was placed in the helmet of her son, and another in the bridle of his horse to help protect him.

Helena left Jerusalem around 327 and died soon after. The relics that she had discovered were stored in her palace in Rome and were later removed to the Abbey of Santa Croce. Over time the cross was cut up and fragments were distributed throughout Europe. One such piece found its way to Queen Margaret and Scotland. It was this piece that was known as the Holy Rood of Scotland. Significantly, King Edward I also stole this relic when he took the Stone in 1296. He had also taken the *croysseneyht* from Wales, which was reputedly another piece of the true cross.

Queen Margaret's brother, Edgar Ætheling, never married and was left without any offspring. Her sister, Cristina, entered the nunnery at Romsey and she too had no children. Therefore, the continuation of the line of descent from King Cerdic and the House of Wessex, the *bretwaldas*, was to continue through Margaret. She married the Scots King, Malcolm III, and continued the bloodline in the Scottish monarchy.

This fact must have aggravated King Edward I of England more than any other when he was seeking to prove his Overlordship of all Britain in later years. The kings from Scotland could claim suzerainty and lay superior, and legitimate, claim to *his* usurped throne and kingship of England, and therefore to all of Britain. Edward must have believed that the Scots kings also continued the tradition of being crowned upon a Stone, just like it had happened at Kingston-upon-Thames. He maybe even believed that the Scots king-making Stone was an ancient relic of the House of Wessex.

Queen Margaret's influence over Scotland has been largely overlooked in history. She possessed her own beliefs, which were predominantly Anglo-Saxon although they must have been influenced by her youth spent in Hungary. She introduced the Benedictine Order to Scotland and helped her husband, King Malcolm III, to found Dunfermline Abbey. She tried, and almost certainly succeeded, in changing the Scottish royal court. She introduced continental modes of government and coupled them with Anglo-Saxon beliefs and traditions. Margaret was responsible for the rebuilding of the monastery on Iona and was a great believer in going on pilgrimage. She is credited with setting up a free ferry service across the Firth of Forth for pilgrims wishing to visit the shrine of St Andrew in Fife. The place names North Queensferry and South Queensferry retain the memory of this service. There is no doubt that Margaret was a very holy and kind person who gave out a helping hand to the poor and the orphaned. As a good Christian she attended mass every night to absolve her sins.

King Malcolm and Queen Margaret had many children, all of whom had Anglo-Saxon names; Edward, Edmund, Ethlred, Edgar, Alexander, David, Edith and Mary. Each saw their Anglo-Saxon heritage as being important to legitimise their authority as the monarchs of Scotland. Margaret and her offspring are held largely responsible for the demise of Gaelic culture in the Scottish Lowlands and Highlands, and it is her influence that would eventually coerce Scotland to turn its back on its Celtic church in favour of coming into line with the Church of Rome.

King Malcolm and his eldest son, Edward, were killed during the Battle of Alnwick on 13th November 1093. The grief must have been too much to bear and Margaret is said to have died from a broken heart three days later. She was eventually canonised in 1258 by Pope Innocent IV on account of her holiness and fealty to the Church. This made her the second Scottish saint to be canonised by the Church of Rome. The first saint canonised was Saint William of Perth, who was canonised in 1256. However, St Margaret was the first Royal Saint of Scotland. A chapel is dedicated to her memory at Edinburgh Castle and is reputed to be one of the earliest buildings in the entire castle, if not the oldest.

The Continuation of the Cerdic Line in Scotland

Following the death of the Scots King Malcolm in 1093, his younger brother Donald Ban claimed the crown at the age of 60 on the grounds of tanistry. Duncan II, Malcolm's son from his first marriage to Ingibiorg, the daughter of the Jarl of Orkney, opposed Donald Ban's claim. Duncan ruled for only a few months in 1094 before his stepbrother, Edmund, and his Uncle, Donald Ban, joined forces to overthrow and kill him. Donald Ban became king again, only this time he ruled alongside Edmund. The two reigned over Scotland together. The Highlands by Donald, and the Lowlands by Edmund. That was until Edmund's brother, Edgar, proclaimed himself a vassal of the English king and with the help of an English army overthrew the pair.

Edgar was the fourth son of King Malcolm and Queen Margaret. He was nicknamed 'the Peaceable'. This was a derogatory term, because he was very submissive to the English crown and encouraged Norman immigrants to Scotland. He did not marry and bequeathed his kingdom to his brothers. Alexander was to become king and David to be his lieutenant. Alexander I, nicknamed 'the Fierce', after dealing ruthlessly with an uprising, subsequently died leaving no offspring. The crown then passed to his brother, David, who was crowed David I, King of Scots, in 1124.

David I (1124-1153)

David was the youngest son of King Malcolm and Queen Margaret. No one expected him to become king, but his reign proved to be an outstanding one for Scotland. He had been a prisoner of his uncle, Donald Ban, but escaped and was brought up in the English court of King Henry I. David was treated well by Henry who arranged a marriage for him to the granddaughter of Earl Siward, who was the heiress of vast Northumberland estates. Through that alliance David had a legitimate claim to a large part of northern England. Henry appointed him as the ruler of Cumbria, thereby increasing his power further still. When Henry died, David took advantage of the confusion and decided to launch an attack into England. He managed to take Carlisle and Newcastle before he was defeated at the Battle of the Standard, also known as the Battle of Northallerton, in 1138. The English king at the time, King Stephen, was not in a position to alienate the powerful Scottish king who had gained control of Northumbria following the second Treaty of Durham in 1139.

David was the Earl of Huntingdon and as such he had to swear an oath of loyalty to the English king. Having been brought up in England, when he returned to Scotland to succeed his brother, Alexander, as King of Scots, he took with him powerful Norman influences that would eventually transform Scottish society. David's Norman friends soon held most of the important positions within the Church and State of Scotland. He gave the Normans lands that meant that they received landowner privileges and authority over the lives of the indigenous Scottish people. In the Lowlands of Scotland, the Celtic ways of tribe and kinship were replaced by a new feudal system of laws and regulations of the English. David influenced language development so that whilst Gaelic was spoken by the Highlanders, Inglis, a Scottish variant of English, was adopted by the Lowlanders. His reign helped to enhance the prestige of the monarchy in Scotland.

Like his mother, David was deeply religious and founded many Abbeys throughout his kingdom. The king assigned lands to the Abbeys and in return gained protection and spiritual support from the abbots, monks and clergy. His only son, Earl Henry, died in 1152. Henry was married to the daughter of the Earl of Surrey and they had three children, Malcolm, William and David. The king appointed his grandson, Malcolm, to be his successor upon his death.

Malcolm IV 'the Maiden' (1153-1165)

Malcolm was known as 'the Maiden' because he never married and maintained a vow of chastity. He was only eleven years old when he came to the throne of Scotland and there were several rebellions during his reign. These were primarily over his succession that was disputed by jealous rivals. It was during his reign that the first references were made in written charters to the 'Kingdom of Scotland' instead of 'Kingdom of Alba'. It has remained the Kingdom of Scotland since that time. Malcolm was forced to renounce his rights to Northumbria when Henry II became king of England. Although this improved Scotland's relationship with England, the Scottish nobles were not pleased. When he died in 1165 his successor was his brother, William.

William the Lion (1165-1214)

William 'the Lion' got his name because of the emblem he adopted on his armour. In those days a knight had to be protected from head to toe in armour, which made them unrecognisable on a battlefield. Each knight had to adopt an emblem for others to know his identity. William chose a "roaring, clawing beast of blood in red on a yellow background" as his emblem – the Lion Rampant, which is still considered today to be as much an emblem of Scotland as the cross of St Andrew.

William ruled for forty-nine years, which made him the longest reigning monarch in Scotland up to that time. His brother, Malcolm IV, had made peace with King Henry II of England, but William led an army to Northumberland to take Alnwick Castle. He was defeated, captured and imprisoned in Normandy. The price of his release was his kingdom, which he subsequently granted to King Henry II, thus making him the Overlord of Scotland. This act was one of the pieces of evidence that King Edward I used to 'prove' his own Overlordship of Scotland in later years.

King Henry II of England died fifteen years after having been made Overlord of Scotland and was followed to the throne by King Richard I. Known as Coeur-de-Lion (the Lionheart) for his excellent military reputation. It was Richard's ambition to go on a crusade to the Holy Land, but he needed a substantial amount of money for such an undertaking. The Scots King William was able to buy back his sovereignty from Richard in 1189 by giving him 10,000 merks to fund the third crusade. This released William, and therefore Scotland, from being a vassal of the English king, but this is something that King Edward I preferred to overlook in later years. William had a son, Alexander, who would reign as King of the Scots following his death.

Alexander II (1214-1249)

Alexander was married to Joan, the daughter of King John of England, and thus became the brother-in-law of King Henry III of England when he ascended the throne. Alexander demanded from Henry the return of William the Lion's dowry, as well as the return of Northumbria. It was the signing of the Treaty of York during the reign of Alexander II in 1236 that fixed the border between England and Scotland on the Tweed-Solway line. Alexander's relationship with England was more diplomatic than warlike. His wife Joan died, and the next year he remarried the French Marie de Coucy. They had a son who would later be crowned Alexander III King of Scots.

179

Alexander II made Scotland stronger than it had ever been. He was determined to subdue the disturbances in the lands of Argyll and prepared a fleet to sail the Clyde in 1221. Unfortunately, he failed to take the stormy September weather and tides into account and was forced to return to Glasgow. The following year he marched his army on foot to Argyll to try to re-establish some semblance of order. To ensure that peace would continue, Alexander transferred the land titles of disloyal nobles to more amenable and reliable subjects.

The Diocese of Caithness, which was under the control of Norway rather than Scotland, witnessed a major event during the lifetime of King Alexander II. The diocese was most probably founded by David I around 1128 when he appointed Bishop Andrew as the Bishop of Caithness. In 1222 the people of Caithness were becoming unruly because Bishop Adam of Melrose had begun to raise the Episcopal taxes. Presumably some of these funds were being sent to the Scottish church rather than the Norwegian church, and this did not please the locals. Whatever the reason, the people of Caithness decided to take matters into their own hands. On 11th September 1222, three hundred Caithness people set on the Bishop at Halkirk (High Kirk) in Caithness and captured the Bishop. They killed Serlo, Dean of Newbattle, and then they then set on Bishop Adam, who they saw as the main instigator. They trapped the bishop in his kitchen, and it is claimed that they decided to roast or boil him alive over his own fire. However, it is more likely that Bishop Adam was trapped in his home whilst it was set on fire and he died in this manner rather than being roasted or boiled alive.

At this time Alexander II was preparing to attack England when news of the event reached his ears. As a Christian he decided that the Norsemen of Caithness could not go unpunished for their unholy actions against a Scottish Bishop and immediately went to Caithness to punish the people for their crimes. He effectively invaded the Norwegian lands of Caithness and those he found guilty were either hung, castrated, or had one or both of their feet removed depending on their part in the killings. He then confiscated half the lands belonging to the Earl of Caithness, because of his lack of assistance to the bishop.

This demonstrates that Scotland as we know it was not unified as it is today. Also, it highlights that Alexander II saw himself as the Overlord of the Norwegian areas in what today comprises northern Scotland, in much the same way that King Edward I saw himself as the Overlord of Scotland later in the century.

Before Alexander died, he also tried to regain the Western Isles (Hebrides) from King Haakon IV of Norway. However, before he could reach them he became ill and died on the island of Kerrera, off Oban on 8th July 1249. It could be that the events in Caithness and the killing of Bishop Adam set the sights of the Scots away from England to the Norse areas of Scotland in the hope of a unified mainland of Scotland, something that was carried on by Alexander's son and successor.

Alexander III (1249-1286)

At the age of just eight years old, Alexander III succeeded his father. The ownership of the Western Isles and the northern areas of Scotland was the first problem he faced after his coronation. This was also the last thing that his father had tried to sort before his death. The Earl of Ross had declared war upon King Haakon of Norway to try to regain possession of the Western Isles. This terrified the local people for they could still remember the fierce Viking raids, which had only stopped in recent years. Haakon sailed from Norway in 1263 with a fleet of over 100 ships of solid oak, each with a golden dragon at the bow and stern. Astronomers predicted that the day after his arrival in the Orkneys there would be a total eclipse of the sun. The Norwegian soldiers considered this eclipse to be a bad omen, but Haakon decided to continue the advance.

Alexander had reinforced all the castles on the shore and gathered a large army at the place where he thought Haakon would land. Here he waited, knowing that there was the strong probability of terrible storms during September and October. As it happened, a great storm did blow through Haakon's fleet of ships. The Norwegians believed that the storm was caused by the magic of Scottish witches, whereas the Scots felt that the storm had been sent by the newly canonised St Margaret to save their country. A battle did take place on land, but

Haakon's fleet had been so decimated by the storms that he decided to retreat and return home. Haakon died shortly after and Alexander III secured a treaty with his successor, King Magnus. This was the Treaty of Perth, whereby Alexander gained the Western Isles by paying 4,000 merks to the Norwegians and 100 merks a year for an indefinite period. The yearly payment continued into the fourteenth century. Orkney and Shetland remained under the control of the Norwegians and it was many years before they too became a part of Scotland.

As an interesting sidenote, there is no mention of the Scots being granted control of Caithness, even though it is widely believed that Caithness was handed over with the Treaty of Perth. If there is no surviving or written agreement stating when Caithness was handed over to the Scots or was conquered, could this mean that Caithness is in fact still a part of Norway?

In 1286 King Alexander III died from falling off his horse at Kinghorn in Fife. His death meant that his successor and closest heir was the young Princess Margaret, Maid of Norway. The death of Margaret in 1290 ended the rule of the House of Canmore. With all direct heirs to the Scottish monarchy now dead, so too was the hereditary honour that had passed through their veins. The line of descent from the House of Wessex, the *bretwalda*, the 'Britain Rulers', had come to an end.

There is no doubt that King Edward I identified himself as a Britain Ruler. Now that the Maid of Norway was dead, and the *bretwalda* bloodline had ceased, there had never been a better opportunity for Edward to make his dream of being the glorified king of a unified Britain a reality – just like King Arthur.

Chapter 8
Celtic Church vs. Church of Rome

At the end of the eleventh century, it was still the Celtic saints who had the biggest following in Scotland, yet it was St Andrew who eventually became the patron saint. Why? It has been suggested that this was purely to stand Scotland in a better light with the Church of Rome at a time when the English church was trying to make the Celtic church subservient. Just as King Edward I of England was trying to subjugate the Scottish crown, so too was the English church pushing for control of the church in Scotland. Only a high-ranking Catholic saint from the line-up of the Church of Rome was deemed suitable for making a stand against the dominating tactics of the English church and crown.

In the twelfth and thirteenth centuries, Scotland was facing problems from not only the English crown, but also from the church in England. Scotland was unlike some of the other Christian countries throughout Europe in that it was not an active follower of the Church of Rome. It is possible that King Edward I was under pressure from the church leaders to instigate a campaign against the Scots with a view of trying to make the church in Scotland subservient to the church in England. This would thus bring all of the British Isles under the same teaching of Christianity.

By the seventh century, Christianity had spread to all corners of the British Isles, but it existed in two main forms. To the north was the Celtic church and to the south there was the Church of Rome. It is widely believed that the Celtic church evolved around the Irish Sea, amongst the lands of the people known to us today as the Irish, Scots, Welsh, Cornish (from Cornwall) and Manx (from the Isle of Man). Essentially, the Celtic church was the name given to various forms of Christianity throughout Britain and Gaul (France) that were outside the direct influence of the Church of Rome and the Papacy. The British Celts each had differing oral traditions and regarded different calendar dates as sacred days, and this was a matter of great contention. Whilst today we accept that the Church of Rome and the Celtic church were different, they were on the whole quite similar in their beliefs and teachings.

Before Christianity became the predominant religion of the Roman Empire, followers of Jesus had been spreading the Gospels to the rest of the known world. The Romans had conquered virtually all of Europe, but there were some regions that were never under their influence. The general perception is that it was in these unconquered regions where the Celtic church flourished under tribes such as the Picts, Norse, Germanic and Irish. However, what is closer to fact, is that the presence of the Romans made very little difference to the religions of the natives even in their conquered lands. The general Roman stance was to allow the locals to continue to operate their own religions and laws as long as it did not interfere with Roman policies. Even when the Romans instigated overtly anti-Christian policies, they were practically useless against areas out-with their control. It was only when the Roman Emperor, Constantine the Great, constituted the Edict of Milan in 313, stating that all religions could be practised throughout the Roman Empire, that Christian preachers were able to spread the Gospels unhindered.

Around the fourth century, history begins to introduce to us the first of the 'Celtic' saints who appear in the areas outside the influence of Rome, often referred to as the 'Celtic Fringe'. The first of these preachers was St Ninian who established a church at Whithorn in the southern part of modern-day Scotland. Some authors have suggested that this is incorrect, due to the fact that the old maps of Scotland were misaligned, with what seemingly is representing southern Scotland actually representing the area around the Firth of Forth, and possibly Fife and the Lothians. By taking into consideration the place names throughout Scotland, St Ninian, or at least his teachings, may even have travelled as far north as Shetland. Another theory proposes that Ninian was in actual fact St Finnian, the same person who supposedly converted St Columba to Christianity and with whom he fought over a Psalter. They suggest that a spelling error in the eighth century made Finnian into Ninian.

It is quite possible that Christian preachers had visited the Celtic Fringe long before St Ninian. It is widely believed that Christians had reached Britain in the first century CE, with some authors even suggesting that Joseph of Arimathea, uncle of Jesus, came to Glastonbury in Britain immediately after the crucifixion.

The earliest recorded saint in Britain was the martyr, St Alban, from the late-second to early-third century CE. Alban was a pagan living near the Roman town of Verulamium. He converted to Christianity and was later decapitated for his beliefs. This happened on a hill near Verulamium, which is the site and origin of the modern-day town of St Albans in Hertfordshire, England. Even though there is no record of St Alban or any of the other early saints operating in the Celtic Fringe at this date, trade routes did exist between the various regions and it is likely that word would have spread about the new religion. It was only when Roman political influence began to crumble, following their withdrawal around 407, that we begin to hear about the origins of 'Celtic' Christianity in Britain. This was when the Roman Legions were recalled and ordered to defend Italy from the Visigothic attacks.

During this period the Irish Sea seems to have become the centre of the Celtic Fringe areas of the British Isles. The spread of the Gospel into these regions did not happen overnight, but took decades, and even centuries, to become established. When the pagan tribes converted to Christianity they still held on to their ancient traditions, many of which simply became Christianised. This allowed the ancient religions to continue to be practised and evolve with the new beliefs, to form what is today regarded as 'Celtic' Christianity. Over the next few centuries these communities in the areas of modern-day Scotland, Ireland, Wales and northern England would flourish into the various Celtic churches of Britain. At the same time the Church of Rome was spreading throughout the rest of Europe and southern Britain, forming what was later to become known as Catholicism, under the direction of the Pope.

The two churches largely remained independent, and it was not until 1066 and the Norman invasion that the Church of Rome began to have a direct bearing over the Celtic church. By the end of the fourteenth century, Celtic Christianity was largely a thing of the past until the revivals of its romanticism in the nineteenth century.

Throughout mainland Europe, and also in England, the Church of Rome established the practice of having one bishop per Episcopal 'See', which is the term used to denote the office of the chief bishop of a particular place. The term See is derived from the Latin word *sedes*, meaning seat, and refers to the *cathedra*, or bishop's throne located in their chief cathedral. This was presumably the intended purpose of the Stone when it was first taken to Westminster Abbey before becoming the coronation Stone of the English monarchs.

Each See could subsequently found (establish) dioceses that were essentially daughter houses that came under the influence of the chief See. In England there were two Sees – York and Canterbury – each of which became very powerful administrative centres in their respective areas. Over time they expected the Celtic areas to submit to their authority. The problem in the Celtic Fringe was that there were not many big towns or cities in which to found a See as the areas were much less densely populated. Therefore, the practice of establishing a chief administrative centre had little purpose. The Celtic system placed more emphasis on operating independently and was based on monastic churches, or monasteries, operated by Abbots. These Abbots were often, although by no means exclusively, descended from royal stock. This ensured that the crown and church were intertwined and often spoke with one voice when decision making on behalf of the country.

With the rise of the Church of Rome across the Celtic Fringe, the Celtic church was required to consecrate bishops in order to conduct the holy orders as directed by the Papacy. However, due to the nature of its establishment the bishops of the Celtic church did not have the same authority as that of their counterparts from the Church of Rome. Their position was regarded as little more than honorary.

The Culdees

Prevalent throughout the lands of modern-day Scotland, Ireland, and to a lesser extent England, from an early date was a rather ambiguous group of people known as the Culdees. No one really knows why, when, where or how they were formed, but they were an ancient religious order that greatly influenced the early Celtic church. The word 'Culdee', or alternatively 'Celi De', loosely means 'Vassals of God' or 'God's Ally'. Whatever the exact meaning of the word it appears to be a term used to identify individual monks or hermits rather than a large group of people.

One theory proposes that the term Culdee was derived from the Rule of Chrodegang, who was the Archbishop of Metz in the northeast of France. After his death in 766, a group of Irish monks are said to have brought back his teachings with them to Ireland. By the ninth century, there are nine places mentioned in Ireland where Culdee establishments seem to follow the Rule of Chrodegang, which was modelled on the Benedictine rule for monastic living.

The fifteenth century Scottish chronicler, Hector Boece, has the Culdee being descended from an Irish religious order of the sixth century that subsequently moved to Iona and Scotland during the ninth century. This would have been roughly the same time period that the Stone was reputed to be on the western coast of Scotland, either Iona or Dunstaffnage, before it was taken to Scone by Kenneth McAlpin in 843. It has even been proposed that the Culdees were the remnants of the ancient Druids of Britain.

Whilst relatively little is known about the Culdees, they are generally portrayed as the Celtic influence that tried to fight what they saw as corruption coming from the teachings of the Church of Rome. They saw it as their mission to keep this 'alien' religion out of their homelands. During this period Scotland had its own high churches under Culdee influence such as Scone, Dunkeld, Lochleven, Abernethy, Brechan, Monymusk and Cell Rigmonaid or Kilrymont (modern day St Andrews). At the end of the eleventh century, Kilrymont had thirteen Culdee monks who were part of the larger Augustinian order. These Culdee monks were regarded as somehow different and who were said to be more interested in their own prosperity than that of the Church.

Much like the rest of Scotland and its traditions, the Culdees were first brought into line under the rule of Queen Margaret when she fled to Scotland in 1068. Margaret and her sons, the future Kings

Alexander I and David I, spent a great deal of effort and money in establishing Augustinian orders into which many of the Culdee were amalgamated. Whether this was by choice or by force cannot be known for certain, but that new abbeys and churches were built upon ancient Culdee sites is widely accepted. This was seemingly a trend that happened to most, if not all, of the Culdee sites in Scotland. By the end of thirteenth century most remnants of the Culdees had been consigned to history. Even the Culdee place names were changed and today there are few places that retain their memory. However, one that does still exist is Kirkcaldy in Fife meaning 'the Kirk (Church) of the Culdee'.

The Synod of Whitby

At a place called Streonshalh, later to be called Whitby Abbey, in Northumbria, a church council, or synod, was held in 664. This was the first synod to be held between the Celtic church and the Church of Rome. It was called to settle a dispute between the two churches over the dating for Easter. This was no new argument and was initially brought up at the first Council of Nicaea in 325 in which it was agreed that Easter would be held on a Sunday.

The Church of Rome wanted to celebrate Easter on the same day each year, Sunday, and by giving Easter a definitive date all churches throughout their sphere of influence could celebrate Easter at the same time. The Celtic church, led by the Ionian monks, followed the dating of Easter more in line with the Jewish calendar, and calculated the date for Easter as being the 14th day after the first lunar month of Nisan (usually March-April period), and then from the 15th to the 21st day was celebrated the Passover. This ensured that the festival of Easter, which is to celebrate the day on which Christ was resurrected, would not clash with the celebrations of the Jewish Passover. Such a clash could happen under the Church of Rome system of dating. However, the Celtic church did allow Easter to be celebrated on the 15th Nisan if it was on a Sunday.

In Britain, some areas outside the church in the Celtic Fringe celebrated Easter as the Spring Equinox, i.e. around 20th-22nd of March by today's calendar. This was because the sun was regarded as symbolic of the dying and rising god that is characterised in Christian teachings as Jesus, particularly with regards to the winter solstice. The equinox is a natural occurrence and could not be determined by anything other than the sun, and some linked this 'pagan' belief with the old Celtic traditions. Similar issues were faced by the Frankish church in Gaul and eventually the Franks adopted the calculations of Rome, as had some churches in southern Ireland.

The Northumbrian church was somewhat split between the Celtic church and the Church of Rome. The main problem was coming about due to the fact that the Church of Rome was rapidly spreading throughout the country. In order to continue expanding they needed to persuade the Kingdom of Northumbria to follow their practices, which had predominately been following the teachings of the Iona Church up to that point. The geographic situation was such that the Northumbrians controlled the east coast of northern England up to the southeast coast of Scotland, as far north as the Firth of Forth. On the other side of the country, the Britons of Strathclyde controlled the west coast of northern England and the southwest coast of Scotland, as far north as the River Clyde. North of the Clyde-Forth line was controlled by the Scots on the west coast and the Picts on the east, both at this time following the teachings from Iona.

At the Synod of Whitby, it was argued by Bishop Colman of Lindisfarne that the Celtic calculations practiced by the Iona Church should be maintained, as it was the one taught by Columba who had followed the practices of St John the Apostle. Bishop Colman was facing opposition from Bishop Wilfred of Hexham, who argued that the Roman calculation was the more holy as it was taught by Rome where the Apostle St Peter had taught and was buried. This was essentially the first time that two churches had pitted saint against saint to establish who was the more senior – St John or St Peter.

It was concluded that whilst Columba had done what had needed to be done during his lifetime, there was now no reason why his followers should not adopt the position of the Church of Rome. To be distanced from Rome was being ignorant of St Peter, over whom no one had authority. He had been given the keys to heaven and was pronounced the Rock on which the Church of Rome had been founded.

With this in mind, the Northumbrian King Oswiu, who was presiding over the synod, eventually agreed that the calculations from Rome would be used for the dating of Easter throughout his kingdom. Following this decision, the Episcopal seat of the Northumbrian church was moved from Lindisfarne, where Colman was no longer welcome to continue his position, and moved to York.

Colman was disillusioned and set up a new monastery at Inishbofin, an island on the west coast of Ireland in the County of Galway, and about as far away as possible from mainland Britain as he could get. This demonstrates the intensity of feeling between the two churches over the dating of Easter and other practices. Most, if not all, of the Ionian Monks in Northumbria were replaced by Irish Monks who supported the Church of Rome. The Synod of Whitby had been a great success for Rome and an utter disaster for the Celtic church. They steadily witnessed their power and dominance throughout the various kingdoms of northern Britain go on a downward spiral until it was virtually consigned to history by the early fourteenth century.

The Coming of the Patron Saint

Those who have even the most basic knowledge about Scottish history will know that the patron saint of Scotland is the apostle St Andrew, and the national flag of Scotland is the Saltire Cross, or the Cross of St Andrew/St Andrew's Cross. What is perhaps not so well known is why this saint was chosen above all others, and especially over the many Celtic saints that were prevalent throughout ancient Scotland, and that had helped to establish the Celtic church.

St Andrew was the brother of Simon Peter, the founder of the Church of Rome, and is sometimes known as the first apostle. He was an apostle of John the Baptist before becoming a follower of Christ. He is believed to have been crucified on an X shaped cross, the same as the Saltire Cross, around the year 60CE. Although it is not certain where he preached the Gospel or died, there is a tradition that it occurred at

Patras in Achaia (modern day Greece), where he spent two days preaching whilst hanging from the cross before he eventually died.

Legend has it that the Roman Emperor Constantius II, the son of Constantine the Great, decided that he would visit the city of Patras in Greece where St Andrew was martyred and was believed to have been buried. Constantius was planning to take the bones of the saint from Patras to be re-interred at Constantinople. Three days before the Emperor arrived in Patras an angel appeared to a man named Regulus, also known as Rule. The angel told Regulus of what was being planned by Constantius. The angel instructed Regulus to go to the sarcophagus in which St Andrew's bones lay and remove three finger bones from the right hand, an upper arm bone, one tooth and a kneecap in order to hide them at a secret place selected by the angel. With some trusted companions, Regulus did as he was commanded and hid the bones in the allotted place. Two days later events proceeded just as the angel had foretold Regulus they would. Constantius arrived at Patras and sacked the city, stealing all of its wealth as well as the bones of St Andrew, albeit without those removed by Regulus. He then returned to Constantinople.

Several years later, the angel reappeared to Regulus and passed on new instructions from God. Regulus was told to remove St Andrew's bones from their hiding place and take them with him on a voyage to a safe place in the north-west region, to the edge of the known world. The angel said that Regulus and his companions would run the risk of being shipwrecked where they were going, but that even if their ship were destroyed, they would survive and should recognise this as a sign that they had arrived at their final destination.

Upon finding this place, Regulus and his companions were to build a holy shrine to St Andrew and revere the sacred place that had been chosen by God. Once the shrine was built Regulus and his followers were to preach the word of God throughout the land, and just as Andrew had done after the crucifixion of Jesus, they too were to preach the Gospel and show the miracles of St Andrew and his relics. Regulus was told that a great nation would rise where the shrine was built, to become a steady and strong anchor of the Christian faith that would be famous for its devotion to St Andrew. Many would travel to this land from all over the world to seek healing and witness miracles. Upon imparting this wisdom to Regulus, the angel disappeared and left him alone to think about all that had been disclosed.

Seeing this as his destiny to fulfil, Regulus did as the angel commanded and prepared to set sail for the unknown destination. He selected wise and trusted friends to help carry out this task, all of whom had been forewarned by the angel that they were to accompany Regulus during his long voyage. Those who followed were the abbots St Damian and his brother Merniacus, priests Gelasius and Chubaculus, deacons Nerius, Elrisenius, Merenus, Machabeus and Silvius, hermits Felix, Sanjanus, Matheus, Mauricius, Madianus, Philip, Luke and Eugenius and three female virgin saints Triduana, Potencia and Emerea – a total of eighteen men and three women.

The ship was loaded with provisions and the relics of St Andrew. All aboard, they set sail across the Mediterranean Sea towards the west and the setting sun, then north until they came to the islands situated at the edge of the world. The crew had been at sea for two long years, through great hardships and unknown seas. They followed the winds and trusted that God would see them safely to their destination, where they were to build the shrine to St Andrew.

Eventually, the ship did crash just as the angel had foretold, and just as promised, all aboard were unharmed and the relics survived intact. The ship had crashed into the east coast of modern-day Fife in Scotland. Seeing this as the sign he was looking for, Regulus knew they had arrived at their final destination. They looked to the sky above them and saw the sign of the Lord's cross, thus confirming that their long voyage was over.

The group found themselves at a place called 'Mucross' in a strange land that the locals, who were of the Pictish race, called Albion. Regulus decided that this was to be the place where he would build the shrine to St Andrew as the resting place of his relics. Regulus met with the Pictish King Oengus mac Fergusa and told him of his mission. Being suitably impressed by the story, King Oengus granted Regulus the land of Mucross upon which he could build his church.

Word soon spread amongst the Picts of what was occurring, and that many great miracles would happen just by touching the bones of the unknown Saint Andrew. Soon people were making pilgrimages from far and wide to touch these sacred bones and cure all sorts of ailments. The blind were able to see, the dumb could speak, and the lame could walk. As word spread, the people from other nations were making the pilgrimages to the shrine of St Andrew on a daily basis. Regulus died at an old age, thirty-two years after having been shipwrecked on Albion. He had completed his mission and established a great shrine to St Andrew in the land appointed by God.

Reigning between 820 and 834 was the Pictish King Oengus II, who granted one tenth of his lands to St Andrew's followers at Mucross, now also being known as Kilrymont meaning 'the church at the king's monad'. This was in return for the miraculous aid that St Andrew had bestowed upon him when he led a campaign against the Saxons in Northumbria. It is said that St Andrew came to Oengus in a dream and told him what to do in order to win at the forthcoming battle against the Northumbrians at Athelstaneford in 832. At a decisive moment of the battle, St Andrew's Cross, the Saltire Cross, miraculously appeared in the sky giving a sign to the Picts of the blessing of St Andrew which would assure them of victory. After the battle Oengus and the Pictish nation adopted the Saltire flag as their emblem. Many years later, when the Kingdoms of the Scots and Picts merged under Kenneth McAlpin in 843, the Saltire Cross was carried as the battle flag of the unified Scots nation. The cross was used on the Seal of Scotland from 1180 onwards and on the Guardian of Scotland's Seal from 1286. However, it was not until 1540 that the Saltire Cross would be officially adopted as the Scottish national flag.

There is another legend that claims the relics of St Andrew were taken to Kilrymont from Hexham in Northumbria, England, by Bishop Acca in the year 732. Bishop Acca was born in Northumbria and served under Bosa, the Bishop of York, and then later served with St Wilfrid in about 678. Acca was somewhat of a treasure hunter and he and Wilfred travelled to Rome on at least two occasions, where the pair were said to have collected many artefacts and relics during their travels.

When they returned home from their second visit St Wilfred became Bishop of Hexham and Acca became an abbot of St Andrew's monastery, also at Hexham. Wilfred died in 709 and Acca took his place as Bishop of Hexham Abbey. He carried on the work of Wilfred and was famous for his theological library and encouragement of his students. Acca gave material to Bede for his *Historica ecclesiastica gentis Anglorium* and in return Bede dedicated several of his works that dealt with the Holy Scriptures to Bishop Acca.

For some unknown reason, in 732 Acca either left his diocese of his own accord or was forced to leave. Some accounts suggest he travelled to Galloway in southern Scotland to become the Bishop of Whithorn, whilst other accounts record that he founded the site of St Andrews in Fife, bringing with him the relics of St Andrew. Whatever the literal truth, which we will never know, he is believed to have been buried at Hexham Abbey and was made a saint soon after his death.

Figure 15: Front view of the Hexham Abbey Frith Stool

There sits in Hexham Abbey today, a seventh century stone seat called 'St Wilfred's Chair' or the 'Frith Stool'. Frith is the Saxon word for Peace, and it is said that fugitives could claim sanctuary at holy crosses that were stationed up to one mile distant from the chair. It was used as the bishop's throne, or *cathedra* of Hexham Abbey.

Legend says that this stone seat was also used to crown the kings and bishops of Northumbria. In relation to our story, it is interesting to highlight that the Kingdom of Northumbria extended up into what is modern day Scotland, as far north as the Firth of Forth. On this basis, the Frith Stool is a very similar artefact to that of the Scots king-making Stone used at Scone. It even resembles some of the early descriptions of the Scots king-making Stone much better than the Stone that was taken to Westminster. It is of polished red sandstone, making it appear like marble, and it has Celtic imagery carved onto its arms, with a rounded seating area to receive the monarch or bishop.

Figure 16: Top view of the Hexham Abbey Frith Stool.

If Hexham Abbey could be moved 100 miles north and renamed Scone, then there would be no doubt about the authenticity of the Scots king-making Stone or what was being described as the Royal Seat. Hexham was even dedicated to St Andrew, Scotland's own patron

195

saint, and legend has it that it held some of his relics for a time. If there were to be a contender for being the 'genuine' Scots king-making Stone then the Hexham Abbey Frith Stool aligns very well with the many theories, even if it's virtually impossible to prove conclusively.

The relics of St Andrew have long since been lost and their eventual fate is unknown. It is widely accepted that they were lost or destroyed during the Scottish Reformation in the sixteenth century when the Protestants destroyed many Roman Catholic churches. They systematically destroyed the relics, statues and other artefacts of saints that were credited with healing abilities or miraculous powers as they viewed them as promoting false idolatry. Priceless artefacts from all over the world, and from all ages, were to be ruthlessly burned or broken up, sadly never to be seen again.

Located in the town of St Andrews today there is an ancient stone sarcophagus widely believed to be the coffin of the Pictish King Oengus I. The carvings on the outside of the sarcophagus depict the famous biblical King David killing a lion, which is in reference to a story from the Old Testament of the Bible. Oengus reigned from 732-761 and is one of the few Pictish Kings who is reasonably well documented. He was involved in a civil war between the Pictish kingdoms that saw him become the 'Chief' King of the Picts. This was essentially a united Pictish front that occurred long before the time of Kenneth McAlpin, who is widely credited with being the first king of a unified Scotland.

In 728 the Pictish nation was in a civil war over their kingship. The situation was brought about because four kings – Oengus, Drest, Nechtan and Alpin – were all in dispute over who should rule. With the time period under discussion, it is important to highlight that the Pictish King Alpin mentioned here is not referring to Kenneth McAlpin who united the Scots and the Picts in 843. However, it is possible that he was of the same lineage. If this is the case, then perhaps Kenneth McAlpin was in actual fact of Pictish descent from his fathers' side and not from his mothers' side as previously discussed. In fact, more and more modern academics are starting to believe that Kenneth McAlpin was a Pictish king before becoming a Scots king, which resulted in uniting the two nations as one. If this is the case, then Scotland's history has been misleading for centuries. It could also explain why Scone, rather than a west coast site like Dunadd, became the Royal centre for the new Scotland.

Figure 17: Stone sarcophagus of the Pictish King Oengus I

Four battles were fought between 728-729 in which it is recorded that Alpin was twice defeated by Oengus, and in which Nechtan subsequently became king. The third battle was fought by Oengus and Nechtan against their enemies at the Battle of Monith Carno (Cairn o'Mount, near Fettercairn) in 729, before they finally defeated Drest in another battle near an unidentified place called Druimm Derg Blathuug in 729. With the four battles won, Nechtan became the ruling monarch of Pictland and it is possible that Oengus arranged a pact with Nechtan to succeed him after his death. With the end of the Pictish civil war, Oengus concentrated on attacking the relatively weak Kingdom of Dál Riata.

Historically, the Kingdom of Dál Riata flourished in what is now known as Argyll, Bute and Lochaber in Scotland, along with County Antrim in Northern Ireland. It is widely accepted that they were skilled at seafaring. They enjoyed the ease of quick travel and navigation in and around the coastal areas of the surrounding kingdoms, thus giving them major advantages in both trade and warfare. The Dál Riata were made up of the Cenel nGabrain (in Kintyre), the Cenel nOengusa (on Islay and Jura), the Cenel Loairn (in Lorne and possibly Mull), and the Cenel Comgaill (in Cowal and Bute). It could be that one or all of the leaders from these areas (Cenel's) were classed as kings, which in turn confuses the kingship of the Dál Riata.

Perhaps the most important settlement of the Dál Riata was at the ancient hillfort and king-making site at Dunadd. The Dál Riata are typically seen as being of Irish-Scots descent and are often credited with having defeated the Picts in the mid-800s under Kenneth McAlpin, and thus becoming the fore-runners of modern-day Scotland. With this in mind we would be forgiven for thinking that this would have occurred at the height of their power, but this does not seem to fit the historical facts. The Kingdom of Dál Riata was at its peak in the late 500s to the early 600s, at least 250 years before the unification of the Picts and the Scots by Kenneth McAlpin. The Dál Riata's power expansion seems to start its demise with their defeat at the Battle of Degsastan in 603 against the Northumbrians. The subsequent attack by Oengus of the Picts in the eighth century meant that many places were captured, including their revered site of Dunadd.

In 741 the Dál Riata were finally defeated, and for a generation at least they disappeared from history with the only surviving accounts of them coming from Irish records. It is possible that this period was the first amalgamation of the Scots of Dál Riata and Picts, and if so, it could explain the confusion over what actually happened between the two kingdoms when outlining the king-making practices in later years regarding the Stone.

The legacy of the Pictish King Oengus I was summed up by the Northumbrian historian Bede, who was perhaps rather biased when he

198

stated, "From the beginning of his reign right to the end he perpetrated bloody crimes, like a tyrannical slaughter."

During the reign of Oengus the principal bishopric seat of the Picts seems to have been at Rosemarkie on the Black Isle, north of Inverness in Scotland. This was at a time when the Picts ruled from the River Forth in the south to the Shetlands and Western Isles in the north. Oengus was a warrior king and for one of his battles he sided with Eadberht of Northumbria to try to overthrow the Kingdom of Mercia (from Middle England) on 10th August 756. Oengus and Eadberht were defeated and although Oengus survived Eadberht was killed along with most of his army. To give thanks for his safe return from the battlefield, Oengus built a church and dedicated it to St Andrew. It is possible that this is what led to the cult of St Andrew appearing throughout the Pictish territory, although this is far from certain.

The Coming of the Political Saint

It is curious that Scotland had an abundance of home-grown Celtic saints whose history is intimately linked to that of Scotland, yet it was decided to overlook all of them in favour of making the patron saint someone that had very little, or indeed possibly even having nothing at all, to do with Scotland. The legend as portrayed above is, perhaps unsurprisingly, just a legend that does not stand up to historical scrutiny.

The bones of St Andrew were supposedly removed to Constantinople during the reign of Emperor Constantius II, who was born in 317 and reigned as Emperor from 337 until his death in 361. By necessity for the legend, this must have occurred during the lifetime of Regulus. We are told that Regulus died at a grand age, and so if we assume that this was aged 80, a grand age even by today's standards, then he would have left Patras at the age of 46, because he lived in Albion for 32 years and spent two years travelling the oceans. Assuming he was at least 18 years old when he hid the bones of St Andrew, and that was the same year that Constantius died in 361, then St Andrew's bones must have been hidden for nearly 30 years. Taking two years to arrive in Scotland means that Regulus would have arrived at Mucross in the year 393 at the earliest. However, there is a problem, King Oengus ruled between 732 and 761 and King Oengus II ruled from 820 to 834. This is about 340-430 years after the arrival in Scotland of Regulus and the bones of St Andrew. There is far too much of an anomaly to be accurate.

The first reference to the legend of St Regulus/Rule was in the tenth century, and St Regulus/Rule's church was built at Kilrymont in 1070. During the reign of Queen Margaret there were two churches at Kilrymont. One was dedicated to St Andrew and followed the teachings of the Church of Rome. This was used by kings and bishops when they visited. The other church was used by the majority of the populace and was dedicated to St Cainnech. This was run by the thirteen Culdee monks present at Kilrymont. This alone speaks volumes about what the lay person living in Scotland thought about the teachings of the Church of Rome at the time, or taken the other way, possibly what the incoming Norman influence thought of the beliefs of the common folk of Scotland.

The story of Regulus coming to Scotland with the bones of St Andrew is dubious and it is perhaps more likely that the cult of St Andrew came to Scotland via Northumbria and quite possibly from Hexham and Bishop Acca. However, this would not be an appropriate story to promote at a time when both the Scots and English crown and church were at war.

We know that before the Romans left Britain around 407 there was already a Christian presence in Britain. However, it could not have been that strong as Pope Gregory the Great sent Augustine, later known as St Augustus, to Britain in 596 on a mission to strengthen the Christian faith in England.

Pope Gregory, later St Gregory, was a devotee of St Andrew and wrote many sermons that were inspired by the apostle. Before becoming Pope he had spent part of his life in Constantinople. It is most likely that this was in the Church of the Holy Apostles, where the remains of St Andrew were believed to have been kept following their removal from Patras in Greece by Emperor Constantius II, presumably minus those bones removed by Regulus in the preceding century.

The Church of the Holy Apostles was sacked in 1204 by the Crusading forces. It was supposed to have been Peter of Capua who saved the bones of St Andrew from the Crusaders and took them to safety to the city of Naples in Italy in 1206. Following the completion of St Andrews Cathedral in Amalfi, also in Italy, in 1210, the relics were placed in the crypt where they still remain to this day. It is said that the relics exude a liquid called 'St Andrew's Manna' and is used to anoint the faithful of the congregation.

Pope Gregory founded a monastery to St Andrew on his own land on Caelian Hill, one of the Seven Hills of Rome, and where Augustine was a Prior before being sent to England. In the year 596/597 Augustine arrived in Kent with the order to convert the Saxons to Christianity. Kent was, at that time, ruled by King Aethelbert/Ethelbert who allowed Augustine to build a Priory on the site of what is now Canterbury because his wife was a Christian. Augustine went on to build the Abbey and was buried there in 604. St Gregory's plan was to build two archbishoprics at the two great cities of the Romans. One at London and the other at York. However, due to Augustine's success at Canterbury, the London archbishopric became Canterbury instead. Augustine's throne/chair was called the *Cathedra Augustini* and was placed at Canterbury. It was made of Purbeck Marble, or Bethesda Marble, and dates back to the sixth century when it is believed that it was used to crown the Saxon Kings of Kent. This was therefore of a similar purpose to both the Hexham Abbey Frith Stool, and of course, the Scots king-making Stone.

Augustine sent Bishop Justus to set up his first church outside Canterbury at Rochester, also in Kent. This church was dedicated to St Andrew the Apostle and Justus was made the first Bishop of Rochester. Bishop Justus was sent to Britain by Augustine from the same church in Rome built by Pope Gregory that was also dedicated to St Andrew. In modern times, Rochester Cathedral is no longer dedicated to St Andrew but to the Blessed Virgin Mary instead.

Inside this Cathedral are the remains of St William of Perth, a Scottish pilgrim who was robbed whilst on a pilgrimage and who, whilst dead, cured a mad woman. So great was his cult around Rochester that the choir was built by the money from the offering plate in 1201 and which allowed the Cathedral to be completed in 1343. St William's following had grown so much that the Bishop of Rochester petitioned his canonisation by Pope Innocent IV in 1256. This was two years before Queen Margaret became canonised, which made St William the first official Scottish saint. During its height the cult of St William was second only to St Thomas Becket at Canterbury. In 1300, the 'Hammer of the Scots', King Edward I himself, donated 14 shillings to the shrine of St William of Perth and many other prominent monarchs and Popes made pilgrimages to the shrine. The Coat of Arms of Rochester bears the Cross of St Andrew, complete with the scallop shell which represents St William of Perth. Rather curiously, here is a Scottish Saint, who is the only true Scot that had been canonised by the Pope, and yet he is not revered or even heard of by the majority in Scotland.

Throughout England in the seventh and eighth centuries there were several churches dedicated to St Andrew as his cult grew in stature. The legend of St Andrew that comes to us from the Scottish version of events, states that he deemed himself as being unworthy of being crucified on the same cross as Jesus and opted to be crucified on a Saltire cross (X) instead. The idea of a condemned man having a say in what instrument he must suffer his fate, never mind him telling the executioner to make a special purpose cross for him, seems very strange. The early writings of St Andrew do not refer to any X shaped cross or of any other cross other than a crucifix or Latin shaped cross (+). This seems to have been either an English or Northumbrian invention that has been continued by the Scots and other nations over the centuries.

It quickly becomes apparent that St Andrew had very little to do with Scotland. The story of his bones being brought there from Patras rests on shaky foundations at best. It is quite likely that the story had been concocted in order to suit some other purpose. With the strong associations of St Andrew at places such as Hexham Abbey, is it possible that his cult came to Scotland via England? If there is a possibility of this, then it is highly probable that the Scots would have seen fit to ensure that this was not known by either Canterbury or York.

This would have necessitated in the Scots concocting a more suitable 'history' for their nation.

In 1192 Pope Celestine III in his papal bull *Cum universi* declared all Scottish Sees, except Galloway (which came under York), as a 'Special Daughter' of the Church of Rome. This meant that they answered to Rome and not to Canterbury or York. It angered the English church leaders who believed that Scotland should come under their rule. Yet it was not until the coronation of King David II in 1329, the son of King Robert the Bruce, when the Scots had the first full rites of anointing and blessing from the Pope at a Scots coronation.

King Robert the Bruce had been acknowledged in his position by the Papacy after the Declaration of Arbroath (1320), although he was never officially blessed. This is partly the reason why King Edward and the church in England did not recognise the Scots monarchy as being legitimately kings in their own right, whether Christian or otherwise. The Church of Rome was unwilling to grant metropolitan status to the town of St Andrews, which by the twelfth century was recognised as the centre of the Scottish church, despite several petitions during the reigns of David I (1124-1153) and Malcolm IV (1153-1165).

St Andrew got his biggest boost in the late thirteenth and early fourteenth centuries at the time when King Edward I of England was making his claims of Overlordship in Scotland. Starting with the English invasion of Dunbar in 1296, and then culminating with the Battle of Bannockburn in 1314, Scotland was in desperate need of support from the Church of Rome.

At the time, Scotland had a population of about 400,000 people and they were well aware that if they did not receive support from Rome in their plight against the English then they could be in serious trouble. Europe had already seen genocide in the form of the Albigensian Crusade in southern France, with some accounts estimating that perhaps 200,000, or maybe even as many as 1,000,000 presumed heretic Cathars were murdered.

Scotland must have been only too aware that if stories were being spun by the English about the heretical savages to the north of Britain, then they too could potentially be the target for another crusade that would pit the Celtic Christian Scotland against Christian England, backed by the Church of Rome. This was especially so, as both Robert the Bruce and the rest of Scotland were excommunicated after 1306.

Something similar had happened in Britain once before with the Pelagian Heresy of the third to the sixth centuries. Pelagius was a monk from the British Isles, possibly of Scottish or Irish origin, who preached that there was no such thing as original sin and therefore the entire principle of being 'saved' through the doctrine of the Church was defunct. According to Saint Jerome (347-420), who was perhaps the biggest critic of the Pelagian Heresy, the teachings of Pelagius essentially denied the role of the Messiah. With the creation of free will from God there was presumably no need for any kind of a redemptive saviour. In response to the Pelagian Heresy, which is described as having been 'epidemic' throughout Britain, Rome sent Palladius, later Saint Palladius, to Britain in order to eradicate it from history. For something to be epidemic suggests that it had a very large following and it is interesting to highlight that the Pelagian Heresy was prevalent throughout Britain, possibly having originated in Scotland, at a time before established history accords there having been any sort of Christianity present in Britain.

The practices of the inauguration ceremonies of the Scots kings could have been deemed pagan by some accounts. Seated upon a sacred Stone and not anointed or blessed by the Pope. It is easy to see how Scotland must have felt backed into a corner, both metaphorically and geographically. If they remained devoted to their home-grown Celtic saints then they would appear distanced from Rome and regarded throughout Europe as followers of a heretical form of Christianity, much like the Cathars. This could have left it open for the English church and their king to petition to Rome to eradicate this heresy once and for all.

The Scottish Reform

During the reign of the Scots King Alexander I (1107-1124) there was mounting pressure, and hence a need to reform the Scottish/Celtic church in order to bring it into line with the teachings of the Church of Rome. Alexander responded to this need by founding new bishoprics with full papal sanction all over Scotland. He even upgraded some of the old Celtic bishoprics.

Each site had to be consecrated by an established Bishop recognised by Rome, of which Scotland had none at the time. The chief seat of the Celtic church was based at Kilrymont, or St Andrews as it was later known, and the question of who would consecrate the Bishop of Kilrymont raised concern amongst the Scots. The only realistic contenders were the Archbishops of York and Canterbury from England, but if either of these were to consecrate the Bishop of Kilrymont it would effectively mean that a Bishop from England would have supremacy over the head Bishop of Scotland. In other words, every church in Scotland would be subservient to the church in England. What was also an issue was the fact that the churches raised taxes for the church *and* crown, and so there was every possibility that some, if not the majority, of taxes collected by the church in Scotland would have gone directly to the crown, as well as the church, in England.

The very idea of this was understandably disliked by Alexander. He knew well that Scotland had an unbroken tradition of Christianity dating back to when Canterbury was still a pagan capital and York a Roman ruin. However, after much debating between Alexander, the Pope and the Archbishops, it was decided that the Archbishop of York would be allowed to consecrate the first Bishop of Kilrymont.

The position fell to a Saxon man named Turgot, who was Bishop of Kilrymont between 1107 and 1115. He had been the confessor to Queen Margaret of Scotland during her reign and wrote *Vita Sancte Margarete* (Life of Holy Margaret). Turgot was followed by another Saxon man, called Eadmer, who came from the Benedictine monastery of Christ Church in Canterbury. Eadmer publicly made the claim that the Archbishop of Canterbury should have primacy over every church throughout the British Isles. This brought all of the old arguments back to the fore and was the beginning of an ongoing conflict between the English and Scottish churches that lasted for centuries. King Alexander saw Eadmer as trouble and intervened so that he could not continue his position as Bishop. This battle between the churches and the King of Scots continued, with appeals to Rome from all sides. Eventually the Pope made each of Scotland's churches a 'Special Daughter' of Rome. In other words, the Scots church now answered only to Rome, which was not to the liking of York and Canterbury in England. However, they had to accept it as they had no real choice in the matter.

Later, during the reign of the Scots King William I (1165-1214), there were many more accusations between both England's crown and church as to who owned what in Scotland. King William was taken prisoner by the English at the Battle of Alnwick and held to ransom. In order to buy his release, he was forced to accept King Henry II of England as his Overlord. The battle between the churches that Alexander I experienced during his reign continued for William. He argued with Rome, trying to prevent any English Bishop from having control over the cathedral of St Andrews and the chief seat of the Scottish church. The English, Scots and Rome each made their proposals as to who should be bishop, but each side vetoed the opposing candidates. The situation was stalemate.

Eventually, the English church sided with the Pope. The next part of the saga saw the Archbishop of Canterbury excommunicating King William I in 1181. A subsequent act from the Bishop of Durham saw the whole of Scotland being excommunicated in the same year. The Pope of the day was Pope Alexander III, who died in August 1181. It is possible that William and Scotland were excommunicated whilst there was no officiating Pope sitting in Rome. Scotland was swiftly welcomed back into the Church following the appointment of Pope Lucius III in September 1181. Lucius sent William the 'Golden Rose' in 1183 as a special tribute to a king of exceptional religious zeal. Another subsequent 'special' relationship was granted to Scotland by Rome in 1192 under Pope Celestine III. This assured the integrity of the Scottish church from England and also allowed the reigning monarch a judgement over any appointments of bishops throughout Scotland, and specifically at St Andrews.

People and political traits rarely change and smear campaigns against the opposition were just as vehement 700 years ago as they are today. Towards the end of the thirteenth century, Scotland was desperately trying to maintain her political and religious independence from England, and specifically from Edward I who was using any and every claim from the preceding centuries to 'prove' the legitimacy of his Overlordship of Scotland. With the Celtic saints not being officially recognised by Rome or England, Scotland really needed something, or someone, who would give them precedence over England. In their plight the Scots were prepared to show a united front with Rome and her beliefs, being willingly prepared to distance themselves from anything that even hinted at separation from the church. It was around this time that St Andrew really began to make his entrance into Scottish history.

During the twelfth century, the Regulus legend was widely publicised by the Scottish crown and church to aid their political motives. The Scottish church had been coming under attack from York and Canterbury. It was trying to maintain its independence by allying itself with Rome, whilst adopting one of its highest-ranking saints as Scotland's very own patron saint. By promoting the story that St Andrew had chosen Scotland in the fourth century, with the assistance of Regulus who himself was directed by angels from God, the Scots were ensuring that Rome could clearly recognise a separate identity from England. To make their statement loud and clear, the Scots dedicated their chief seat of the Celtic church, Kilrymont, to the brother of Peter, founder of the Church of Rome and one of the most influential apostles of Christ – St Andrew.

At this time England had St Edmund as its patron saint, who was far behind St Andrew in the rankings of popularity, and therefore closeness to God. Few others from the Christian line-up could rank higher than St Andrew. The cult of St George, patron saint of Soldiers/Warriors, arrived in England after the crusades of the twelfth century. It was during the reign of King Edward III (1327-1377) that St George replaced St Edmund as the patron saint of England. It would seem that the holy patrons and protectors of countries could be changed at will and without the need of God or the Papacy's approval. By choosing St Andrew as its patron saint Scotland was making its position well known to England.

By 1144 the place name 'St Andrews' was in use and the construction of St Andrews Cathedral started several years later in 1160. It was twenty years after this, in 1180, that the earliest representation of St Andrews Cross, or the Saltire Cross, were used on the Chapter Seal of St Andrews. The Cathedral was eventually finished in 1318, 158 years after its construction began.

Figure 18: St Andrews Cathedral today

At the end of the eleventh century, it was still the Celtic saints who had the biggest following in Scotland, yet it was St Andrew who became its patron saint. St Andrew could be used as a shield by the Scots against the English claims of Overlordship coming from both their crown and their church. The main problem with St Columba or any of the other Celtic saints is just that – they were Celtic, and therefore not 'Christian' in the Roman sense of the word. To continue following them could have been deemed heretical if the Pope could be persuaded that this was the case.

Many modern historians do not see a Celtic church that fought off the Roman church and lost, but rather one that was forced to submit its authority to survive. There were many different Christian religions in and around Europe between 300 and 1300. One by one they were either destroyed, lost or amalgamated into more dominant established religious organisations, with the Church of Rome being at the top of the pile. The Celtic church probably consisted of numerous churches in Britain and France, each speaking variant forms of Gaelic rather than Latin. It could also be that each 'church' followed the teachings and practices of a different saint, such as the Irish who followed St Patrick, and the Picts who followed the teachings of St Columba.

In Britain today, we have the Church of Scotland, the Church of England and the Roman Catholic Church among many others, and yet they all are Christian churches supposedly following the same teachings of Jesus. Whilst the Roman Catholic Church is comprised of just one church, the Protestant movement consists of the Baptist Church, the Church of England, the Church of Christ, the Episcopal Church, the Lutheran Church, the Methodist Church, the Presbyterian Church, the Salvation Army, the Quakers and many more. It could be argued that the Protestant church runs in a similar vein to that of the long forgotten Celtic church, where each offshoot has a slightly different practice and teaching. Even today, with a reduction in congregation attendance across most of the Christian churches, some of the smaller churches are looking to amalgamate or risk dying out. It could be that this was similar to the Celtic church of the past. They were obliged to amalgamate into the Church of Rome or risk obliteration.

It should be remembered that when the Stone from Scone was first taken to Westminster the original intention was for it to be used as the *cathedra* for the bishop. This suggests that it was perhaps more important for Edward to have relics associated with the ancient Celtic church rituals of Scotland rather than the king-making ceremony. Taking the Stone has always been assumed to be about subjugating the

Scottish crown, but what if it was instead more about subjugating the Scottish church?

It was not until the signing of the Declaration of Arbroath in 1320 that St Andrew was openly proclaimed as the patron saint of Scotland. It therefore becomes very interesting to learn that on the eve of the Battle of Bannockburn, just six years prior in 1314, King Robert the Bruce demanded two sets of relics to be brought before the Scots troops and prayed to for victory. The first were the relics of St Columba, carried in the Breac Bannoch, or Monymusk Reliquary. The second was a reliquary containing the arm-bone relic of a saint less well known in the present day, but potentially he is the most important saint in Scottish history – St Fillan.

Chapter 9
The Baghel and the Belle

Just a few years after the Stone was taken from Scone by King Edward I in 1296, the English poet Piers Langtoft, who died around 1307, wrote his *Langtoft's Chronicle*. This was distinctly anti-Scottish in content and contained nine 'songs' that were supposedly taunts used by the English and Scottish soldiers before battle. These 'songs' were possibly chanted on the battlefields of Stirling Bridge in 1297 and Falkirk in 1298, not to mention all of the other lesser skirmishes during the long years that made up the Wars of Scottish Independence. It is unlikely that the majority of the populace in Scotland or England knew anything about the king-making ceremony in Scotland, let alone that it involved seating the monarch upon a Stone in order to have the rights of kingship conferred upon them.

A modern example of this might be Scottish Football supporters, who sing an unofficial national anthem, 'The Flower of Scotland', before each football match. If we were to ask a random selection of supporters what the song is about, the chances are that they would reply that it was when the Scots defeated the English in battle. But ask them which English king did the Scots defeat, and at which battle, then many would perhaps get the answers wrong. They know the words to the song, but they do not need to understand the history in order to sing or chant them to the opposition, especially if that opposition is the English. It is surprising how little changes over more than 700 years!

One of the songs written about by Langtoft seems to suggest that it was believed in Scotland that what Edward took was not only the wrong Stone, but that what he was really after had subsequently been taken and hidden away. The verse of particular interest is as follows:

Thair kings Scet of Scone
Es driven ovir doune
To London i led.

In town herd I telle,
The Baghel and the Belle,
Ben filched and fled.

This could be interpreted as:

Their Kings Seat of Scone
was taken down to London, I'm led [to believe]
In town I heard a tale
that the Baghul and the Belle
have been taken and hidden

Alternative interpretations of this verse could imply that it was Edward who filched (stole) the 'baghul and belle' along with the king's seat of Scone and also took them to London, although there is no evidence, verbally or written, to suggest that this is what happened. What are the baghul and the belle?

A *baghul* is the Irish Gaelic term for a crosier, or staff, that was carried by a saint, and a *belle* is, rather unsurprisingly, a bell. Many of the early Celtic saints are attributed with owning each of these items, some of which are still in existence. Such relics were used for the swearing of oaths. It was believed that an oath sworn on the relic of a saint was more sacred than one sworn on the bible. The veneration of these relics, particularly in pre-reformation times, and their importance to daily life should not be underestimated.

The English chronicler Langtoft was probably unaware of the significance of what he was recording. As far as he was concerned, the genuine 'king's seat of Scone', i.e. the Stone, had presumably long since resided at Westminster Abbey. However, this is a rather curious poem to be released just a few years after the supposed humiliating theft of the most priceless relic of Scotland. Why should the poem mention that a crosier and a bell have been taken and hidden somewhere, and especially as a taunt just before a battle?

When outlining the history of Scotland during the late thirteenth century, it must be remembered that this was only a few hundred years after the merging of the Irish-Scots of Dál Riata and the Picts under King Kenneth McAlpin in 843. Both Pictish and Scottish traditions would have been passed down through the generations. Their influence would still have been felt in all spheres of life, and especially in the everyday language of the common folk and place names. This has largely been forgotten by the history books which regard Scotland as a completely unified nation. However, this simply was not the case.

A point of interest to the Stone of Destiny story are the key differences, and similarities, in the language of the Picts and the Scots. Although the Pictish language is relatively unknown to historians, it is assumed that its closest equivalent is that of the Welsh Cymraeg language, with similarities being found in the place names of the eastern parts of Scotland such as Aberdeen and Aberdour. 'Aber' meaning 'river mouth' in Welsh. The western parts of Scotland, speaking in Irish-Scots Gaelic, is very different from the Welsh, even though some of the words are pronounced the same.

What is interesting in relation to the Stone is that there is a very subtle difference between the words for 'stone' and 'bell' in their Welsh and Irish translations. In Welsh, *cloch* is a bell which is represented by *clog* in Irish, and vice versa. In Welsh, *clog* is a stone, represented by *cloch* in Irish. In Scone, the ancient Pictish capital and therefore potentially closer to the Welsh dialect, a *cloch*, or *clach/clag* as it is also pronounced, would have meant a bell and not a stone. Could it be possible that the Gaelic-English translators working for King Edward I mistranslated the word *cloch/clach* for an artefact that was present at the coronation of John Balliol, and all of the previous Kings of Scots, as a *Stone*, when perhaps they should have translated it from the Pictish (Welsh) word for *Bell*? It is worth emphasising that there are no known written references to any coronation ceremony or king-making Stone being used in Scotland until after it was taken by Edward from Scone.

If an artefact is not known to be of special reverence by the English, then the chroniclers who wrote about the coronations many years after the event would perhaps not even have known that a bell was included as part of the ceremony. If they did, then they might not have recognised it for what it was. Similarly, if the Scots knew that Edward had taken the wrong artefact as a result of a simple mistranslation, then they would more than likely have taken every opportunity to further his humiliation by making it widely known at every opportunity, such as the chanting between the troops just before a battle.

As previously mentioned, there were English appointees at the coronation of John Balliol in 1292 who would have presumably witnessed the king-making ceremony in full. Perhaps they were the ones to convey to Edward, after the ransacking of Scone in 1296, that the Stone now in his possession, and presumably being held at Edinburgh Castle until 1303, played no significant part in the ceremony. Is this why Edward decided to return to Scone in 1298 and pull the Abbey apart? Was he driven by embarrassment to look for the genuine king-making bell?

The poem written by Langtoft shortly after Edward took the Stone suggests that it is plausible that the genuine 'Stone' of Destiny may have been a 'Bell'. If true, when Edward realised, he must have felt great embarrassment and irritation for demanding that the Abbots at Scone hand over the 'Stone' and was given one. Are there any historical clues to indicate a suitable candidate for a king-making Bell?

The Eve of Bannockburn

It is from the Scottish chronicler, Hector Boece (1465-1536), that we learn about a peculiar event that happened the night before the Battle of Bannockburn in 1314. King Robert the Bruce was in his tent praying for strength in battle and for the victory of his country over the invading English. He was praying to God, naturally, and to an old Celtic saint that is largely unknown or forgotten by the majority of the populace today – St Fillan.

Bruce had requested the arm-bone relic of St Fillan to be taken to Bannockburn and placed by the altar in his tent for safekeeping. Whilst deep in prayer, the silver reliquary for the arm-bone relic was heard to open and then subsequently click shut. Fearing that an opportunistic thief may have just stolen the prized relic, Bruce went to inspect the inside of the reliquary. Thankfully the arm-bone was inside, but this confused Maurice, Abbot of Inchaffray, whose duty it was to bring the relic of St Fillan to the battlefield. The Abbot was forced to confess to Bruce that he feared for the success of the Scottish army against so many English troops, and in order to stop them getting hold of the relic after their inevitable victory he left it for safe keeping at Inchaffray Abbey. He then told Bruce that he had only brought with him the empty silver reliquary in the hope that no one, especially the king, would find out. Somehow the arm-bone of St Fillan had journeyed the great distance from Inchaffray Abbey and placed itself back inside its protective housing to be present at the battle. It was surely a miracle!

Although Bruce was furious at the doubting Abbot, the saint was clearly making his good fortune known and victory for the Scots was assured, by the power of God and his trusted St Fillan. The relic was subsequently paraded before all of the Scots troops as a sign that God and St Fillan were on their side. Victory was virtually guaranteed for the Scots before the battle had even begun.

Inchaffray Abbey, or Insula Missarum, as it was called in the Middle Ages, means Isle of the Masses. It was founded as a priory in 1198 by Gilbert, Earl of Strathearn, and was upgraded to the status of Abbey in 1220 or 1221 under King Alexander II as a daughter house of Scone Abbey. This meant that it was an extension of Scone and was governed under the jurisdiction of its abbots. Inchaffray was an Abbey much like the multitude of others that appeared in Scotland during the twelfth and thirteenth centuries and it plays a rather minor role in much of traditional Scottish history. It is only Abbot Maurice, as the keeper of the relic of St Fillan at Bannockburn, that gains Inchaffray popular recognition. By implication of the story, Inchaffray was most likely a safe house for the relics of St Fillan at one stage in its history, and it is therefore possible that it was also a haven for other relics too from time to time.

The validity of the account of Boece in describing the relic of St Fillan being present at Bannockburn is somewhat uncertain. He wrote his version of events almost 200 years after the battle took place. As was the custom of the day, Boece drew inspiration from the works of earlier authors, such as John of Fordun, and expanded them in more creative ways to present them as his own. It cannot be said with any certainty whether a relic of St Fillan really was prayed to by Bruce before the battle, but it is quite likely that there were prayers of some sort or another said to the guardian saints of the day, whether St Columba, St Andrew, St Fillan or even as one legend states, St Magnus from Orkney.

It was very much the tradition in the Middle Ages, and particularly so in Scotland, to carry relics of saints into battle to pray for their blessing and to aid victory. That some relics of one saint or another would have been taken is almost beyond doubt. It is also believed that the Breac Bannoch, or Monymusk Reliquary, which carried some of the bones of St Columba, was also taken to Bannockburn and paraded before the troops, but again there is no conclusive proof.

John Stuart (1876-78), who presented his study of the authenticity of Boece's account of Bannockburn to the Society of Antiquaries of Scotland, believes that it was the *Quigrich* relic of St Fillan that was taken to Bannockburn and not the arm-bone, of which he could find no hard evidence of ever having existed. The *Quigrich* was the name given to the crosier, or staff of St Fillan, which is the same as a *baghul* from the Irish terminology. Stuart argues that it is probable that a story would have survived to the day of Boece regarding the influence of St Fillan and his relic over King Robert the Bruce at Bannockburn, even though there was no written evidence to verify the claims.

Who was St Fillan?

Fillan, alternatively spelt Feolan, Faolan and Fáelán, is said to have originaly come from Ireland. The legends ascribed to him are very similar to many of those attributed to the early Celtic saints that voyaged from Ireland to convert the ancient pagan tribes that were the original inhabitants of modern-day Scotland. We are told how Fillan was born with a stone in his mouth, and that his father threw him into a lake when he was just a baby. Angels came to watch over the infant until he was subsequently found by Bishop Ibar who brought him up as his own child.

Fillan was instructed by Ibar into the Christian faith, and as the years passed he saw it as his mission in life to convert the heathen tribes of Pictland to the one true faith. His name, meaning 'Little Wolf', may have resulted from the story that one day Fillan was ploughing a field for the harvest when a wolf came and killed one of the oxen that the saint required to do the work. Fillan invoked the power of heaven for retribution, and upon doing so the wolf returned and helped pull the plough in place of the ox to work the fields.

There is another story about the life of St Fillan that is perhaps the origin for the belief that there was an arm-bone relic for the saint. Certainly, there are known to have been arm-bone relics for other early Celtic saints and so it is quite likely that there really was such an artefact for St Fillan.

Tradition claims that one night Fillan was in his cell, possibly the cave of St Fillan at Pittenweem in Fife, when a lay brother came to inform him that supper was ready. Not receiving a response, the brother was curious to know what St Fillan was doing in his cell. He looked through a chink in the wall and to his amazement he saw that Fillan was writing his manuscript by the aid of a light that was emanating from his left arm. The next day the brother lost his sight when a crane (a large bird) that was being looked after by the holy fraternity pecked out the eye of the spying man. The brethren pleaded with St Fillan to heal the sight of the poor man, which he subsequently did. St Fillan is said to have received the monastic habit from St Mundu, a companion of St Columba, whilst he was working with him at the monastery of Kilmun in Argyllshire.

It is often stated that St Fillan was a leper, but this is possibly confused by the translation of the Gaelic word *anlobhar* which could alternatively mean that he was a stammerer. It is widely believed that St Fillan lived in the sixth century due to the fact that records inform us that one of his teachers, Ailbe, is said to have died in 541. However, there are references in the *Martyrology of Tallaght* (preserved in the Book of Leinster) to seventeen or eighteen Irish saints called Fillan, but only two of whom can be linked directly with Scotland. One of these

Fillans is from from the early sixth century and the other from the late eighth century.

The sixth century St Fillan was the disciple of Ailbe and preached around Loch Earn in central Perthshire. His feast day falls on 20th June. The later St Fillan, who was responsible for preaching in the area of Glendochart, also in Perthshire, is supposed to have died in 777 and his feast day is 9th January. His mother is said to have been Kentigerna and his uncle Comgan, each of whom are also celebrated Celtic saints. The author, Simon Taylor, in his excellent work titled *The Cult of St Fillan in Scotland* examined this confusion in great detail. He comes to the conclusion that the two supposedly distinct St Fillans are in actual fact referring to one and the same person. He suggests that the confusion between the two saints occurs because earlier writers were picking and mixing detail from other saints to fill out their stories. In doing so St Fillan becomes linked with eighth century Leinster instead of sixth century Munster in Ireland.

St Fillan is said to have built his priory in Glendochart. This was the borderland between the Kingdom of Dál Riata to the west and the Kingdom of the Picts to the east. King Robert the Bruce restored this chapel in 1318 and its ruins can still be seen to this day. It has even been suggested that St Fillan is buried here under a slab in the centre of the ruined chapel.

In later times when coronation ceremonies occurred at Scone, this area of Glendochart was one of the main throughfares between east and west of Scotland. It was even on the processional burial route of the ancient Scots kings. When the presiding king died his body was taken from Scone and transported along this route, past St Fillan's Priory, for burial on Iona. The tradition of being buried on Iona has its origins from the Irish-Scots kings of Dál Riata who were buried there long before the uniting of the two kingdoms by Kenneth McAlpin in 843. Even when Pitctish Scone was made the capital of the new united Kingdom of Alba, the monarchs still made it their wish to be buried alongside their ancestors on Iona. Due to the mountainous terrain the only viable route would have been through Glendochart.

There is another link between St Fillan and the Pictish monarchy that warrants mention. The ancient stronghold hillfort of Dundurn, next to the modern-day town of St Fillans, was possibly a king-making site prior to the use of Scone. At the top of this hill is a natural stone 'chair' known as 'St Fillan's Chair'. We mention it to highlight further some of the long-forgotten links between the veneration of artefacts associated with St Fillan that were present at ancient royal locations throughout Scotland. The potential relevance of it being a 'chair' made of 'stone' should not go unnoticed. The Pictish royal centre at Dundurn eventually moved to Scone. It would be impossible to physically move St Fillan's Chair, so it is possible that an alternative was made.

Indeed, the idea of the king-making ceremony being less about a one-and-only Stone, and more about the significance of sitting on a stone, any-stone, during the ceremony was discussed by Caldwell (2003). He states that:

> "The important thing may have been that the new king sat on a stone, not a particular one, and if the previous stone got lost or broken, or was deemed of the wrong size for the new king or a more developed ceremony, then a more appropriate stone could be produced. Perhaps this would be a better model for accommodating several stones rather than assuming there would have been one for each new king."

When the Pictish royal centre moved from Dundurn to Scone, it is possible that a new Stone had to be made using the local stone from the area of Scone. If correct, this could explain both the historic traditions of the Stone being transported from different locations and also why the Stone taken by Edward has been identified as coming from the Scone area. What is the link with St Fillan?

The Reverence of the Bruce

For King Robert the Bruce to choose to pray to God and St Fillan above all of the other saints from the Celtic line-up is very interesting. There are several theories as to why he held a special reverence for this particular saint. The most basic theory is the belief that both Bruce and Fillan suffered from leprosy. Tradition has it that Bruce visited the ancient church dedicated to St Fillan in Aberdour, Fife, after the Battle of Bannockburn to give thanks to the saint for the victory and that he did so through the leper squint opening in the church's west gable. As previously discussed, there is confusion as to whether St Fillan was a leper or a stammerer. If he did suffer from leprosy then perhaps the king could empathise with the saint for their shared affliction and this is perhaps why Bruce revered him.

Another theory, that is perhaps more credible, revolves around a battle that Bruce had whilst in the vicinity of St Fillan's Priory in Glendochart. This was against the men of Alasdair MacDougall, Lord of Lorn, known as the Battle of Dalry, or Dal Righ. MacDougall was married to the daughter of John Comyn, Lord of Badenoch, the enemy of Bruce that he killed in Greyfriars Church in Dumfries in 1306 – an act that saw Bruce excommunicated. Wanting to avenge the murder of his father-in-law, MacDougall marched with a thousand men intent on ambushing the king as he passed through Glendochart.

Bruce managed to hear of the impending attack and met MacDougall at the Kings Meadow, Dalry, by the bank of the River Dochart, about a mile south from the town of Tyndrum. Bruce is said to have had an army of roughly 500 men, including his brother, Edward, Earl of Atholl, and Sir Niel Campbell of Loch Awe. Seeing that his army was outnumbered, Bruce advised a retreat further south across the river and away from danger. It is said that Bruce brought up the rear the troops, bravely fighting off any opportunistic attackers looking to pick off stragglers in the retreating party. Enraged that Bruce was escaping, three of the men most loyal to MacDougall swore they would pursue the king to slay him or die.

They chose to set an ambush at a point along the river where Bruce could not turn his horse and escape, known as Lochan-nan-arm (Loch of the Weapons), near Dalry. The first man jumped at Bruce and grabbed hold of the bridle of the king's horse, but soon had his arm cut off at the shoulder with one blow. The second man rushed at Bruce on

220

his horse but was quickly slain. The third man seized hold of Bruce's leg, but the king soon retaliated and killed the final assailant. One of the men held onto Bruce's mantle in his dying moments and pulled it from the shoulders of the king. Attached to the mantle was the famous Brooch of Lorn. This artefact has been kept in the MacDougall family as a memento of the famous battle.

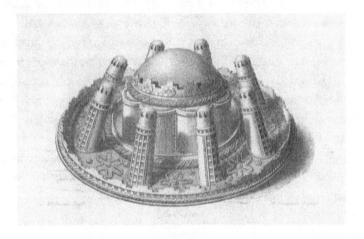

Figure 19: The Brooch of Lorn

Bruce had somehow escaped what should have been certain death. He was outnumbered three-to-one and he believed his miraculous victory was in part down to the guardian saint of the area – St Fillan.

If St Fillan was not known to Bruce before this event then it is more than likely that he would have come to know of him and his relics during this campaigning in the area of Glendochart. Bruce would have remained thankful to St Fillan for the protection afforded him during this against-the-odds encounter with MacDougall. At Bannockburn, eight years later, it is highly probable that Bruce would have remembered the good fortunes of St Fillan in helping him when outnumbered at Dalry in the hope that protection could once again be summoned. His prayers were answered.

The Relics of St Fillan

There are five relics traditionally associated with St Fillan, namely the Quigrich, the Bernane, the Mayne, the Meser and the Fergy. Of the first two relics, we know a great deal. They are still in existence and on full public display, but of the remaining three there is open conjecture as to what exactly they were.

Each of the five relics were assigned a custodian, or guardian, that in Gaelic is known as *deoradh*. This was a hereditary title whose original meaning is somewhat akin to a guardian, but can also mean stranger, exile or pilgrim. From *deoradh* we receive the modern name Dewar. Historically, the Dewars have been the principle sept of Clan MacNab who themselves are the descendants of the hereditary Abbots of Glendochart. The title of *deoradh* was not reserved solely for the guardian of the relic, but even to the relic itself from the fact that it was carried as a 'stranger' for special purposes to distant districts to bring healing and protection to the people. In this sense each of the relics of St Fillan was regarded as a Palladium of Scotland.

The Quigrich

The crosier or staff of St Fillan was given the the Gaelic name *Coigreach* (Quigrich), which also means stranger, or foreigner, due to the fact that it was carried to distant places for the recovery of stolen property. The Quigrich is a silver reliquary that is delicately ornamented with various Celtic patterns. On the front is a large clear crystal. The history of this relic is well documented. It remained in the possession of its hereditary keepers until 1877 when it was gifted to the National Museum of Scotland in Edinburgh, "there to remain in all time to come for the use, benefit, and enjoyment of the Scottish Nation" and where it still resides to the present day.

When the Quigrich was being cleaned in preparation for being placed on display it was noticed that the silver reliquary was much heavier than an object of its size should have been. After carefully prizing it open, a much older bronze crosier from an unknown date was found inside. It was the original crosier being housed in a protective silver reliquary.

222

The Quigrich is recorded in a royal charter of King James III dated 6th July 1487. The charter acknowledges that it has been in the keeping of Dewars since the time of King Robert the Bruce and before. It was the belief of Alexander Dewar, the last of its hereditary custodians, that his ancestor was selected as its keeper at the close of the Battle of Bannockburn, because of the special military services rendered to his royal master on that eventful day. This statement is curious, because there is no record of a St Fillan's crozier having been taken to Bannockburn, only the arm-bone relic, so could this be true?

Figure 20: St Fillan's Baghul, known as the Quigrich

The Irish Gaelic for 'arm' is '*Bachlainn*' and the Welsh for staff/crozier/crook is '*Baglan*'. This sounds not too disimiliar to the the Irish word for crozier '*Bachal*' or '*Baghal*'. Perhaps someone mistook, or misheard, from the Welsh (Pictish) word '*Baglan*' and believed it to be the Irish Gaelic '*Bachlainn*' and in this way it's possible the crozier relic became an arm relic.

In 1336, twenty-two years after Bannockburn, there was a letter of confirmation of the lands of Ewich in Glendochart in favour of

"Donald M'Sobrell, dewar Cogerach". This document was found in the Breadalbane Papers and was reprinted in the *Proceedings of the Society of Antiquaries* in 1876-1878. They confirm the ancient heritage of this relic and whilst it can never be proven, it is possible that a relic of St Fillan really would have been carried on to the fields of Bannockburn.

The most authoritative work on the Quigrich was by Dr Joseph Anderson in his book *Scotland in Early Christian Times*. Anderson suggests that some of the artwork on the outer casing of the Quigrich is also to be found on the privy seal of King David II, the son of King Robert the Bruce. This assigns to it a date of the fourteenth century. Much of the ornamentation that now decorates the outer casing was originally housed on the older crosier. This may also have included the large crystal stone on the front of the crosier but this is not known for certain. It is stated that there are zoomorphic features on the base of the Quigrich. However, there are no detailed drawings or images of this and so it is merely noted here for reference.

Figure 21: Close up of the Stone on the front of the Quigrich

One of the legends associated with the Quigrich relate to its powers of healing. Tradition asserts that if water was poured through the Quigrich and then drunk its healing properties would cure scrofula, which is a form of tuberculosis. In the Middle Ages it was believed that the disease could also be cured by the 'royal touch', which was the touch of the sovereign of England or France. It was therefore also known as the 'Kings Evil'. The kings were thought to have recieved this power by descent from Edward the Confessor, who, according to some legends, received it from Saint Remigius.

The Mayne

References to the Mayne are scarce, with the first mention appearing in a rather bland document from 1640 called the Retour of Robert Campbell of Glenurchy. The mention is simply:

> "Three crofts of land undermentioned, viz, Deweris croft in Suy, called Dewar-Vernons croft, a croft in Auchlyne called Dewar-na-fergs croft, and a croft in Killin called Dewar-na-man's (mayne's) croft."

The Dewar-na-Maynes Croft was situated on a small island on the River Dochart at Killin. On this site there still exists a cemetary for the McNab family who were likely the dewars of this relic. Some authors suggest that the Mayne was the left arm-bone relic of St Fillan that miraculously illuminated itself so that the saint could see to write his manuscript. This is supposedly what was taken to Bannockburn.

Dewar-na-Man/Mayne could also been spelled Dewar-na-Manes, and this opens up an interesting observation considered by the historian, researcher, and late-friend of the authors, Robert Brydon. Commonly found inscribed on ancient Roman gravestones is the inscription D.M. This stands for '*Dis Manibus*' and translates as 'for the Manes'. The 'Manes' were said to represent the soul, or their 'shade', thus describing the spirit of the dead person residing in the underworld. D.M. was inscribed on the graves to remind the sacriligious not to desecrate the grave which was being guarded by the departed. What is perhaps implied by the use of the term 'Mane' is that particular reliquary in which resided the 'Manes' of St Fillan, which could also have perhaps contained that persons' ashes, corpse, or other remains, such as the arm-bone.

Another theory is that maybe instead of Man/Mayne/Manes, it should be written *Maen*. As discussed previously, the old Pictish tongue is perhaps most similar to the ancient Welsh Cymraeg language and so an amalgamation of the two languages is likely to have occurred. In the Welsh language, the word *Maen*, which is similar in pronunciation to 'Mayne', is another word for 'Stone'. It is therefore possible that the Dewar-na-Mayne was the keeper of a relic of St Fillan that was a stone.

We are told in one of the original legends for St Fillan that he was born with a stone in his mouth, and on the front of the Quigrich there is a small crystal stone of unknown provenance, but clearly of importance. To surmise that there might have been a stone relic of St Fillan is not beyond reason.

There are eight 'Healing Stones' attributed to St Fillan still in existence, and it is possible, albeit not provable, that collectively these are the 'Mayne' relic. For centuries these were held in the old mill next to the Dochart Falls section of the river at Killin. The mill was subsequently turned into the Breadalbane Folklore Centre where visitors could see and touch the stones, even in modern times. When the Folklore Centre closed in mid-2000s the stones were moved to the parish church for safekeeping. Tradition claims that the stones were blessed by St Fillan towards the end of the 7th century and are the last of his relics to be preserved in the area where he lived.

In 1836 the stones were in the custody of an old woman whose ancestors had been in charge of them for centuries. Each stone was said to represent a part of the body and the healing power of St Fillan was performed by using the relevant stone on the afflicted part of the body. For example, the practice for a head pain would use the stone that looks most like a skull. This stone was rubbed on the head, three times one way, then three times the other way, and finally three times right round the head. The stones exhibiting circular 'sockets' were reputedly "applied to the nipples of the breasts of women who had pectoral inflammation" (Gillies, 1938).

In a private collection there is what is reputedly a ninth Healing Stone of St Fillan. It exhibits similar circular impressions to those on some of the better-known stones. How this stone got to be in a private collection is unknown. There is a mention from MacMillan (1884) to some of the healing stones going missing from the mill at Killin and possibly taken to a nearby site known as *Cladh Davi*, where similar stones were kept for healing purposes. However, there is no modern tradition or claim that there were more than eight stones.

Perhaps significantly there is a tradition of a St Fillan healing ritual that utilises nine stones collected from St Fillan's Holy Pool, near the vicinity of St Fillan's Priory near Tyndrum, Glendochart. This maybe explains the origin of the mysterious ninth stone.

Figure 22: A possible ninth Healing Stone of St Fillan

On 9th August 1798, an Englishman was travelling in the Glendochart area and recorded in his diary what he witnessed. His account is reproduced in full in the book *In Famed Breadalbane* (Gilles, 1938). He writes:

"Each person gathers up nine stones in the pool and after bathing walks to a hill near the water, where there are three cairns, round each of which he performs three turns, at each turn depositing a stone, and if it is for bodily pain, a fractured limb, or sore that they are bathing, they throw upon one of the cairns that part of their clothing which covered the part affected."

It is possible that the ritual of collecting nine stones from St Fillan's Holy Pool aligns with the extant nine healing stones we see today, albeit one got separated from the others at some point in history. Collectively, these could be the Mayne/Maen/Man relic, and it should not go unnoticed that a tradition connecting St Fillan to stone veneration is perhaps relevant to our story about the Stone of Destiny.

The Meser

As with the Mayne relic there are scant references to the Meser. It is first mentioned in a document from 1468 in a claim for rent from Lady Margaret Stirling against John Molcallum McGregor. On 9th February 1468 the court of the Bailie of Glendochart, held at Killin, heard McGregor publicly state that he did not hold his lands of Corehynan from Margaret, but from the 'Deore of the Meser'.

There is no documentation explaining what exactly was being described and guarded by the Dewar. It has been suggested that it was the manuscript written by St Fillan with the aid of his illuminated arm, although how and why is not explained. As with the Mayne we would like to present an alternative theory.

In the Middle Ages a Mazer was a communal drinking bowl typically used for ceremonial purposes and was passed from guest to guest during the feasting. An excellent example of this is the Bute Mazer that was made soon after the Battle of Bannockburn and is now on display in the National Museum of Scotland in Edinburgh. Again, there is no documented proof that the Meser relic of St Fillan was a communal drinking bowl but 'Meser' and 'Mazer' are very close to being the same word, if indeed they are not representing the same word. We present this theory purely as speculation, but in light of there being no documented proof as to what the Meser actually was, we believe our theory to be a plausible suggestion.

The Fergy

History leaves us few, if any, clues as to what the Fergy relic of St Fillan actually was, although some have believed it to be some sort of portable altar or shrine of St Fillan. Another theory suggests that Fergy means 'wrath' but this does not help to understand what the relic was or how the term was derived. It is first mentioned in a document from 1549 when the Prior of Strathfillan, Hew Currie, tried to make a claim on behalf of the church for the Quigrich, Bernane and Fergy to be handed over by their respective Dewars. It seems that even the church could not over-rule the importance that was placed upon the hereditary keepers of the relics of St Fillan. The church claim to the relics was subsequently dismissed. Without any documented facts about what the Fergy relic was, we can only hazard a guess.

We have already discussed how there was reputedly an arm-bone relic of St Fillan, potentially taken to Bannockburn, albeit this was perhaps a mistranslation for the Irish word for crozier. In mid-2000s, a carving was found that suggests there may very well have been an arm-bone relic of St Fillan. Researcher Niall Robertson unearthed an ancient stone slab at St Fillan's Priory in Glendochart that had the image of a left arm carved onto it. The Priory was rebuilt in 1318 by King Robert the Bruce in commemoration of the Scots victory at Bannockburn four years previously. We do not know the date of this stone or when it was carved, but its very existence, and especially so by being in the graveyard of St Fillan, would suggest that it is a direct reference to the arm-bone relic and St Fillan.

There is also record of another physical remnant of St Fillan. In the Stirling of Keir Charters from 1560, St Fillan's 'Tooth' relic is recorded as belonging to the Lany family along with a 'little sword'. It is referenced in *Strathendrick and its Inhabitants from Early Times* (Smith, 1896):

"I find in the beginning the Lanyis of that Ilk hes bruikit that leving without ony infeftment, except ane litill auld sourd gauin to Gillesicmvir be the King, and ane auld relict callit *Sant Fillanis twithe*, quhilke servit thaim for thar chartour quhyle Alexander his dayis."

The other relic mentioned in the text, the 'little old sword', was gifted to Gillespie Moir by King Culenus, who reigned as King of Alba from 967-971. The existence of this sword, and the hereditary rights associated with it, was confirmed in a charter during the reign of King Alexander II in 1227. Guardianship of this sword, and presumably too that of St Fillan's Tooth, was a hereditary honour passed down through the generations. The last record of the sword was in 1789 when antiquarian Robert Ridell recorded it in his diary along with a drawing. Unfortunately, even by this date the tooth relic had disappeared. Now, sadly, both are lost.

Figure 23: Carved slab from St Fillan's Priory in Glendochart, showing a left arm
© N. Fergusson

The Fergy was kept at a place called Dewar-na-Fargs-Croft in Auchlyne, Glendochart, which is a site that was used by the Campbells of Auchlyne as a burial ground in later times. The ruins of the croft are remarkably still standing, but no archaeological work has been conducted.

In light of the various comments and suggestions for the Mayne and Meser relics, we would like to suggest that the Fergy was the name given to either the arm-bone relic and/or the tooth relic of St Fillan. Perhaps it was a name given to the keeper of both? This supposition is based on nothing more than having a relic without a name and a name for an unknown relic and matching the two together.

The Bernane

The Bernane, or Bell of St Fillan, is one of the more curious relics that is known to exist. This too can be found in the National Museum of Scotland in Edinburgh, placed alongside the Quigrich. Bernane means 'little gapped one' and was a name frequently appplied to the hand bells of Irish saints. The bell is 12 inches high and has a quadrangular mouth. It is made of bronze, was cast in one piece, and is believed to date to sometime in the ninth century. The bell in the museum has a crack in it that happened at some unknown time in history. An iron clapper was added to the inside of the bell at an unknown date. A replica is known to have been made at the turn of the twentieth-century by the Marchioness of Breadalbane and this is now in a private collection.

The exact origins of the bell are unknown. One of the first written records of the bell mentions the Dewar-na-Bernane (or Vernan as it is also spelled), who was summoned alongside the Dewar-na-Quigrich and Dewar-na-Fergy in 1549 by the Prior of Strathfillan, as previously described. Interestingly, this is one of very few ancient documented references to the bell.

Perhaps the earliest reference occurs in 1488 when King James IV specifically requested the presence of St Fillan's Bell at his coronation at Scone. In the Lord Treasurer's accounts there is an entry for a payment of 18 shillings "til a man that beyris Sanct Fyllanis bell at the kingis commande."

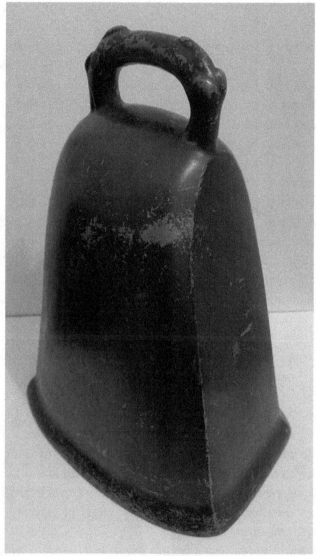

Figure 24: Replica of St Fillan's Bell.

In later times the bell was used as part of a healing practice in order to help cure lunacy. The unfortunate victim was tied with rope at the waist and thrown into St Fillan's Holy Pool, about a mile north from the Priory in Glendochart. The Pool was renowned for its healing virtue and was said to be at its most powerful towards the end of the first quarter of the moon. The 'pool' is actually part of the River Dochart, but it is not until it reaches the point of a rocky promontory that it was said to have been imbued with the healing powers of the saint.

Having been suitably submerged, the 'patient' was pulled out of the water and taken back to the Priory and placed in a large stone with a hole carved into it just large enough to hold him or her. They were then held down by a wooden framework and St Fillan's Bell was put upon their head. They had to remain like this throughout the night. If in the morning they had managed to loosen the bonds and struggled free, then it was deemed that St Fillan had been favourable and they were cured. However, if they remained tied to the wooden framework then there was no help to be found. For the rope or leather to have loosened enough for the 'patent' to become free they would surely need a miracle for when the bonds dried out it would have shrunk and resulted in the rope tightening, making it harder to ever escape without assistance. The best they could pray for, along with the aid of St Fillan, was a night of rain to help loosen the bonds further.

The bell was kept on a stone in the open Churchyard of the Priory for these practices, and it was said that if it were ever removed it would fly through the air and return to that very same spot. The crack that can now be seen in the bell is supposed to have occurred when a soldier, seeing this bell flying through the air, shot at it in a panic to try to bring it down. Exactly when this is supposed to have happened is unknown. However, on 9th August 1798, it appears that the bell had lost its ability to fly.

An English traveller visited the Priory and decided to put the flying bell to the test. He stole the bell and took it south with him to England. Here it remained until 1869 when, purely by chance, Bishop Forbes, author of *Kalendars of Scottish Saints*, visited the Earl of Crawford at Dunecht and met a man who informed him that the bell of St Fillan was in the posession of a relative of his in Hertfordshire, England. The Bishop made contact with this gentleman and soon had the bell returned and secured for the Society of Antiquaries of Scotland. It was placed alongside the Quigrich in the National Museum of Scotland, which was perhaps the first reunion of the two relics of St Fillan in a very, very long time.

The only distinctive markings on the bell occur on the handle. There are two schools of thought as to what these represent, and both pose very curious questions. The first suggests that they are two animal heads, perhaps representing dolphins, or the 'Pictish Beast'. This is a common feature on many of the standing stones carved throughout the ancient kingdom in Scotland. However, to date the image has not been found on any other artefact from the period. Why this symbol should appear so frequently in Pictish carvings is unclear, and it has been suggested that it could denote either an important individual or concept in Pictish mythology and/or a political symbol. If St Fillan's Bell is depicting the Pictish Beast, then it is the only non-carved depiction known to exist from that era which makes it hugely important.

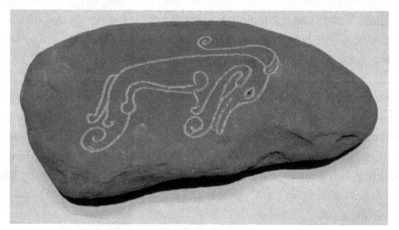

Figure 25: Depiction of the Pictish Beast

The other viewpoint is that the handle is portraying phallic symbolism. This is perhaps even more curious, especially for a supposedly Christian relic. Such thinking led Maclagan (1882) in his book, *Scottish Myths*, to suggest that the bell, and the wider reverence and importance of Fillan, is actually pre-Christian in origin. He proposes that the phallic symbolism of St Fillan's Bell perhaps links it back to early pagan beliefs and practices.

Figure 26: Close up of the handle of St Fillan's Bell.

Maclagan provides a great deal of evidence to support his claims, even though it can be difficult to follow his arguments with full comprehension. He suggests that the originally clapperless bell might have been held upside down, like a chalice, to be used for a more important purpose than just making a sound. He discusses the idea that it could have been used as part of some kind of ancient ritual or divination ceremony, somewhat akin to the drawing of lots. Presumably this implies the bell acted as an oracle of sorts, helping to determine matters of national importance, such as who is the rightful king.

This might explain why succession by tanistry was prevalent through the ancient kingdoms of modern-day Scotland. Could the next king have been chosen, and power conferred, by interpreting the 'casting of lots' emanating from a sacred relic, such as the bell? Is this why it was said that the Stone of Destiny would 'shout' (perhaps 'ring'?) when touched by the rightful heir to the throne? Interestingly, the Welsh word for 'shout' is 'dolefain' which sounds very similar to 'dolphin' which is potentially what is being depicted on the handle of the bell.

Either way, that the bronze bell of St Fillan has been held in veneration for centuries is without doubt. However, there is another, presumably older, iron bell of St Fillan in existence, known as the *clag buidheann,* or Yellow Bell.

The Yellow Bell

This bell is much older than the bronze bell, possibly dating to the sixth century or before. It too has an interesting history. It ended up as the church bell in the parish of Struan in Perthshire, just north of Scone, until 1939 when it was bought by a private collecter and donated to the Perth Museum where it remains on display. This is a wrought iron bell of about a foot high and also has a quadrangular mouth. The iron was coated with bronze and it is one of very few early Celtic bells still in existence.

This particular bell of St Fillan was known in Gaelic as the *'Clag Buidheann'*, or 'Yellow Bell'. In the late 1800s there were still people who remembered traditions of the Yellow Bell from around the west coast near Loch Etive, and more specifically in the region called Balmhaodan. This is near Dunstaffnage and where Boece tells us that the king-making Stone was kept at one stage in its history. The legends associated with this bell are identical to those attributed to St Fillan's Bell in Glendochart, namely that it was held in high veneration by the people for its curative powers and taken to the sick in other parishes. Also, if it was not immediately carried back home after accomplishing its benevolent errand it would take the matter into its own hands and fly through the air to its home.

That the bell should have originated from around a supposed location of the Stone, near Dunstaffnage, is most interesting and the similarities with the legends about the Scots king-making Stone do not stop there. We can read in *Saint Modan of Rosneath: A Fragment of Scottish Haigology* by Robert Story (1878) of a mysterious bell referred to as the *clag buidhe*. It is possible that he is referring to the tradition

236

of some other bell that is assigned the same name and attributes as St Fillan's Bell, but this is perhaps unlikely. He states:

> "The bell at last was taken away to Scone. Not long afterwards the people of Balmhaodan heard a din and jangling in the sky above them, and lo, there was the Clag buidhe flying home, but instead of its former grave sweet melodies, it was clanging out a novel rhythm which shaped itself into the harsh words, '*an rud nach buin duit, na buin da*'; 'don't you meddle with what meddles not with you'. It was removed a second time to Scone, and never returned to desolate Loch Etive.
>
> The legend of the bell's removal to Scone also points...to a very early date. Kenneth Macalpin...originally king or regulus of Dalriada, became in the tenth century king of Scotland, and fixed his capital at Scone. I imagine that the return of the yellow bell with such a change of note must speak of the Argyll men going to Scone for some favour, which procured for them a snubbing from their old friend, now independent of them."

St Fillan's Bell, now on display at Perth Museum, known as the *clag buidheann,* or yellow bell, is perhaps being described as making the same journey from the Dunstaffnage area to Scone, which is the same as in the legend associated with the king-making Stone. Passage from Dunstaffnage to Scone passes right through Glendochart, where the cult of St Fillan flourished. The date for this earlier bell corresponds with the approximate date for the 'first' St Fillan – early sixth century, whereas the later bronze bell is early ninth century – if not significantly older. It is possible that the later bronze bell of St Fillan was cast to commemorate the uniting of the Picts and the Scots with Kenneth McAlpin in 843. The bell aspect relating to the Irish-Scots traditions from the Kingdom of Dál Riata and their reverence for saintly bells, and the Pictish beast included on the handle of the bell for the Pictish aspect of the unification. The ancient traditions thus being continued with a new unification bell following the joining of the kingdoms of the Scots and the Picts.

Figure 27: St Fillan's Bell, the clag buidheann, on display in Perth Museum
© Perth Museum and Art Gallery, Perth & Kinross Council

What is an interesting side-note that may be relevant, even if impossible to prove is directly connected, is that in ancient China, supposedly originating from 239 BCE, a 'primal tone' was determined for each new Emperor known as *huangzhong*. This means 'yellow bell', so called after the Chinese deity known as Huangdi, or 'Yellow Emperor', who is regarded as the initiator of Chinese culture. The 'yellow bell' tone was used as the basis to determine the musical scale intervals, and by resetting this for each new Emperor it ensured that their reign was in tune and harmony with the universe.

The idea of the bell being tuned to a specific frequency is further postulated by John Purser, who examined the tone of the bronze bell of St Fillan in his book *Scotland's Music* (1992). He says that two bronze bells may have been commissioned by Kenneth McAlpin in 848-849. He also concludes that depending on where the bell is struck it produces a frequency that is equivalent to a musical note of either A, B or C.

It was previously discussed how there could have been a confusion with the translations for the words *cloch* and *clog*. Welsh Cymraeg is assumed to be the closest match to the now extinct Pictish language. *Cloch* means bell in Welsh and stone in Irish, whereas *Clog* means stone in Welsh and bell in Irish. The *baghul* and *belle* (crosier and bell) were mentioned in a poem by Langtoft from 1301, alongside the 'King's Seat of Scone', referring to the Scots king-making Stone that was taken to Westminster Abbey in 1296. It is possible that this poem is perhaps meant to be highlighting that the Stone that King Edward I took from Scone was of little significance to the Scots, and the real king-making relics were the *baghul* and the *belle*.

The idea of the 'Stone' of Destiny actually being a 'Bell' was first proposed by Maclagan in his book *Scottish Myths* in 1882. He went on to write a further publication for private circulation to those in Clan Maclagan titled *The Clan of the Bell of St Fillan*. 'Fillan', he contends, was not so much a physical person, but more of an association with ancient and pagan rites. These practices were followed by certain tribes of Britain before, during, and after the Roman occupation of Britain. These pre-Christian practices and belief systems gradually evolved through the occurrence of interbreeding between the Roman soldiers and the natives of Britain. Over time, these beliefs were made more acceptable by assigning Christian symbolism, and hence saintly association.

Maclagan provides a very interesting theory for why Fillan specifically was so revered. In an earlier chapter we discussed King Cassivellaunus and how he fought, and won, against Caesar. The battle is said to have occurred somewhere near the mouth of the River Thames, presumably near *Caer Lud* (London) in England. From here, and following subsequent invasions of Britain, the Romans moved further north. They built Hadrian's Wall between the Tyne and Solway (122-130CE) and the Antonine Wall between the Forth and Clyde (142-144CE). Prior to this, between 70-80CE, and further north still, the Romans established a fortified land frontier known as the 'Gask Ridge' in modern-day Perthshire, Scotland. This would be approximately 125 years after Caesar's invasion and would have been sufficient time for there to have been an amalgamation of various religious rites and practices as tribes, soldiers and traditions moved around the country. This post-Roman invasion, and pre-Christian period, is suggested as the basis for the phallic symbolism appearing on St Fillan's Bell, and why Fillan's relics, particularly the *belle*, were perhaps used as part of an ancient king-making tradition.

Although it can never be proven beyond any shadow of doubt that the 'Stone' used during the coronation ceremonies of the Scottish monarchs was a 'Bell' it certainly makes for an interesting theory. What is perhaps most striking of all is that there are no written references to there being a Scots king-making Stone until what is taken in 1296 is in the hands of the English.

What is more intriguing is that the name Cassivellaunus, presumably a *bretwalda*, appears to be made of two separate words, *cassi*, meaning tin or bronze, and *vellaunus,* meaning chief. In Gaelic there is no letter 'v', and so it would be substituted for 'f', thus *vellaunus* becomes *fellaunus* – Fillan – the chief, or perhaps more rightly, the king.

Chapter 10
The British-Israelites

When the various tests on the Stone were being performed in the mid-1800s, Arthur Stanley, Dean of Westminster, wrote his *Historical Memorials of Westminster Abbey* (1868). Stanley was instrumental in the foundation of the Palestine Exploration Fund in May 1865. This enterprise was set up to conduct archaeological excavations of biblical and post-biblical sites around the Levant, which was the old name for the area now roughly comprising modern day Israel, Palestine, Syria and Jordan. The Palestine Exploration Fund was intended to be non-religious and non-political in nature. Whether this could ever have been achieved during the mid-nineteenth century, let alone today, and especially regarding biblical matters, is highly debatable.

The aim was to archaeologically prove that the events and locations portrayed throughout the Bible were literally correct. If the findings of the Palestine Exploration Fund did not quite fit with their theories, or even worse if they proved them to be wrong, then they were largely ignored in favour of those that did help to substantiate the legitimacy of the Bible. Many of the places that we recognise today as being the Biblical locations of thousands of years ago were only identified as such following the findings of the Palestine Exploration Fund just over 150 years ago. The archaeologists and historians of the Palestine Exploration Fund were creating an ancient history for Palestine that concurred with the biblical version of events, rather than taking the evidence as they uncovered it and then forming their conclusions. The common phraseology for their activities was that they had 'the Bible in one hand and a spade in the other.'

It was Arthur Stanley who requested Professor Ramsey to examine the Stone and give his opinion when he suggested that it looked like it had been "originally prepared for building purposes." The idea that the Stone might have been a building block was of interest to Stanley, because there was a growing belief in Britain that the Stone in Westminster, identified as Jacob's Pillow, was again mentioned in later chapters of the Bible. In The Book of Psalms (118:22) it says, "The stone which the builders refused is become the head stone of the corner."

Around this time, if not slightly earlier, the Stone was also beginning to appear in Freemasonic rituals where it was often identified as either the Capstone or Foundation Stone of the Temple of Solomon in Jerusalem. This has been referred to as 'Jacob's Stone' and was supposedly saved from the destruction of the Temple by the Babylonians in 586BCE. This Stone was supposedly taken to Ireland by the prophet Jeremiah.

The movements of Jeremiah are not known for certain following the destruction of the first Temple. Rather curiously, his departure coincides with the arrival of a certain Ollamh Fódhla in Ireland. He was reputed to be a wise prophet and was the person who convened the first assemblies at Tara.

Ollamh Fódhla is, in some accounts, identified as being the prophet Jeremiah. Some traditions claim that Jeremiah brought with him both the Ark of the Covenant and the Lia Fáil, or Jacob's Pillow, following the destruction of the Temple in the sixth century BCE. He is also reputed to have travelled with the daughter of Zedekiah, the last King of Judah, and the last king in the line of David. His daughter was believed to have been called Tea Tephi and it is from her that Tara is supposed to have derived its name.

It is claimed that she married the Irish King Érimon and so continued the line of Judah in the Irish monarchy. Érimon is said to have built a fort in her honour on top of the greatest hill in Ireland and named it after her as Tea-múr meaning 'the wall of Tea'. Over time, this became known as Temair, or Tara. She is sometimes even referred to as the Maid of Destiny, because she travelled with Jacob's Pillow, also known as the Stone of Destiny. The site of Tara that was established by Ollamh Fódhla was seen as a 'School of the Prophets' and some have even commented that the word Tara may be derived from the Hebrew word Tora, meaning 'doctrine' or 'teaching'.

The Twelve Tribes of Israel

As discussed in a previous chapter, the patriarch Jacob is believed to have rested his head on the Stone when he received the covenant from God about the legacy of his offspring. Jacob had twelve sons, whose descendants became known as the Twelve Tribes of Israel. After many generations, the twelve tribes had become hugely populated and had forcibly, with the assistance of God, gained control of the land which He promised to Jacob. They subsequently renamed it Israel.

God had instructed Jacob to change his name to Israel, which in Hebrew means 'he will rule (as) God', and so the naming of the land was in commemoration of the posterity of their father. The land was divided into twelve parts so that each tribe had their respective piece of land holding in the Promised Land. Over time, conflicting interests between the tribes caused a split that created the establishment of two factions. The southern kingdom of the House of Judah, which was comprised of the tribes of Judah and Benjamin (also including a minority from the tribe of Levi), and the northern kingdom of the House of Israel that consisted of the remaining ten tribes.

Following the Assyrian captivity of the Israelites in Babylon that began in 710BCE, it is widely believed that only the House of Judah returned to Israel, leaving the remaining ten tribes to disperse elsewhere. The whereabouts of their dispersal has been the cause of many a controversy ever since. It is due to this uncertainty that they are commonly referred to as 'the Lost Ten Tribes of Israel'.

The Israelites were a simple farm folk, and it is reasonable to suggest that they did not return southwest from Babylon to the desert land of Palestine, because the land was very hard to work and earn a living from. With more fertile lands to the north, it would have made sense for them to have headed in that direction. Regardless, the House of Israel as a distinct entity from the House of Judah is not spoken of much more throughout the rest of the Bible. Even though they are commonly portrayed as being one and the same, this is not technically correct. It is also important to highlight that before the split the term 'Jew' was not used, and it does not signify the people from all twelve tribes. 'Jew' is a term that was only used to signify those of the House of Judah who returned to Palestine following their captivity by the Assyrians.

The Brith Society

In the mid-1800s, a movement began to appear in Britain known as the Brith Society. 'Brith' is the Hebrew word for 'Covenant'. The basic tenet of the Brith Society was that the British people were descended from the ten tribes of Israel who did not return to Palestine after the Assyrian captivity in Babylon. Instead, it is said that they ventured to the 'isles afar off' (as stated in Isaiah 66:19), which in the Brith interpretation of the Bible implied the British Isles.

The Brith Society is also commonly known as the British-Israel Society or The Covenant Society, signifying a racial link between the British people and the 'lost' descendants of Jacob. The Covenant on which they base the name of their society was that made by God to Jacob when he rested his head upon the Stone and was told about the legacy of his offspring. The British-Israelites believe in the literal truth of the legend of Jacob's Pillow.

The bringing of the Lia Fáil and Tea Tephi to Ireland by Jeremiah/Ollamh Fódhla was regarded as having been for the continuation of the Davidic royal line of Israel in the British Isles. The similarities between Jeremiah and Ollamh Fódhla are interesting to say the least and throughout history there have been those who believe, without hesitation, that the two characters are literally one and the same person. The British-Israelites believe that as a result of this transposition the ancient kings of Ireland, Scotland and subsequently England, that were crowned upon the Stone, are also descended from the tribes of Israel.

The Brith Society believes that the promises made by God to Jacob whilst he rested his head on the Stone apply to all twelve tribes and not exclusively to the Jews. Biblical prophecy played a major part in their belief system and so they looked to the world around them for indications that there was a greater purpose to their lives, and that their beliefs were well founded. The British influence around the world was opening up the civilisations of the ancient past to people from all walks of life that were proud to be part of the British Empire. The Great Pyramid of Giza was even regarded as confirmation of Bible events, with its internal and external dimensions supposedly corresponding with major events throughout history indicating that it was a timeline from which the future of the world could be determined. Believing in prophecy and the literal truth of their interpretation of the Bible, the Brith Society set out to prove that the ancestry of the British people was intimately linked with that of the lost ten tribes of Israel. When Jacob rested his head upon the stones, God had promised him:

> "...thy seed shall be as the dust of the earth, and thou shalt spread abroad to the west, and to the east, and to the north, and to the south; and in thee and in thy seed shall all the families of the earth be blessed."
>
> **Genesis 28:14**

The British Empire was at its strongest when the Brith Society was gaining popularity. The saying that 'the sun never sets on the British Empire' was, to many, all the proof that was needed that God was making true His promise that the descendants of Israel would rule over the Earth. Even the name of the land itself, Britain, was claimed to be proof of the ancient Israelite heritage by signifying its inhabitants as the 'Covenant People'. The British-Israelite interpretation of the word 'Britain' suggests that it was comprised of two Hebrew words, 'Brith' (Covenant) and 'Am' (People) thus spelling 'Brith-Am' which vulgarly got pronounced over time as 'Brit-An'.

The Brith Society proposed and promoted the 'seven times' punishment of God as affirmation of their beliefs to any would-be doubters. The 'seven times' punishment was given to the Hebrews who disobeyed the commands of God, as described at length in the Book of Leviticus chapter 26. God speaks to the Hebrews and instructs them of how they must behave in order to keep the Covenant that He made with Jacob as he rested his head on the Stone. If they did not follow His instruction then they are repeatedly told that they will be chastised 'seven times' in various different ways for their defiance.

245

In calculating the duration of the seven times punishment the British Israelites overlooked the lunar year (354.25 days) and the solar year (365.25 days) in favour of the prophetic year (360 days). The length of a prophetic year was based on a reference in the Book of Revelation 11:2-3 which says:

"But the court which is without the temple leave out, and measure it not; for it is given unto the Gentiles: and the holy city shall they tread under foot forty and two months.
And I will give power unto my two witnesses, and they shall prophesy a thousand two hundred and three-score days, clocked in sackcloth."

Revelation 11:2-3

'Forty and two months' is equal to three and a half solar years (42/12 = 3.5). A 'thousand two hundred and three-score' (1,260) days divided by 3.5 therefore equals 360 days per prophetic year, and it is upon this calculation that the British-Israelites based the length of a 'time'. They equate each day for a year based on a reference in the Book of Ezekiel 4:6 in which God says, "I have appointed thee each day for a year." Thus, when a day is used prophetically that day indicates a year, but only if God is chastising a nation. If He is chastising an individual, then a day actually means a day. To confuse things further, if God is speaking of Himself in prophetic terms then according to 2 Peter 3:8 "one day is with the Lord as a thousand years, and a thousand years as one day." The 'seven times' punishment that the Hebrew nation was to endure for their national pride and disobedience of His laws was therefore equal to 2,520 years (7 x 360).

Biblical dates are very difficult to cite with any certainty. However, the date of the Assyrian invasion of Israel is widely believed to have started in 740BCE and ended thirty years later in 710BCE when the Assyrians came up against all the defended cities of Judah and captured them. The collapse of Judah was to be seen as a sign that the people had disobeyed God and their 'seven times' punishment was to begin with the start of the Assyrian captivity.

Believing that the Hebrew people were to be punished for 2,520 years, the Brith Society calculated that the end of their punishment would occur sometime around the early 1800s, possibly 1810, at which time the Hebrew people would be able to make good on the promises of God to spread to the west, east, north and south. For many, there was no more proof needed. With the defeat of Napoleon at Waterloo in 1815 there was no other serious contender to rival the British Empire in strength and dominance throughout the world to the west, east, north and south. God had made good of his promise to Jacob. The sun would never set on his chosen people or their nation – the British Empire.

The Search for the Ark of the Covenant

The British-Israelites promoted a plethora of 'evidence' to substantiate their claims of British descent from the Lost Ten Tribes of Israel. The society found itself a large and influential following throughout the British Isles. Adherents to this belief system came from all backgrounds and walks of life. Historians, clerics, archaeologists, and of course the common laymen, all wanted definitive proof of their divine heritage. They certainly believed that the Stone of Destiny was one and the same as Jacob's Pillow, and as it formed a basis for their truth, they set out to find more tangible artefacts that rightfully belonged to the British tribes of Israel.

In 1899 a group of Brith Society archaeologists had pieced together enough information to propose a hypothesis that the prophet Jeremiah was one and the same as Ollamh Fódhla, and he had indeed settled at Tara in Ireland. They also believed that as he fled Jerusalem at the time of the destruction of the Temple of Solomon, he must have brought with him the Ark of the Covenant. According to tradition, the Ark had also been housed in the Temple. When the Temple came under attack by the Babylonians in 586BCE Jeremiah was believed to have taken the Temple treasures and Princess Tea Tephi with him to Tara. It was believed that he hid the Temple treasures at the sacred site.

The Brith Society archaeologists were so convinced by this that they approached the landowner of Tara and requested his permission to carry out extensive archaeological excavations. Their objective was to recover the Ark and any other Temple treasure that may have been buried at Tara. There was uproar from those who did not follow their line of thought, thinking that to debase such an ancient site as Tara was sacrilege in itself. Even the famous Irish poet, William Butler Yeates, visited Tara to protest about what was happening. In a letter to *The Times* newspaper on 24th June 1902, Yeates, Douglas Hyde and George Moore wrote of the excavations:

> "This is not being done through any antiquarian zeal, but, apparently, that the sect which believes the English to be descended from the Ten Tribes may find the Ark of the Covenant.
> Tara is, because of its associations, probably the most consecrated spot in Ireland, and its destruction will leave many bitter memories behind it."

The landowner said that he would shoot any 'trespassers' who tried to stop the British-Israelites, but this was perhaps more bravado than a real threat. No-one who came to the site in protest was ever shot. With the sole intention of finding the Ark of the Covenant, a thorough excavation and recording of findings was never created and perhaps many important artefacts were simply destroyed or deemed too unimportant to log. The holes that were dug were simply filled in when no Ark was found and no known records were kept. One of the concerned landowners in the region, Sir John Dillon, visited the site regularly to keep up to date with any findings from the digs. He offered his assistance in an effort to try to limit the overall damage to the area. On one of his visits he found an ancient bracelet in one of the holes that had been dug. It was made of either gold, or some alloy of gold, and he handed it to one of those concerned with the excavation for his perusal. When the gentleman saw that it was not the Ark of the Covenant, he simply threw the bracelet of priceless antiquity into the nearby River Boyne and it was lost forever. The excavations continued for several years with protests and public condemnation of the work. Eventually all work was stopped by the autumn of 1902.

Their main interest was focused around the 'Rath of the Synods' at Tara. This was believed to be the site of preaching by Adomnan, author of the *Vita Columbae*. The Ark of the Covenant was never found. Without doubt the British-Israelite archaeologists, whose actions would suggest they were only amateur at best, did find many interesting features at the site. Unfortunately, they were never recorded nor properly analysed and so they have potentially been lost forever.

Britain = Israel?

The work and beliefs of the Brith Society began to permeate into the subconscious of many intelligent people. At the turn of the twentieth century new ideas based upon their thought processes began to surface. Although these can perhaps seem to the modern reader as being simply outrageous to even be considered, that they were believed, and still are in some circles, should provide the open-minded reader with enough intrigue to hear the evidence.

One such theory was written about in 1946 by William Comyns Beaumont in his book *Britain: The Key to World History*. Beaumont puts forth the theory that the events portrayed in the Bible actually happened in Britain and not in the Middle East. Therefore, the 'lost' ten tribes never left mainland Britain in the first place. More specifically, he introduces the idea that the site of ancient Jerusalem was actually the site of the modern-day city of Edinburgh in Scotland and not thousands of miles away where modern-day Jerusalem is located.

Beaumont's theory revolved around some rather interesting observations. For example, the Romans were actively pursuing a military campaign in Scotland in 140CE, the same time as the destruction of Jerusalem and the renaming of the city to *Aelia Capitolina* by the Emperor Hadrian. At the same time, one of the Legions stationed in Britain was awarded the use of the imperial name *Aelia,* in commemoration for some successful military campaign. In addition, the Roman cartographer, Ptolemy, had recorded on his map of Britain that there were twelve Pictish tribes in Scotland – the same as the number of tribes of Israel. It was also alleged that the guttural intonations of the Hebrew language could find their closest counterpart in the lowland Scotch tongue. The similarity between '*Gewissæ*' and '*Jew*' as a chosen people was noted in an earlier chapter.

Beaumont presented an entirely new version of biblical history and used a great deal more evidence to try to substantiate his claims. It is not for this book to examine all of those claims, but it does serve to highlight that *if* there is indeed any basis or foundation of fact in his work, then much of the fighting that has been raging for the past two millennia in the Middle East could perhaps have been avoided.

The Bible has been interpreted in so many different ways, with each new religious movement using the same text to 'prove' whatever pre-conceived ideas they require verifying. Beaumont simply did the same thing. He took the events portrayed in the Bible and using the same bibliography as many other writers, such as Josephus, Ptolemy and others of the Roman era, he came to an entirely different conclusion regarding the physical locations of where certain events are believed to have happened. What is perhaps most unsettling of all, is that to dismiss his claims outright is very easy, but to prove them false is much more difficult.

The Freemasonic Legends

During the 1800s it was widely accepted by many societies, not just the British-Israelites, that the Stone of Destiny was synonymous with Jacob's Pillow. When coupled with the idea that the Ark of the Covenant may have found its way to the British Isles, it aroused much interest, not least of all in Freemasonic circles. In certain aspects of Freemasonry, the Stone was also known as the 'Cubical Stone'. This is an important emblem in the ritual of the Royal-Arch and the Rose-Croix as well as some of the other higher Masonic degrees.

The Cubical Stone is often referred to as 'the stone the builders rejected'. This is continually referred to in the Bible and especially in the book of Revelation. According to one Masonic tradition, the Cubical Stone, believed to be one and the same as Jacob's Pillow, is also reputed to be the Stone upon which Adam made his offerings to God in the Garden of Eden. There is another Masonic tradition which claims that the Stone was deposited in a secret crypt in the Temple of

Solomon, where it remained until its discovery during the rebuilding of the Temple by Zerubbabel. The Cubical Stone of the Freemasonic traditions is said to be a white stone and this is another reason why some contend the genuine Scots king-making Stone was white marble.

The traditions of a white Stone can be directly related to the Bible. In reading the passage that is of interest to the Mark Mason degree (Revelations 2:17), we learn that a name appears on the Stone which is similar to the king-making Stone being used to proclaim the rightful king:

> "He that hath an ear, let him hear what the Spirit saith unto the churches; To him that overcometh will I give to eat of the hidden manna, and will give him a white stone, and in the stone a new name written, which no man knoweth saving he that receiveth it."

Revelation 2:17

The British-Israelites drew inspiration from all over in order to try to satiate their quest for the truth regarding the origins of the British people. In doing so, along with Freemasonic traditions, they managed to confuse many different stories and versions of events in trying to piece together one complete picture. This created a minefield for later historians who would find themselves having to explain away traditions and associations of the Stone of Destiny that were unfounded, such as it being a white stone and not sandstone. To emphasise this further, in the book *Westmonasterium* by John Dart (1723), the Stone at Westminster is described as, "the Marble-Stone whereon our Saviour stood at his Ascension, and which bare the Marks of his Footsteps." This claim has not appeared anywhere else, yet it clearly originated somewhere and when first written was presumably sufficiently well established as a theory to warrant including in that comprehensive record of Westminster Abbey.

Figure 28: The White Cubical Stone, as depicted on a Templar teaching board

These were traditions based entirely from the need of groups, such as Freemasons and the British-Israelites, to firmly root the Stone to the events portrayed and prophesised throughout the Bible. To believe in something can be harmless enough, but as a belief finds more followers suddenly the sacred can come under threat from the hands of over-enthusiastic fanatics whose primary concern is to prove themselves, and their beliefs, infallibly correct.

The Rapture and the Apocalypse

At the same time as the Brith Society was reaching its peak in Britain, so too were many other schools of thought regarding biblical prophecy. One such group was the Plymouth Brethren, founded by John Nelson Derby in 1825. Derby promoted to his followers that they should not have any contact with anything ungodly and that the second coming of Christ was imminent. Derby was responsible for creating the idea of the 'Rapture' which is tied to the Apocalypse and the End of Days, as prophesised in the Book of Revelation. In the twenty-first century, the idea of the Rapture has found many adherents, especially in the so-called 'Bible-belt' of the United States of America. In a 2002 survey by *Time Magazine* and CNN, it seems that 60% of Americans believe that the events portrayed in the Book of Revelation will literally happen. In addition, maybe as many as 50 million American citizens believe in the Rapture and think it will occur within their lifetime. Belief in the Rapture is to believe that before the End of Days all true Christian believers will literally dematerialise in an instant and then ascend to heaven to be with Christ. Those who remain on Earth will face the Tribulation. That will last seven years and would then culminate with the biblical Apocalypse.

The Rapture movement that was created by Derby played on the ideas being promoted by the Brith Society, whose own beliefs similarly supported those of Derby. They believed that the end of the 'seven times' punishment might very well coincide with the start of the Apocalypse, which could only come about following the second coming of Christ. It was as if the strength and success of the British Empire had damned the world to oblivion, with only the British Christians having any chance of being saved!

There have always been those who are predicting the end of the world. They are correct, in that it will come. The world *will* die eventually. The real question is, when? Dates have been cited for centuries, with the modern predictions being 1975, 1984, 1999, 2000, 2001, 2006, 2012...and so it goes on.

As the years passed and the End Times did not materialise, followers grew old and died, meeting their maker in the most time-honoured way. However, many of the followers of the Rapture movement relocated to America and continued to promote their beliefs on that side of the Atlantic. With a new world and new opportunities before them, the old ideas took root and have flourished into something that gives promise to the American believer today, exactly as the British believer of yesteryear was promised when the British Empire was at its height. History repeats itself and unfortunately lessons have not been learned. Bizarrely, the Stone of Destiny is an artefact that is right at the heart of making their dreams come true.

The idea of the British being a 'chosen people' may seem laughable to the majority of the world's population today, never mind in Britain. But throughout history the strongest Empires of the day have believed in a similar concept. Beaumont's work came at a time when the world had gone mad, and millions had lost their lives in the name of Freedom. In its basest form, World War II had pitted the British Empire against Nazi Germany, and yet each was overshadowed by the new superpowers of the United States of America and the Soviet Union. The story of the Nazi belief in superiority and the so-called 'Master Race' can also trace its roots in similar beliefs to those of the Brith Society. The major difference being that in some Nazi circles it was believed that the 'wandering tribe' story should be attributed to their Saxon ancestors, by whom some of Britain had been populated. Hence the term Anglo-Saxon when sometimes describing the English. In British-Israelite circles it is often stated that, "Israel's grave is the Saxon's birthplace." Such an idea should perhaps lead us to consider re-examining why the Nazis so hated the Jews.

The creation of the state of Israel in 1948 was to give to the Jewish community what God had promised to Jacob when he rested his head on what was believed by many to be the Stone of Destiny. Finally,

254

the nation-less race would have a homeland that they could call their own.

As the British sailed the oceans and colonised new and far-flung lands at the height of the Empire, it had been the common practice to take as many relics as possible from countries such as Ethiopia, Egypt, India and many others. These relics were to adorn such institutions as the British Museum, as well as British castles and palaces and were nothing more than what could be described as plunder.

It was not just the British who helped themselves to the possessions of others. The cities of London, Paris and Washington each have an Egyptian obelisk in pride of place, showing and celebrating their conquests of the past. However, in the modern day a change in sentiment has started and many countries are demanding the return of their 'stolen' relics. The state of Israel is one such country seeking the return of its artefacts. It has even taken to asking the Vatican to return any and all of the Jewish relics and papers that are in its possession. Perhaps unsurprisingly, the Vatican is reluctant to do so for fear of losing vast amounts of its archives – or perhaps alternatively for what might be uncovered?

Following the destruction of the Temple of Herod in the year 70CE by the Roman Emperor Vespasian and his son Titus, several Temple treasures are believed to have been taken from Jerusalem to Rome. The most notable of these relics was the golden candelabrum, known as the Menorah. The Arch of Titus in Rome was erected to celebrate the Menorah and other treasures being triumphantly carried from the Temple by the Romans. There are those who believe that the Menorah remains in the Vatican and they are making loud noises for its return to Israel, even though its possession is flatly denied.

With this in mind, what of the Stone of Destiny and the claim of it being Jacob's Pillow? The legend states that the Stone originated from Bethel in Israel, yet it is now on display in Scotland. Would Israel now be within its rights to ask for it to be handed back to its rightful owners? After all, if there is even a shred of evidence to the claim that it originated in Israel, then the Stone is perhaps one the most important religious relics on public display, and it could very well be the Covenant Stone of the Israelites.

Before the Apocalypse can happen it is prophesised that there must be a new Temple built on the Temple Mount in Jerusalem. There are calls from some angles, such as an organisation known as the Temple Mount Foundation, for the return of the Stone of Destiny to Israel, so that it can be used as the foundation Stone of this new Temple. What is perhaps most alarming of all, is that in order for the Temple to be built, the area must first be 'cleared' of the Al Aqsa Mosque that is presently sited there. The mosque is more commonly known as the Dome of the Rock. It was built around 690 by the 9th Caliph (leader of the Islamic community), Abd al-Malik. Situated inside the middle of the Dome of the Rock is what many refer to as the 'Foundation Stone' and according to the teachings of Islam it is from this rock where the prophet Muhammad, accompanied by the archangel Gabriel, ascended on a journey to heaven for one night in 621CE.

On this journey, Mohammad is stated to have met Abraham and Moses, among several other prophets, and is reputed to have been given the Islamic prayers before descending back to earth. In Jewish teachings, the site of the Dome of the Rock is where God tested Abraham when he ordered him to sacrifice his son, Isaac. Some have even speculated that this may be the site where Jacob received the covenant with God when he rested his head on the Stone. This could therefore imply that the Stone that is housed in the Dome of the Rock is the real Jacob's Pillow. If the Dome of the Rock were to be destroyed in order to build a new Temple in preparation for the Apocalypse then there would rightly be outrage from the Islamic community, not to mention the vast majority of the global population, about the destruction of one of Islam's most sacred sites. Possibly this act could be the start of another World War, which would surely be just as vehemently violent as any biblical Apocalypse.

Whilst the Stone that is currently on display in Scotland is, to some, nothing more than an unimportant piece of red sandstone, to others it represents a means to bringing forth the Apocalypse as prophesised in the Book of Revelation. It was discussed earlier how the legend of the Stone being Jacob's Pillow appears to be nothing more than a political creation by the English in 1327. Even if this could be proven beyond any shadow of doubt, there would still be those who would disregard the facts in favour of supporting their long-established beliefs. The Brith Society was able to 'prove' their beliefs based on the global power that the British Empire held at the time. History seems to be repeating itself today in the USA. The End Time/Rapture religious movement present in the USA believes in the literal word of the Bible and they are doing everything in their power to bring about the Apocalypse within our lifetime. Many of these people do not know that it is an idea that was started in 1825 in Plymouth, England. The same can be said of the Temple Mount Foundation in Israel that is trying to build the new Temple on the site of the old in Jerusalem in preparation of the coming of the new Kingdom of God on Earth.

All of these ultra-religious groups, and there are very many of them throughout the world, are 100% sure that their beliefs are correct. They generally see the Bible, or some other religious book, as the literal word of God. They will claim that it justifies and proves their beliefs – however outlandish and irrational others may see them to be. But what if the Brith Society and William Beaumont were correct? Can we say without a shadow of a doubt that they are wrong? Global history and politics would have to change overnight and maybe it would be for the better. Time will tell.

Conclusions

Today we typically regard stone as something that is 'just there', but to ancient man it was held in a much higher regard. From the moment that man first picked up a stone in his hand and used it for some practical purpose as a tool, a weapon, or even as jewellery, we have acknowledged the importance of stone as being paramount to the existence of humankind. As a tool it has provided us with shelter, the ability to eat hitherto inaccessible foods such as nuts and shellfish, we have become aware of flint which allows us to make fire, we can cut down trees and many more functions which are impossible without a stone in the hand. As a weapon we crafted stone into spearheads and knifes, allowing us to hunt for food and protect our families from predators. And as jewellery we have adorned ourselves with the beauty of nature as a testament to one fundamental fact. Without stone we could not exist.

The great stone palaces and temples from the oldest civilisations have stood the weathering of time and conflict and still amaze with their beautiful architecture, precision of craftsmanship, and overall magnificence. Perhaps the greatest stone achievement of mankind is the Giza Plateau in Egypt that incorporates the last of the Seven Wonders of the World – the Great Pyramid. If these structures had been made of any other material than stone, then it is unlikely that they would still be standing. It is like the story of the three little pigs who each built a house to protect themselves from the big bad wolf. The houses of straw and sticks are easily blown down after some intense 'huffing and puffing', but the house of stone can withstand his attack. This practical application of stone as a form of permanent shelter eventually led to it being viewed in more spiritual terms.

Over time the use of stone became synonymous with certain aspects of king-making ceremonies in most, if not all, of the ancient cultures of the past 6,000 years or more. In the British Isles perhaps the best example of an ancient reverence for stone is Stonehenge. Even in the modern day we cannot fully explain how and why such a thing was built 4,000 years ago. The most common form of ancient stone in the British Isles are what are called "Petrosomatoglyph". This derives from Greek *petros* (stone), *soma* (body) and *glyphein* (to carve), or in other words to carve a part of the body on a stone. Probably the most common form is the carving of a foot or feet. This is a form which has been used from the southern coast of England all the way up to the northern shores of Scotland. Perhaps the most popular carved footprint in Scotland is that which is at the ancient hill fort at Dunadd in Argyll. The traditions associated with this king-making site place it as a pre-cursor to the arrival of the Stone of Destiny on the shores of mainland Britain.

It is unlikely that we will ever know what exactly the genuine Scots king-making Stone really was, what it looked like, or why it was so revered. Is it the Stone taken, stolen, then returned to Westminster in the 1950s, or is that a decoy or replica, and is the real one hidden somewhere and guarded until some future time? Did it originate in Israel, Egypt, Spain, Ireland, Iona, Dunstaffnage, Scone, or some other place? Is it the Frith Stool at Hexham Abbey? Indeed, we may never know for certain whether it was originally a 'Stone' or 'Bell'? Perhaps the real question is whether or not it particularly matters in the present day, given that for over 700 years a block of sandstone has been used as the coronation Stone of the English and British monarchs. 700 years still gives it quite some historical significance!

From 1296 onward the legends about the Stone that Edward took began to spread like wildfire throughout both Scotland and England. To this day, a large proportion of Scots believe that it was the wrong Stone that was taken. The actions by Edward immediately after its removal from Scone could certainly lead one to come to a similar conclusion. Today in Scotland, rather than being the celebrated relic of a glorious past the Stone of Destiny is regarded by many as being a worthless lump of rock. Yet if this is the case, why should it still form a major part of the coronation ceremony of the British monarchs?

In its current home of Edinburgh Castle, until its move to Perth in 2024, the visitor is told relatively little about its supposed origins – even from the point of view of it being a very ancient Scottish palladium. The legend of the Stone of Destiny has had over 700 years to be perfected and yet it is still open to a vast amount of conjecture. The Stone is, without doubt, an important artefact. It *was* stolen in 1296 and it *has* been used as the coronation Stone for most of the English and British monarchs since that time. But even so, few can bring themselves to believe in its vast, oft-told history. Why?

A fable is usually about a mythical something, and yet the legend as portrayed was really believed by some to have happened to a genuine tangible artefact. The Declaration of Arbroath was a petition to the Pope sent in 1320 by the Scots seeking recognition of their independence from England. It claimed very similar origins for the Scots race which match the supposed travels of the Stone. A study into the origins of Celtic DNA that was published in the *American Journal of Human Genetics* in 2004 is virtually confirming that the migration story of Celtic blood from Spain to Ireland, and thence to Scotland, is *true*, so why not that of the Stone? DNA was certainly not known about 700 years ago and yet we are starting to discover that all of the old fables could in fact have been accurate in their portrayal of events.

There are always at least three sides to every story – the winners' side, the losers' side, and then the unknown. If a large portion of the Scottish people believe that the Stone taken to Westminster is not the genuine Scots king-making Stone then why were there such jubilant scenes throughout the country when it was brought back to Scotland in 1951? This was after it had been stolen, or reclaimed if you prefer, from Westminster Abbey by Ian Hamilton and three other Scottish Nationalists on Christmas Day 1950. Surely there must be a kernel of truth embedded in the subconscious of the nation that really wants it to be the genuine Stone to help appease 700 years of apparently unfair treatment by the English. When the Stone was on Scottish soil in 1951 a letter was written to King George IV by Hamilton and his co-conspirator, John MacCormick, asking that the Stone remain in Scotland and not be returned to England. The request was ignored and any calls for its return in subsequent years were treated in a similar fashion.

Aside from the coronation ceremony of Queen Elizabeth II on 2nd June 1953, nothing much happened to the Stone at Westminster

Abbey over the next 40 years. However, in the year of the 700th anniversary of its theft from Scone by King Edward I of England, an announcement was made at Parliament in Westminster. The Stone was to be returned to Scotland!

The year was 1996. The announcement was made by the Conservative Party government and many sensed an ulterior motive. The Conservatives were continually seeing poor electoral results in Scotland and it was thought by many Scots that the return of the Stone was nothing more than a token gesture to try to win over the hearts and minds of the Scottish populace. The fact that it would still have to return to Westminster Abbey in England for every succeeding coronation was, to some, just another insult. The Stone is on 'loan' to Scotland and under strict instruction that it must be returned to Westminster Abbey for the coronation of the next and every succeeding monarch of the United Kingdom of Great Britain.

What is interesting is that from 2024 the Stone will be on display in Perth Museum, which will be the same location as the iron 'yellow bell' of St Fillan. This could be the first time the king-making 'clach' and 'clog' have been in the same vicinity since the coronation at Scone of King John Balliol in 1292. Perhaps there should be a petition to also move the 'baghul' to Perth as well?

Since 1996 and the return to Scotland of the Stone, the Scots once again have their own parliament. The Scottish National Party (SNP) has been in Government since 2007, pushing the agenda of complete political separation from England. In 2014 there was a 'once in a generation' referendum in Scotland on its independence from the United Kingdom. It was a narrow win for the Unionists with 55.3% of the votes, meaning that 44.7% of the Scottish population did want independence.

Following the further divisive vote for the UK to leave the European Union in 2016, known as Brexit, the SNP have been using this as the basis for a second referendum on Scottish independence. 62% of Scots voted to remain in the EU against a 'leave' figure of 38%. These figures are widely used to promote the idea that "Scotland voted overwhelmingly to remain in the EU", however if we look at the actual numbers of votes it tells a slightly different story. 55.3% of votes for 'Scotland to remain part of UK' is actually 2,001,926 people, whereas 62% of Scottish votes for 'UK to stay in the EU' is 1,661,191 people which, coincidently, is almost exactly the same number of people that voted for Scotland to be an independent country (1,617,989 votes). It could be argued that Scotland voted more overwhelmingly to remain part of the UK. The situation is complex and the outcome far from certain.

If independence is voted for by Scotland, would a completely separate and independent nation allow the Stone to travel to England for the coronation of the monarch on 'foreign' soil? Likewise, what would then happen if the Israeli Government decided that they were going to seek the return of the Stone to its 'original' homeland in Israel?

The Stone of Destiny is, was, and always will be about politics.

Epilogue

To explain the foundations for how this book was written we need to go back to 2002 when the authors were invited to join a research group with the aims of finding the 'real' Stone of Destiny. The driving factor for such a quest was the persistent theory that the Stone that was returned to Scotland in 1996 was not the same as the one used for Scottish coronations prior to it being taken in 1296. Aside from the possibility that the Stone on display in Edinburgh Castle was not the genuine Scots king-making Stone that tradition claimed it to be, the team had no pre-conceived ideas about what the Stone actually was or in what direction our research would take us.

It was not political consideration that inspired us forward, but rather the chance to get a bit closer towards an answer to the question of whether it is possible that Edward really was duped in 1296, and if so, what could have happened to the genuine Scots king-making Stone?

Each member of the team came from a different background and none of us could be classed as an authoritative historian or archaeologist. We had each researched different aspects of history and cumulatively we had a good foundation upon which to base our research. Whilst it might not have been the most professional body ever to walk the fields in Scotland, we could certainly lay claim to being one of the most enthusiastic. It was our aim to visit all the sites in Scotland associated with the Stone of Destiny, and whilst we ended up in some rather strange places, with seemingly little or no relevance, each trip helped to clarify what it was that we were seeking.

We used any and every means at our disposal to try to find the Stone, including those used by the Police when the Stone was stolen from Westminster Abbey on Christmas Day in 1950. The police had enlisted the help of a dowser to try to locate the missing Stone, which resulted in them dredging the Serpentine in Hyde Park, London. They were unsuccessful in finding the Stone, yet we were perhaps more fortunate.

Our research had caused us to look into the legend that the Stone was at one time in its history on Iona. It was decided that we would hire a helicopter to transport the team to the island for further investigation. The traditional story is that the Scots king-making Stone was one and the same as St Columba's Pillow. One member of the team had come to the conclusion, by dowsing, that the king-making Stone and St Columba's Pillow were two separate items. According to the interpretation of the dowse, St Columba's Pillow was still hidden somewhere on Iona and the team took it upon themselves to try to find it. It is worthwhile to highlight that there is a stone on full public display on Iona called 'St Columba's Pillow', but this was found in a nearby field and was so named due to no other reason than having a stone without a name and a name without a stone. This is not what we were looking for, nor believed to be St Columba's Pillow.

Iona is a beautiful island, located off the western coast of Mull, itself off the west coast of mainland Scotland. It is said to be from Iona that Christianity had originated in Britain, with St Columba preaching to and converting the heathen, pagan Pictish tribes to a form of Celtic Christianity. It was a glorious day and the views from the air of the surrounding countryside were simply stunning. When we arrived at Iona our helicopter landed in a nearby farmer's field creating quite a stir amongst the locals and visitors to the island – this obviously didn't happen too often!

We started to look for what the dowsing had indicated was hidden somewhere on the island – St Columba's Pillow. We found a secluded part of Iona Abbey and hidden out of sight, but clearly on purpose, we found a Stone lying exactly where the dowsing rods had indicated it would be. There were no markings or distinguishing features on the Stone, and it was similar in shape and size to some of the very old gravestones that were in use on Iona. It was positioned in a slated 'coffin', the likes of which can be found in ancient settlements throughout Scotland, as though it had been placed there as its final resting place. Quite what the Stone was, none of us could be sure, but that it was, and probably still is there is beyond doubt. *Something* had been found that had been purposefully hidden. Was this St Columba's

Pillow, or was it merely by chance that we had found a Stone? We can never answer that question, but the experiences and events witnessed as a result of the dowsing experiments have left us with a real sense of appreciation for the unknown, along with many unanswerable questions.

Later in the year the team visited Scone Palace to see if we could glean any information on the potential whereabouts of the 'genuine' Stone of Destiny. As we walked around Moot Hill we postulated about the idea of the Stone never having left the area and wondered if it may still be hidden somewhere in the grounds. We even considered the possibility that it had been built into the fabric of the Murray mausoleum that was built in 1624. This is located on top of Moot Hill where the coronation ceremonies had supposedly taken place. Our logic, if it can be so called, was that the centre of Moot Hill would have been a good place to hide the Stone. By installing it into the framework of the building it would have been where it rightly belongs, in full view, and the chances of anyone removing it would be slim. We reasoned that the south-east octagonal pillar of the mausoleum, that we had determined to be the exact centre of Moot Hill, would have been as good a place as any for the Stone to have been hidden – right at the heart of the ancient king-making site at Scone.

We spoke with a guide of Scone Abbey and told him of our postulations. We were informed that it was a popular theory by the locals that the Stone was still somewhere in the vicinity of Scone. Although we had no evidence upon which to base the idea that it was built into the mausoleum, it seemed as plausible as some of the other theories we had read about. However, with no way of being able to prove or disprove it, the team decided not to mention it anymore.

On 25th August 2007 the authors of this work revisited Scone Palace to relive some of the adventures that we have had in our quest for the Stone of Destiny and whilst researching this book. We joked about our naïve postulations of the Stone being hidden in one of the four octagonal pillars of the mausoleum on Moot Hill and then went to the bookshop to see what books were for sale on the Stone of Destiny. We were amazed to find none. We then asked someone to take a picture of us crouched next to the replica Stone that is sited on Moot Hill, thinking it would make a good photo for this book.

On the way back to the car park we spoke to the guide that we had spoken to at the beginning of our quest and asked him about any recent developments at Scone. We learned that there had been a team of archaeologists from Glasgow University who had recently conducted geophysical ground surveys of the area surrounding Moot Hill. They are believed to have found the foundations Scone Abbey. This would have been the very place that the Stone was held and from where Edward would have taken his Stone. We were told how the latest thinking was that the Stone could very well still be hidden in some underground cavity in the ruins of the Abbey, but that major archaeological work and finance would be needed. It would take years to have approval granted, and this may never happen.

We were then told about some of the other theories of the location of the Stone. What we were told is that a 'team of archaeologists' had come to Scone several years previously and concluded that it was located in one of the pillars of the mausoleum on Moot Hill. We looked at each other in amusement, for what we were being told was something that we had been involved with creating. Completely by accident, we had created a theory that was now being told to thousands of visitors to Scone Palace as part of the legend of the Stone of Destiny. We felt this was worthy of mention at the end of the book to help highlight just how easy it is for legends to evolve and grow. We also wondered how many times something similar had happened throughout the 700 years that the legend of the Stone had been developing.

On our travels we came into contact with people from all over the world, each with their own story to tell us about their thoughts on the whereabouts of the 'real' Stone of Destiny. In total we were informed of the whereabouts of four 'genuine' Stones. One of which had made its way to Nova Scotia and was at the bottom of a pond, another was in the vicinity of Loch Awe in Argyll, one was found near Alloa and was now in their garage, and the last was still kept hidden by its Templar guardians somewhere in Scotland. The intensity of belief that each of these people 'in the know' held was quite amazing, and any suggestion that their facts were not as watertight as they would have liked was met with instant dismissal.

Whilst the reader might see some of the above as being eccentric and irrelevant, we prefer to see it as entertaining and informative. Most of the people we met totally believed what they told us, and who were we to criticise? There is a large proportion of Scots who believe that King Edward I took the wrong Stone, which must therefore mean that somewhere there is the 'real' Stone of Destiny. We chose not to exclude any of the theories or 'real' Stones put to us as potential red herrings, preferring instead to follow the claims through as best as we could.

The Stone of Destiny is an amalgamation of stories and legends surrounding mythical king-making Stones and a tangible artefact whose history is largely unknown. The Stone that was taken from Scone in 1296 could very well be the king-making Stone of the Scottish monarchs. Likewise, it could be nothing more than a block of stone that was handed to the English in desperation. Without doubt passions will run high when attempts are made to return it to England each time there is a coronation ceremony. Even if it is not what King Edward I intended to take, the Stone has over 700 years of history to back up its provenance.

What is the truth of the Stone of Destiny? The simple answer is that the truth is what you, as a reader, decide it to be. The British-Israelites had their truth. The Scots have theirs and the English theirs. Everyone has an opinion, but it is impossible for anyone to know what really happened over 700 years ago. We have tried to be as unbiased as we can when writing this book, but no doubt new information will come to light in the future which may negate much of what has been written in these pages. We actually welcome that, because we will be informed as much as anyone else.

What is the truth of the Stone of Destiny? The truth is we shall never know.

Figure 29: David Bews (left) and Mark Naples next to the replica Stone of Destiny at Moot Hill, Scone (25th August 2007)

Bibliography

Addison, J. D. (2006, April 19). *Arts and Crafts in the Middle Ages*. Retrieved September 22, 2007, from The Project Gutenberg eBook: http://www.gutenberg.org/files/18212/18212-h/18212-h.htm

Aitchison, N. (2000). *Scotland's Stone of Destiny*. Gloucestershire: Tempus Publishing Ltd.

Anderson, J. (1881). *Scotland in Early Christian Times (Extract Quoted from Gillies, In Famed Breadalbane, 1938)*. Edinburgh: David Douglas.

Bahn, P. (2001). *The Penguin Archaeology Guide*. London: Penguin Books.

Baker, G. P. (2001). *Constantine the Great and the Christian Revolution*. New York: Cooper Square Press.

Barber, R. (1999). *Myths and Legends of the British Isles*. Woodbridge: Boydell & Brewer Ltd.

Beaumont, W. C. (1946). *Britain - The Key to World History*. London: Rider and Company.

Blarney Castle: A Souvenir Guide Book. Dublin: John Hinde.

Bourke, C. (1983). The Hand Bells of the Early Scottish Church. *Proceeding of the Society of Antiquaries of Scotland Vol. 113* , 464-468.

Bower, W. (1993). *Scotichronicon Vols: 1-9*. Edinburgh: The Mercat Press.

Breeze, D. J. (1996). *Roman Scotland*. London: Historic Scotland.

Breeze, D., & Munro, G. (1997). *The Stone of Destiny: Symbol of Nationhood*. Edinburgh: Historic Scotland.

Brown, C. (2002). *The Second Scottish Wars of Independence 1332-1362*. Stroud: Tempus.

Bryant, A. (1963). *The Age of Chivalry*. Norwich: The Reprint Society Ltd.

Brydon, R., & Ritchie, J. (1996). *Shadow of a Dream* in *Chapman* , 6-11.

Caldwell, D.H. (2003). *Finlaggan, Islay – Stones and Inauguration Ceremonies* in Weander, R., Breeze, D. J., & Clancy, T. O. (2003).

Capt, E. R. (1977). *Jacob's Pillar: A Biblical Historical Study.* California: Artisan Sales.

Carew, M. (2003). *Tara and the Ark of the Covenant.* Dublin: Royal Irish Academy.

Service, J. (2013). *Chinese Music Theory.* Retreived at: http://www.hcs.harvard.edu/soundingchina/Service.html

Connon, F. W. (1951). *The Stone of Destiny.* London: The Covenant Publishing Co. Ltd.

Cowan, E. J., & McDonald, A. (2005). *Alba: Celtic Scotland in the Medieval Era.* Edinburgh: John Donald.

Cowan, I. B. (1976). *Inchaffray Abbey.* Edinburgh: Royal Commission for Ancient and historical Monuments of Scotland.

Dallison, C. N. (2000). *Hexham Abbey.* Shropshire: RJL Smith & Associates.

Dewar, P. B. (1991). *The House of Dewar 1296-1991: The Fortunes of Clan Dewar.* Private Publication.

Dunlop, E. (2005). *Queen Margaret of Scotland.* Edinburgh: NMSE Publishing.

Farmer, D. (2003). *Oxford Dictionary of Saints.* Oxford: Oxford University Press.

Forbes, A. P. (1872). *Kalendars of Scottish Saints, with personal notices of those of Alba, Laudonia, & Strathclyde.* Edinburgh: Edmonston & Douglas.

Fowler, C. (1951). *The Amazing History of the Stone of Destiny.* Droitwich: Frank Donald Ltd.

Gerber, P. (1997). *Stone of Destiny.* Edinburgh: Canongate Books Ltd.

Gillies, R. W. (1938). *In Famed Breadalbane: The Story of the Antiquities, Lands, and People of a Highland District.* Perth: The Munro Press Ltd.

Grosset, G. &. (1997). *Ancient Egypt Myth & history.* New Lanark: The Gresham Publishing Company.

Hall, U. (2006). *The Cross of St Andrew.* Edinburgh: Birlinn.

271

Hamilton, I. (1992). *The Taking of the Stone of Destiny.* Reading: Corgi Books.

History of La Coruña. (n.d.). Retrieved August 18, 2007, from Tour Spain: http://www.tourspain.org/coruna/history.asp

Holy Bible: King James Version. Harper Collins Publishers.

Hunter, J. (1856). *King Edward's Spoilations in Scotland in A.D. 1296 – The Coronation Stone – Original and Unpublished Evidence* in *Archaeological Journal Vol. 13* p.245-255

Hodge, A. (2019). *The Medieval Documents: Edinburgh Castle Research.* Edinburgh. Historic Environment Scotland

Hughes, D. (2017). *Chronicle of the Kings and Queens of Britain from the Earliest Times to the Present.* Heritage Books, USA

Innes, J. (2004, September 9). *DNA shows Scots and Irish should look to Spain for their ancestry.* Retrieved December 20, 2007, from The Scotsman: http://www.scotsman.com/scotland/DNA-shows-Scots-and-Irish.2562906.jp

Jarrold, W. T. (1937). *Our Great Heritage with its Responsibilities.* London: The Covenant Publishing Co. Ltd.

Jones, G. and Jones, T. (1968), translators, *The Mabinigion*, New York, Dent & Sons

Josephus, F. (1987). *Antiquities of the Jews.* Peabody: Hendrickson Publishers.

Kagarlitsky, B. (2006, September 14). *The Problem of 2008.* Retrieved November 1, 2007, from Transnational Institute: http://www.tni.org/detail_page.phtml?page=archives_kagarlitsky_2008

Keating, G. (n.d.). *The History of Ireland (BOOK I-II).* Retrieved from CELT: The Corpus of Electronic Texts: http://celt.ucc.ie/published/T100054/index.html

Kingsley, S. (2006). *God's Gold.* London: John Murray.

Knight, C., & Lomas, R. (1999). *Uriel's Machine.* London: Century Books Limited.

Lamont, A. (1976). *William Blake and the Stone of Destiny.* Penicuik: The Scots Secretariat.

Luard, H.R. (ed). (1890). *Flores Historiarum.* Rolls Series 95, III. London (p.101)

Lynch, M. (1991). *Scotland: A New History.* London: Pimlico.

Macalister, R. A. (1931). *Tara: A Pagan Sanctuary of Ancient Ireland.* London: Charles Scribner's Sons.

MacGibbon, D. a. (1896-7). *Inchaffray Abbey.* Edinburgh: Royal Commission for Ancient and Historical Monuments of Scotland.

Mackenzie, K. R. (1877). *The Royal Masonic Cyclopædia.* London: John Hogg.

Mackenzie, W. M. (1913). *The Battle of Bannockburn: A Study in Medieval Warfare.* Stevenage: The Strong Oak Press.

Maclagan, R. C. (1879). *The Clan of the Bell of St Fillan.* Edinburgh: Private Circulation.

MacLagan, R. C. (1882). *Scottish Myths.* Edinburgh: MacLachan and Stewart.

MacLagan, R. C. (1909). *Religio Scotica.* Edinburgh: Otto Schulze & Company.

MacLagan, R. C. (1913). *Our Ancestors: Scots, Picts and Cymry and What Their Traditions Tell Us.* London & Edinburgh: T. N. Foulis.

McKerracher, A. (1984). *Where is the Real Stone?*, in Scots Magazine

McKerracher, A. (2000). *Perthshire in History and Legend.* Edinburgh: John Donald Publishers.

Moffat, A. (2000). *Arthur & The Lost Kingdoms.* London: Orion Books Ltd.

O'Shea, S. (2000). *The Perfect Heresy: The Life and Death of the Cathars.* London: Profile Books.

Pettit, S. (1989). *Blarney Castle: The Story of a Legend.* Cork: Litho Press Co.

Pohlsander, H. A. (2004). *The Emperor Constantine (2nd Edition).* London and New York: Routledge.

Prestwich, M. (1980). *The Three Edwards: War and State in England 1272-1377.* London and New York: Routledge.

Purser, J. (1992). *Scotland's Music.* Edinburgh: Mainstream Publishing Company (Edinburgh) Ltd.

Ralls-MacLeod, K., & Robertson, I. (2002). *The Quest for the Celtic Key.* Edinburgh: Luath.

Reese, P. (2000). *Bannockburn: Scotland's Greatest Victory.* Edinburgh: Canongate Books Ltd.

Rodwell, W. (2013), *The Coronation Chair and the Stone of Scone,* Oxford, Oxbrow Books

Rutherford, D. W. (1973). *St Fillan's Church Aberdour.* Church Guide Book.

Scotland Votes No (n.d.). Retreived from: https://www.bbc.co.uk/news/events/scotland-decides/results

Simpson, W. D. (1958). *Dunstaffnage Castle and the Stone of Destiny.* Edinburgh.

Skene, W. F. (1868-70). *The Coronation Stone* in *Proceedings for the Society of Antiquities of Scotland Vol: XIII* , 68-99.

Slavin, M. (1996). *The Book of Tara.* Dublin: Merlin Publishing.

Smith, J. G. (1896). *Strathendrick and its Inhabitants from Early Times.* Glasgow. James MacLehose & Sons (p.290)

Squire, C. (1919). *Celtic Myth and Legend.* London: The Gresham Publishing Company Ltd.

St Andrew. (2005, September 30). Retrieved October 28, 2007, from The National Archives of Scotland: http://www.nas.gov.uk/about/051124.asp

Stong, J. (1995). *The New Strong's Exhaustive Concordance of the Bible.* Nashville: Thomas Nelson.

Story, R. H. (1878). *Saint Modan of Rosneath: A Fragment of Scottish Hagiology.* Paisley.

Stuart, J. (1876-78). Historical Notices of St Fillan's Crozier. *Proceedings of the Society of Antiquities of Scotland Vol: 12* , 134-169.

Taylor, S. (2001). The Cult of St Fillan in Scotland. In T. R. Liszka, *The North Sea World in the Middle Ages* (pp. 175-210). Dublin: Four Courts Press Ltd.

The Burial Route of the Kings. (n.d.). *Historic Hill Routes and Argyll & Lochaber No: 2* , 12-13.

The Declaration of Arbroath. (n.d.). Retrieved from
http://www.geo.ed.ac.uk/home/scotland/arbroath_english.html
The London Stone. (2002, July 22). Retrieved September 1, 2007,
from h2g2: http://www.bbc.co.uk/dna/h2g2/A791101
The Moot Hill. (n.d.). Retrieved September 21, 2007, from Scone
Palace: http://www.scone-palace.net/palace/moothill.cfm
The Stone of Destiny. Retrieved December 29, 2020, from Scottish
Government website: https://www.gov.scot/news/the-stone-of-destiny/
The Stone of Scone/Destiny. (n.d.). Retrieved from
http://www.martinfrost.ws/htmlfiles/gazette/stone_destiny.html
Thomas, C. (1997). *Celtic Britain.* London: Thames and Hudson Ltd.
Thompson, P. W. (1936). *Britain in Prophecy and History.* London:
The Covenant Publishing Co. Ltd.
UK Votes to Leave the EU (n.d.). Retreived from:
https://www.bbc.co.uk/news/politics/eu_referendum/results
Weander, R., Breeze, D. J., & Clancy, T. O. (2003). *The Stone of
Destiny. Artefact & Icon.* Edinburgh: Society of Antiquaries of
Scotland. Monograph Series Number 22.
Wessex. (n.d.). Retrieved September 2, 2007, from Wikipedia:
http://en.wikipedia.org/wiki/Wessex
White, M. (2006, August). *Selected Death Tolls for Wars, Massacres
and Atrocities Before the 20th Century.* Retrieved October 27, 2007,
from Twentieth Century Atlas:
http://users.erols.com/mwhite28/warstat0.htm#Crusades
Wilson, D. (1876-78). Notices of the Quigrich or Crozier of St Fillan
and of its Hereditary Keepers. *Proceedings for the Society of
Antiquities of Scotland Vol: 12*, 122-131.
Wilson, J. (1876). *Lectures on Our Israelitish Origin.* London: James
Nisbet & Co.
Yeoman, P. (1999). *Pilgrimage in Medieval Scotland.* London:
Historic Scotland.

Index